# ON TRANSLATING FRENCH LITERATURE AND FILM II

**Rodopi Perspectives on Modern Literature**

**22**

Edited by
David Bevan

# ON TRANSLATING FRENCH LITERATURE AND FILM II

Edited by
Myriam Salama-Carr

Amsterdam - Atlanta, GA 2000

The paper on which this book is printed meets the requirements of "ISO 9706:1994, Information and documentation - Paper for documents - Requirements for permanence".

ISBN: 90-420-1451-2 (bound)
©Editions Rodopi B.V., Amsterdam - Atlanta, GA 2000
Printed in The Netherlands

**Table of Contents**

Introduction — i
(Myriam Salama-Carr)

1. "Why Retranslate the French Classics? The Impact of Retranslation on Quality" — 1
(Isabelle Vanderschelden)

2. "In Search of the Foreign: A Study of the Three English Translations of Camus's *L'Étranger*" — 19
(Michel Ballard)

3. "The Translator's Intervention: Dialogue in *Strait is the Gate*" — 39
(Myriam Salama-Carr)

4. "When is Losing Finding? Translating Surrealism" — 51
(Mary Ann Caws)

5. "Tactics and Non-Tactics: The Experience of a Translator of Modern Poetry" — 59
(Michael Bishop)

6. "Rhyme's Wrongs: Dealing with Verlaine's Rhymes in English" — 73
(Martin Sorrell)

7. "Equivalence and Adequacy in Translation: Are They Equivalent? Are They Adequate?" — 89
(María Sánchez-Ortiz)

8. "Translating the Past: *Before the War*, The English Version of Robert Brasillach's Memoirs *Notre avant-guerre*" — 99
(Peter Tame)

9. "Translating Sartre's *Situations, V*" — 111
(Stephen Brewer and Terry McWilliams)

10. "Subtitling and Dubbing, For Better or Worse?    129
The English Video Versions of *Gazon maudit*"
(Jean-Pierre Mailhac)

11. "Adventures Across Time: Translational Transformations"    155
(Susan Bassnett)

12. "Translating Stereotypes in the Cinematic Remake"    171
(Lucy Mazdon)

13. "Can Intertextuality Be Translated? Baudelaire's    183
'Le Guignon' and 'Le Flambeau vivant' in English"
(Emily Salines)

14. "Back to the Original: Translating Maghrebi    201
French Literature into Arabic"
(Said Faiq)

15. "The Imaginary Quay from Waterloo Bridge to London Bridge:    219
Translation, Adaptation and Genre"
(Terry Hale)

# Introduction

"Norms do prevail but translators govern norms as much as their behaviour is governed by them" claims Daniel Siméoni[1]. This reassertion of the translator as an agent who has assumed power in the formation of literary canons, a repositioning on which much of contemporary Translation Studies focuses, underpins many of the essays in the present volume.

This collection of essays, which has its beginnings in the second Conference on Translating French Literature and Film organised by the European Studies Research Institute of the University of Salford, together with the Henri Peyre French Institute, University of New York Graduate Center,[2] bears witness to the centrality of the translator's presence, whilst, at the same time, confirming the diversity of approaches in the field. Beyond the three-pronged thematic organisation of the volume — translation of French Prose, of French Poetry and of French Film — plural relationships that hold between the various parts of the whole can be seen to emerge. Unifying principles such as the creative nature of the translator's work, the impossibility of neutral intervention, and the role played by translations — and therefore translators — in the creation of genres, should not lead us to overlook the diversity of constraints which bear upon their work.

Isabelle Vanderschelden's discussion of the various factors which come into play when literary classics are retranslated, and Michel Ballard's comparative analysis of three English translations of Camus's *L'Étranger* highlight the complexity of translation norms, from which the translator's subjectivity cannot be excluded. Myriam Salama-Carr examines how the translator's intervention, as far as the handling of dialogue in the English version of Gide's *La porte étroite* is concerned, can be explained by a combination of stylistic constraints and options, the latter resulting in both transparency *vis-à-vis* the source text, and naturalisation.

The intensely personal experience of translating surrealist poetry and poetics is recounted by Mary Ann Caws as both creative and (de)constructionist, whilst Michael Bishop reflects on his own practice as a translator of Modern Poetry, which he maps onto Willis Barnstone's *ABC* of the translator. It is also on his own practice of translating that Martin Sorrell bases his discussion of various English versions of Verlaine's verse, highlighting in the process the changes of norms that affect the translation of poetry, and his own subjective preferences.

The concept of equivalence, that many in the field have come to love to hate but on which a significant number of discussions still hinge, is critically reviewed by María Sánchez-Ortiz in an attempt to achieve some terminological consistency. And it is perhaps with Anthony Pym's tentative definition in mind, namely that the notion of equivalence could refer to "a relation operative not between a source text and a target text but between the target text and the reader prepared to believe and trust its status as an 'equivalent' of an unseen source"[3] that we ought to look at the problems discussed by Peter Tame as translator of Brasillach's Memoirs, *Notre avant-guerre*, together with those problems identified by Stephen Brewer and Terry McWilliams whilst working towards an English version of Sartre's *Situations, V*, when ideologically laden texts are made available, across time and culture, through translation.

It cannot be denied that the translator of cinematic material is faced with specific constraints. However, this form of translation is increasingly taken into account by mainstream research in Translation Studies, partly due to the way the latter is extending its subject boundaries. Film translation usually refers to the practices of subtitling and dubbing, and the controlled environment where these methods are applied. This is the focus of Jean-Pierre Mailhac's article which examines the pros and cons of each of the subtitled and dubbed versions of the French film *Gazon maudit*, and questions the received wisdom according to which subtitling is often deemed preferable. But film translation, as discussed by Susan Bassnett, can operate at an intersemiotic level when a book, in this instance Jules Verne's *Voyage au centre de la terre*, is made into films, a process which raises the issues of authenticity and invariance in a context of adaptation. Lucy Mazdon looks at yet another form of film translation, that of film into film, as in the case of cinematic remakes, posited as a form of rewriting which casts doubts on the immutability and supremacy of the "original".

This supremacy is further thrown into question when issues of intertextuality arise. In Emily Salines's paper, the English translators of Baudelaire's "Le Guignon" and "Flambeau vivant", works which are themselves based on translations from English to French, stand at the heart of a complex network of *Correspondances*, and their choices range from restoring the English original (Poe's text) to retranslating the French poems. "Back to the original" is indeed the title of Said Faiq's essay which looks at the problematic translation (into Arabic) of a French text, Ben Jelloun's *La nuit sacrée*. This novel can itself be seen as a stereotyping translation from the Arabic. The notion of the original and the author/translator dichotomy, as the two agents become one, is further questioned as both "original" and translation are viewed here as inherently manipulative, and representative of a different, subaltern trend.

Finally, Terry Hale, starting from the viewpoint of French influence on the creation of genre in nineteenth-century Britain, questions the traditional divide that exists between translation and adaptation, and he calls for the latter to be more explicitly recognised in theoretical accounts of translation.

As these essays show, the increased visibility of translators in translation discourse and paratexts is paralleled by the development and refinement of the theoretical apparatus that they have at their disposal when reflecting on their work. This can only help to reduce the traditional, and perhaps fictitious, divide between theory and practice, and between "observers" and "insiders".

Myriam Salama-Carr

### Notes

1 Daniel Siméoni (1998) "The Pivotal Status of the Translator's Habitus", *Target, International Journal of Translation Studies*, 10:1, 23-24.
2 "Translating French Literature and Film, II", European Studies Research Institute, University of Salford, 9-11 October 1998.
3 Anthony Pym, *Method in Translation History,* Manchester: St Jerome Publishing, 1998, 107.

**ACKNOWLEDGEMENTS**

The Editor wishes to thank Louise Graham for her invaluable help in the preparation of the camera-ready copy for the present volume, and Geoffrey Harris, the former director of the European Studies Research Institute of the University of Salford, who organised the Conference on Translating French Literature and Film which inspired this book, for his support.

# 1.
## WHY RETRANSLATE THE FRENCH CLASSICS? THE IMPACT OF RETRANSLATION ON QUALITY

In the context of world literature, a translation can be questioned and challenged at any time, which may lead to its revision or even complete retranslation. This applies to literary classics which have been defined as texts "that allow each age to reinterpret [them] anew deriving from it a powerful experience".[1] Some classics in translation have been well established in the target language (TL) and culture (TC) for many years, such as John Florio's Montaigne, Scott-Moncrieff's Proust, or Nancy Mitford's *Princesse de Clèves*, but as the history of these examples shows, it is just a matter of time before a literary translation is challenged or replaced by another. Many factors may influence the retranslation of a book: the quality of the translation, a different interpretation, or the fact that the target text (TT) has a specific function. Little research has been carried out to analyse and evaluate retranslation so far, apart from empirical comparative assessments, but all discussion on the subject involves, at some stage, a degree of value-judgement.

This article examines the impact of retranslation in its various forms, enabling us an insight into the procedure itself. Secondly, we will consider some of the reasons advanced in justification of retranslation. Finally, we will elicit the implications that retranslating has upon quality assessment and discuss the extent to which it can be argued that retranslation improves quality in literary translation. A variety of examples drawn from classics of French literature, and their English translations, will be used, and we will occasionally refer to the testimony of literary translators, reviewers and scholars to clarify matters.

### Revising A Translation

Revision is often the first step towards retranslation, and it involves making changes to an existing TT whilst retaining the major part, including the overall structure and tone of the former version. This can embrace a wide variety of alterations ranging from simple copy-editing to extensive rewriting, and it normally takes place if the existing version contains a limited number of problems or errors, such as inaccuracies, mistranslations, or stylistic infelicities. The TT has flaws, but it is still worth 'recycling'.

Translated classics, in particular, may require modernisation or, at the least, updating before a reprint, in order to make them more accessible to their readership, taking into account the evolution of the TL and TC over a period of time. In the case of a commissioned translation, not yet published because it is deemed unsatisfactory, this may be a cost-effective solution for a publisher. It is preferable to revise it, even quite extensively, rather than to retranslate completely. Similarly, if there is a demand for re-publication, it is often easier and cheaper to revise a classic for which a translation exists, rather than commission a new translation. To take a specific example, even though Proust's work has now been partly retranslated, the first move towards amending Scott-Moncrieff's canonical 1920s translation was Terence Kilmartin's revision in the early 1980s, when Proust fell out of copyright.[2]

The revision of *Remembrance of Things Past* was in itself an enormous task: the six volumes, about four thousand pages in all, required more than ten years work, and Kilmartin died before he could complete the task. D.J. Enright was then asked to re-revise Kilmartin's version in which several misunderstandings had been corrected but "several others [had] slipped through." Eventually a new revised version entitled *In Search of Lost Time*, was published in Britain in 1993 by Chatto and Windus.[3] The numerous episodes of revision and partial retranslation of Proust's works were commented upon by literary reviewers:

> [It is] a version which not only embodies important textual changes, but eliminates many of Scott-Moncrieff's misjudgements. And now, following Kilmartin's death and the publication of a new Pléiade edition, [...] D.J. Enright has produced a revision of Kilmartin's text.[4]

After these revisions, Scott-Moncrieff's translation remains the English version of Proust which is most widely available in British and American bookshops and libraries.

If revision is acceptable by publishers in certain cases, it is often seen from the translators' viewpoint as the worst option. Most revisers are given little credit for their work, and it is often felt that the results obtained are unsatisfactory. If accuracy of detail is easily corrected, it becomes more difficult at text level for reasons of overall cohesion.[5]

It can sometimes be difficult to distinguish between revision and retranslation if the amendments made are substantial, whilst the difference between retranslator and reviser is clearly indicated on the title page, where the reviser comes third after the author and the former translator. Leonard Tancock's revision of *La Princesse de Clèves*, which had been translated by Nancy Mitford in 1950, is a pertinent example:

> Nancy Mitford herself made no pretence of strict academic accuracy, and I was fortunate that shortly before her death she gave permission for me to revise her work for Penguin Classics [...]. The problem therefore has been to rectify errors, omissions, additions, or unduly broad paraphrases while respecting Nancy Mitford's English wherever possible and refraining from 'improvement' for its own sake.[6]

It is apparent from Tancock's preface to the revised edition, that he has only made carefully selected modifications to Mitford's text. This is not a retranslation, as he has tried to retain Mitford's style, and he suggests that if he had carried out a complete retranslation, the TT would have been different but not necessarily as good. Revision is justified for minor adjustments, or if the publisher has to balance economic viability and the availability of an important text in the TT. Whether or not it really improves quality is debatable, as the procedure can be perceived as a minimal cost revamping exercise, in the same way as it can be considered an updating of the TT in order to improve its quality. However, if the revision work becomes too extensive or has a negative impact on the TT, retranslation becomes necessary, if costly.

### Justifying Retranslation

The advantages of retranslating rather than revising an existing text are obvious for the translator. (S)he receives credit for the new version, but, more importantly, has full control over the translation process. The only constraint is the source text (ST) and possibly its context, image and reception. Translators do not have to consider earlier versions, although they can refer to them, if they so wish. Their work is free-standing, and meant to supersede the existing translation(s), as French translator Sylvère Monod explains:

> Il peut s'agir aussi de l'autre grande catégorie: la retraduction entreprise en vue de produire un texte entièrement nouveau, sans s'appuyer sur les traductions anciennes, que l'on vise à supplanter, non à améliorer.[7]

In the case of a retranslation, the literary work already has a place in the TL polysystem, as it has been published in translation before, and has therefore been introduced to the target readership. This implies that, whether or not the translator is influenced by previous translations, both TL readers and critics have a direct means of comparison. Five main arguments have been put forward to justify retranslation:

*The existing translation is unsatisfactory and cannot be revised efficiently.*

This is not necessarily due to liberties taken with the ST or numerous errors of comprehension, but it can also result from changes in perception or of TL norms over the years. A number of French classics were modified and embellished in their initial translations into English, and it was one, for example, of the priorities of the Penguin Classics Series created in 1945 by E.V. Rieu, to return to a more faithful but readable approach to translating. New translations of Zola, Balzac, Flaubert and Voltaire were published mostly in the 1950s, and 1960s, and are still available in bookshops and libraries today, even if, in some cases, they have been superseded by more recent versions published in the same collection.[8]

*A new edition of the ST is published and becomes the standard reference.*

One of the reasons given for some of the shortcomings of Scott-Moncrieff's translation of Proust was that he was not working on the definitive edition, as he was translating whilst the French ST was not even completed. A study of some of Vizetelly's early English translations of Zola's books carried out by Geoff Woollen indicates a similar situation.[9] We will reconsider this at a later stage.

*The existing TT is considered outdated from a stylistic point of view.*

It is often assumed that translations age more than their STs and that it is normal to retranslate a classic for each generation, that is every twenty or thirty years. Retranslation in this light corresponds to historical updating, in the form of modernisation of the TT, to accommodate the evolution of linguistic norms and changes in idiomatic usage. Voltaire's *Candide*, for instance, has been translated into English many times since its publication in France, and retranslations of *Madame Bovary* have also appeared at regular intervals since it was first published in 1852.[10]

The need for retranslation is more likely to be met if the work has been canonised in the TC or if it is often used for educational purposes. For example, as a favourite text for French *A Level* in Britain, Maupassant's *Une Vie* has had many retranslations and bilingual editions over the years.[11]

*The retranslation has a special function to fill in the TL.*

European plays in translation have known a revival in Britain and the United States as the number of successful recent productions show. This has led to the commissioning and publication of new translations of classic authors such as Molière, Racine, Corneille, as well as Marivaux and Beaumarchais. In such cases, the director may want to use a new translation which will focus on specific elements emphasised in the production or which will take the intended audience into account. It is not unusual for translators of plays to be dramatists as well, and there are cases when translator and director are one and the same.[12] Such translations have a specific aim, therefore the translation strategies can vary according to factors which are external to the ST, including the translator's convictions. Neil Bartlett is an example of this:

> I'm a theatre artist rather than an academic or professional translator, and I don't come from that branch of theatre whose Lynch-pin is the speaking of the iambic pentameter. [...] The translator must always be thinking of the stage rather than the page.[13]

Another application of the notion of special function is specific to the English language and concerns the frequent synchronic co-existence of two TTs, one for the British market and another for the American one. This can be imputed to geographical and cultural variations of the

English language, particularly at idiomatic and lexical levels. *La Nausée* and *Les Mots* have two English versions made in the same period, one for the British market, one for the American one.[14]

*A different interpretation of the ST justifies a new translation.*

The translator's interpretation constitutes the second justification of synchronic nature for retranslating. There are several examples of two English versions of the same French classic published in the 1980s and 1990s in Britain, which seems to indicate that translators support the notion of multiple interpretations and readings of a text. We have already mentioned established classics like *Candide, Madame Bovary,* and *La Princesse de Clèves* which have been the subject of recent retranslations.

It does however take some time for a literary text to establish itself as a classic abroad, and it is still unusual to find retranslations of Post-war twentieth-century classics. Camus's *L'Étranger* (1942) is thus an exception in the retranslation market, in that it was first translated by Stuart Gilbert in 1946, then retranslated by Joseph Laredo in 1982. Both TTs aim primarily at a British audience and have the same publisher, which seems to indicate that the retranslation is to supersede the initial TT. An American translation by Matthew Ward was also published in 1988 (see Michel Ballard's discussion in this volume). However, most leading twentieth-century French authors have not yet had the privilege of being retranslated.[15] There can be more than one reason for retranslation, but is improved quality the main concern?

## Retranslation and Quality

A new translation is often associated with quality, but what are the factors which guarantee that retranslating actually improves the quality of translation? Quality in translation does not follow objective universal criteria, and those involved in literary translation have different priorities, let alone their own personal convictions on what constitutes a good literary translation. The more a literary text is analysed and canonised, thereby attaining the status of a classic, the more the quality of the TT is likely to be questioned.

TL readers do not normally have a source-oriented approach to retranslation. They usually consider above all the quality of the TL text, using TL norms, because they do not know the ST. Their perception is therefore TL-oriented, and they will respond primarily to quality criteria such as the readability, fluency and accessibility of the TT. The translation may also have a special function, e.g. a simplified adaptation for a children's edition. They will also consider the style of the TT, but will not normally be able to assess its faithfulness to the original. Reviewers, on the other hand, whilst considering the factors mentioned above, are sometimes tempted to make a detailed comparative study of the translations against the original. Their preoccupations may vary according to the function of their review, but their main criterion tends to be accuracy, linked to faithfulness to the original and a rendering "close to the original", a phrase which is ambiguous as it depends on the meaning and definition of *closeness* adopted.

From a commercial viewpoint, retranslations can contribute to the revival of interest in a forgotten literary text, and publishers often use new translations as a positive marketing device. For example, the *World Classics* series by Oxford University Press launched a successful programme of retranslations in the 1980s, clearly advertising on the book covers that these were new translations.[16]

Whilst the publishers' blurb often values readability, accessibility and, to a lesser extent, accuracy as quality criteria, the translators' views on quality tend to relate more to their individual interpretation of the original. The choices that they make (or would make) in their own version of a given ST, are governed by their interpretation of the ST and their own views of translation as a process. Whether translators are aware of it or not, their perception of quality will also be influenced by the language of their time of translation, as Tilby emphasises:

> [...] new translations, whatever their authors' active aim, will almost invariably modernize the text, rendering the original in a form of English that belongs at every level to the translator's own age.[17]

Their perception of quality is influenced by the historical and socio-cultural context, as well as the norms in which both retranslator and target text (TT) are inscribed. Whether a given translation is acceptable in the light of these norms will also become the major criterion of quality applied by TL readers. On the other hand, if some retranslations are controversial, it may be due either to a radically different interpretation of the ST, or to contrasting translation strategies. Given the number of quality criteria, it is difficult to provide an objective quality assessment model for retranslations. The presupposition that retranslation improves the quality of a literary translation cannot be confirmed nor dismissed, even if it is usually the main argument put forward by retranslators' prefaces and publishers' advertisements. Other arguments for retranslating the classics may have to be proposed.

### First and Great Translations, Hot and Cold Translations

Retranslators often benefit from a better overall view, due to the interval between the publication of the ST, the first translation, and the time in which the retranslation takes place. This is an advantage, but it implies, notwithstanding what was said earlier, that the translator cannot be unaware of the way in which the original was received in the TC, even though (s)he may choose to ignore it. Geoffrey Wall's introduction to his recent translation of *Madame Bovary* illustrates this point:

> Translating afresh the already translated classic text, the translator is drawn into dialogue with his or her precursors. Though I was working on different principles, and though I found that I eventually disagreed with some of their most cherished effects, I have profited from the posthumous conversation of three previous translators of *Madame Bovary*: Eleanor Marx, Alan Russell and Gerard Hopkins.[18]

A more general distinction between first translation and retranslation is at the centre of Antoine Berman's work on retranslation in "La Traduction et la lettre ou l'auberge du lointain":

> Il est tout à fait essentiel de distinguer deux espaces (et deux temps) de traduction: celui des premières traductions, et celui des retraductions. La distinction de ces deux catégories de traduction est l'un des moments de base d'une réflexion sur la temporalité de traduire. [...] Celui qui retraduit n'a plus affaire à un seul texte, l'original, mais à deux ce qui dessine un espace spécifique.

original                    première traduction

re-traduction(s)

> La re-traduction a lieu pour l'original et contre ses traductions existantes. Et l'on peut remarquer que c'est dans cet espace qu'en général, la traduction a produit ses chefs-d'oeuvre. Les premières traductions ne sont pas (et ne peuvent être) les plus grandes.[19]

The notion of "first translation" is associated with "défaillance" (deficiency), in other words a relative failure of the first attempt at translating a text due to anti-translating forces and a resistance to the translation process.[20] Claude Demanuelli, makes a similar distinction between first translation and retranslation, using the metaphor of "hot" and "cold" translations to illustrate the special context underlying retranslation:

> [...] lorsqu'on traduit de façon contemporaine la publication originale, il est toujours très difficile, surtout si c'est une grande œuvre, de savoir comment elle évoluera. Il y a une série de paramètres qu'on ne peut pas prendre en compte si on commence à traduire l'oeuvre en même temps que se fait l'écriture première. [...] Et on constate, je crois, que la retraduction, c'est comme une opération à froid. Le premier traducteur opère à chaud, le deuxième opère à froid avec le recul et la distance qu'autorisent finalement vingt ou trente ans, ainsi que tous les travaux qui sont faits sur la traduction et la théorie de la traduction.[21]

As we saw earlier, Scott-Moncrieff was working on a "hot" translation, when he translated Proust. He did not benefit from the overall view considered indispensable for the cohesion and unity of any translation. Similarly, Gilbert's version of *L'Étranger* in 1946 was based on the first edition of the French. As a result, he was criticised for a tendency to elaborate on the ST and remove its ambiguity. He was working on a "hot" translation, and did not have the knowledge of the two 1980s retranslators, regarding the critical reception of the book and the fact that it became a modern classic, as well as access to the definitive French version. Matthew Ward explained his objective in his 1988 preface to his 'first American' translation thus:

> There is some irony then in the fact that for forty years the only translation available to American audiences should be Stuart Gilbert's 'Britannic' rendering [...] As all translators do, Gilbert gave the novel a consistency and voice all his own. A certain paraphrastic earnestness might be a way of describing his effort to make the text

intelligible, to help the English-speaking reader understand what Camus meant. In addition to giving the text a more 'American' quality, I have also attempted to venture farther into the letter of Camus' novel to capture what he said and how he said it, not what he meant. In theory, the latter should take care of itself.[22]

Retranslation, especially if it takes place forty years later, is conditioned by the reception that the foreign book first had in the TL culture, and by the evaluation of the previous translation(s). Laredo's retranslation (1982) tends to correct the "hot first translation", whereas Ward's (1988) provides a TT aimed more specifically at American readers. Both of these can be considered as "cold" translations.

As Ward points out, it is often suggested that retranslation is a more source-oriented process.[23] His preface to *The Stranger* announces an attempt at translating what Camus says, not what he means. Before considering this hypothesis more generally, it is important to note a major exception, namely the case of plays for which other factors prevail. These may lead to retranslations which are more like adaptations. Ted Hughes's translation of Phèdre recently performed in London is just one example, and represents yet another reason for a retranslation to be published, namely the fact that the translator is an established author in the TL culture.[24]

Both Berman and Demanuelli have noted an evolution from a TL-oriented text in a first translation to a return to closer rendering of the source-text in retranslations.[25] For Berman, a first translation is "blind and hesitant", and it is only in retranslation that a TT can become more "accomplished". In other words, the first (hot) translation often favours readability, the naturalisation of culture-specific elements, explanation and even simplification. The more a text is retranslated, the more it seems to return to the ST literally, in an attempt to preserve its structures and style.[26] This is made possible by the fact that the text has already been translated and therefore a distance has been created and could be understood in different ways: it could be used in support of a more literal translation, as Berman does, but, on the other hand, it could also help to explain why adaptations are also made from classic STs, such as plays transposed into a modern environment, or Jules Verne's books made accessible for children.

Berman places retranslation within a "horizon" or perspective with a corresponding specific justification for retranslation, on historical, interpretative and reception-oriented grounds. It is in this perspective of retranslation that "great translations" become possible. A "great translation" refers to a TT which has acquired a long-term status in the TL. According to Berman, this is partly due to the fact that it has come at an appropriate time.[27] A "great translation" can only be made possible by a "great translator" who has the necessary "translating force", and benefits from "the minimum distance making the translating process possible". In Berman's terms, "great translations" are defined by "abundance", instead of the traditional notion of loss:

> [C'est] une abondance spécifique: richesse de la langue, extensive ou intensive, richesse du rapport à la langue de l'original, richesse textuelle, richesse signifiante, etc.[28]

This concept has strong qualitative connotations. It suggests that first translations have little chance of being perennial, as they are "deficient" in many respects. Berman provides some criteria which must coexist to provide "great translations".[29] These, in particular, illustrate the attempts made by translators to find a balance between contradictory constraints involving the ST and the TL, using the knowledge derived from former translations and the status acquired by the work in the TL. Retranslators often work in a less constricting environment, and they can make decisions which would not be judged acceptable or appropriate in the case of a first translation. Not all retranslations will be considered as "great translations". The latter, as defined by Berman, are abstract concepts, remote from the commercial and linguistic arguments which underlie retranslation. There are definitely different forces at stake, here, and they result in different priorities regarding retranslation.

## Interpretation and Plural Readings

Variations in priorities tend to show that several interpretations of a given text may coexist according to different readings of the ST by the translator, which follows recent developments in contemporary literary theory regarding the interpretation of texts. This is one reason why retranslation does not necessarily arise from a judgement on the quality of earlier versions. It can derive from a diachronic procedure, as explained above, but it can also be due to personal interpretation. Reviewing two versions of *Madame Bovary* available on the market, Steegmuller's and Wall's, Roger Huss explains that "the differences are significant enough for neither to be redundant". He provides a detailed comparison and concludes thus:

> Which of the two translations should be preferred? To hook a first-time reader, I would recommend Steegmuller, but prescribe Wall for a more lingering second reading. Subsequently, stereoscopic study of the two versions with their complementary qualities can be relied on to provide insight into many of the complexities of the untranslatable original.[30]

Retranslation is, in this case, a synchronic procedure in which two or more versions of the same text are different and complement each other. Similarly, two retranslations of *La Princesse de Clèves* published at the same time, one by Terence Cave, the other by Robin Buss, have been the subject of a comparative review by Peter France. He sees different functions for the two TTs: one is more suitable for students looking for a precise academic translation, the other is more accessible to the general reader.[31] In this respect, the decision to retranslate the book arose from a personal interpretation of a work, regardless of the commercial need for a new translation or a commission.

Examples of this type are rare because the cost is often prohibitive and discourages competing publishers. However, they do illustrate Barthes' theory of "plural reading", which gives an active role to the reader — or translator — as an interpreter of the text:

> Mais pour nous qui cherchons à établir un pluriel, nous ne pouvons arrêter ce pluriel aux portes de la lecture: il faut que la lecture soit elle-même plurielle, c'est-à-dire sans ordre d'entrée [...] Il n'y a pas de première lecture, même si le texte s'emploie à nous en donner l'illusion [...] Si donc, contradiction volontaire dans les termes, on relit tout de suite le texte, c'est pour obtenir [...] non le vrai texte mais le texte pluriel: même et nouveau.[32]

Although linguistic accuracy or readability can be assessed, it is more difficult to evaluate the interpretation of the ST, and to give an objective value-judgement on the choices or decisions of the translator. Irina Mavrodin, Proust's Romanian translator, summarises the main issue around retranslation, using the notion of "plural reading" that she attributes to Paul Valéry:

> Il y a plusieurs manières de lire un texte et on peut fournir d'excellentes traductions qui se valent tout en étant très différentes. Si la traduction est une lecture possible parmi d'autres lectures, alors on pourrait intégrer la théorie de la traduction à une théorie de la lecture plurielle telle que Valéry la conçoit, et par conséquent, à une théorie de la réception.[33]

The concept of "plural reading" may offer a more relevant justification of retranslation than could the various arguments around quality improvement. It caters for the need to retranslate on historical and temporal grounds, as well as for the more synchronic existence of several self-standing translations of a classic in a given language.

It is possible to draw some conclusions on the impact of retranslation on the quality of classics in translation. Except for a few special cases of incompetence, and lack of rigour, which can be resolved by revision, the very existence of retranslation, generation after generation, suggests that no clear-cut distinction between right and wrong or good and bad can be made in literary translation. The criteria of quality applied to retranslations cannot be defined in generic universal terms, nor can they avoid temporal changes. The historical dimension discussed above helps to clarify the reasons why classics represent the most common targets for retranslations. Norms of language and literary translation change, and they govern the evolution of quality criteria, which explains in part the need for new translations. In this light, the comparative study of several translations of the same ST can provide an insight into the historical evolution of translation as a process. For example, it could establish whether or not the common notion that retranslations are more ST-oriented than first translations is justified, but so far, this type of descriptive research is lacking, it is not possible to confirm this plausible hypothesis. Retranslation also has a synchronic dimension in the sense that the potential for interpretations and the possible renderings in translation are infinite. We are now moving toward a perception of retranslation as another reading of the ST, with another potential interpretation, another readership, another function in the TL.

If these conditions occur simultaneously, the environment may be appropriate for the production of a "great translation" which will, in time, become established and take its place in the literary heritage of the TL. But on a more practical note, the publication of any retranslation of a classic in English depends largely on publishers' willingness to take a commercial gamble, and it needs to be encouraged as an enriching event in the TL culture, promoting the plural reading of classics. Whether or not a TT becomes a great translation can be decided at a later stage.

Isabelle Vanderschelden

**Notes**

1 Michael Tilby, "Classics in translation", *French Cultural Studies*, Vol. 5, 1994, 209-213.
2 See Terence Kilmartin, "Translating Proust", in *Grand Street*, Vol. 1, 1, 1981, 134-146, for a detailed history of the revision process. See James Grieve, "On Translating Proust", in *Journal of European Studies*, Vol. 12, 1, 55-67, for a reflection on the revision of Proust and on reviews such as Stuart Jeffries, "Making up for Lost Time" in the *Guardian* 16 November 1992, 4-5, George Craig, "Fine-tuning Proust", in the *TLS*, 22 October 1993, 24, or Jonathan Coe, "A Proust for our Times" in the *Guardian*, 12 May 1989, 29. An English translation of *À La recherche du temps perdu* is C.K. Scott-Moncrieff's *Remembrance of Things Past*, London: Chatto & Windus, 1923-1932; revised edition by Kilmartin, Penguin, 1981; subsequently revised by D.J. Enright as *In Search of Lost time*, London: Chatto & Windus, 1993.
*Du côté de chez Swann* was translated as *Swann's Way* by James Grieve, Melbourne: National University of Australia Press, 1982; and by Richard Howard in 1989.
3 See Jeffries' review, 4.
4 See Craig's review, 24.
5 This point was argued by James Grieve in 'On Translating Proust', which analysed the shortcomings of revision, namely omissions, solecisms and syntax problems. He gave many examples and concluded by wishing that a new translation had been commissioned. He himself produced a retranslation of *Swann's Way* shortly after (see note 2).
6 From the preface to the revised edition, Penguin, 1977, 24.
Madame de la Fayette, *La Princesse de Clèves*, trans. Nancy Mitford, London: Euphorion Books, 1950, and Penguin (revised) 1962; revised by Leonard

Tancock, Penguin, 1978; trans. Terence Cave, Oxford: OUP, 1992; trans. Robin Buss, Penguin, 1992.
7  *Assises de la Traduction Littéraire en Arles 90*, Actes Sud, 1991, 57: "[the translation] can also be the other main category: a retranslation undertaken with a view to produce a completely new text, without referring to previous translations as the aim is to replace them not improve them." (My translation). *Assises 90* is a convenient way of referring to discussions on retranslation held at the *Assises de la Traduction Littéraire en Arles 1990*, to which we will refer.
8  See for example various translations of Zola made by Leonard Tancock, or versions of Flaubert's *Madame Bovary* listed in note 10. Tancock's prefaces also highlight the priorities of the Penguin Classics collection in the 1950s and 1960s for example, *Germinal*, Penguin, 1954.
9  D.J. Enright's version (1993) which was partly a retranslation as a second edition of the original came out in the prestigious La Pléiade Collection. Geoff Woollen, "The E. Vizetelly Translations of Zola", unpublished paper, Burns Conference, 1994.
10 The following is a selection of English (re) translations of French Classics mentioned here: Flaubert, *Madame Bovary* (1857): trans. Eleonor Marx-Avelin, London: Vizetelly and Co, 1886 and regularly re-published by various houses until 1949; trans. Gerard Hopkins, New York: Hamish Hamilton, 1948, and Oxford: OUP, 1959, revised OUP, 1981; trans. Alan Russell, Penguin, 1950; trans. Francis Steegmuller, New York: Everyman, 1957; trans. Paul de Man, New York: Norton, 1980; trans. Geoffrey Wall, Penguin, 1993.
Voltaire, *Candide* (1759): trans. Tobias Smollett used in many pocket editions e.g. London: Wordsworth, 1993; trans. Richard Adlington, London: Routledge, 1927; trans. John Butt, Penguin, 1947 and 1990; trans. Lowell Blair, New York: Bantam, 1959; trans. Robert A. Adams, New York: Norton, 1966; trans. Joan Spencer, Oxford: OUP, 1966; trans. Roger Pearson, Oxford: OUP, 1990.
11 For Maupassant, see David Coward "Traduire Maupassant" in *Maupassant, Conteur et romancier*, Lloyd, Christopher and Robert Lethbridge (eds), University of Durham, 1994, 3. Coward found 13 versions of *Une Vie* and 12 of *Bel-Ami*.
12 For examples, see Johnston's interviews of drama translators, *Stages of translations*, Bath: Absolute Classics, 1996. See also translators' prefaces of recent editions of various French plays which are also of interest, e.g. *Landmarks in French Classical Drama*, London: Methuen, 1991, in which feature *The Marriage of Figaro* translated especially by William Gaskill for a performance at the Crucible in Sheffield and *Le Cid* in a new translation by David Bryer which "simplifies many of Corneille's rhetorical devices in the interests of speed and clarity", xxvi.

13 Kevin Jackson's interview with Neil Bartlett and Sian Evans on the translatability of Racine into English, "Getting to the Roots", *The Independent*, 3 February 1990.
14 *Words*, trans. Irene Clephane, Hamish Hamilton, 1964, and Penguin, 1967; *The Words* trans. Bernard Frechtman, New York: Vintage, 1981. *Nausea*, trans. Robert Baldick, Penguin, 1965; trans. Lloyd Alexander, Hamish Hamilton, 1962.
15 Translations of Camus's *L'Étranger*: *The Outsider*, trans. Stuart Gilbert, Hamish Hamilton, 1946 and Penguin 1961; *The Outsider*, trans. Joseph Laredo, Hamish Hamilton, 1982 and Penguin 1983; *The Stranger*, trans. Matthew Ward, Knopf, 1988 and New York: Vintage, 1989.
Translations of Sartre's *La Nausée*: *Nausea* trans. by Lloyd Alexander, Hamish Hamilton, 1962; trans. by Robert Baldick, Penguin, 1965.
16 See Tilby's review, 1994, 213.
17 *Ibid.*, 210.
18 *Madame Bovary*, "A Note on the Translation", Penguin, 1992.
19 Antoine Berman, "La Traduction et la lettre ou l'auberge du lointain", in A. Berman et al., *Les tours de Babel, essais sur la traduction*, Mauzevin: Trans-Europ-Repress, 1985, 116: "It is absolutely essential to make a distinction between two spaces (and two times) of translation: one for first translations, and one for retranslations. This distinction constitutes one of the crucial bases for a reflection on the temporality of translation. [...] The retranslator is no longer confronted by one text, the original, but by two, which creates a specific space — original, first translation, retranslation(s).
Retranslation takes place in favour of the original, but against existing translations. And it is worth noting that it is within this space that, in general, translation has produced masterpieces. First translations are not (and cannot be) the greatest." (My translation).
20 Antoine Berman, "La retraduction comme espace de la traduction", *Palimpsestes*, vol. 4, 1986, 4: "Toute traduction est défaillante, c'est-à-dire entropique, quels que soient ses principes. Ce qui veut dire: toute traduction est marquée par de la «non-traduction. Et les premières traductions sont celles qui sont le plus frappées par la non-traduction». Tout se passe comme si les forces anti-traductives qui provoquent la «défaillance» étaient, ici, toutes puissantes. [...]. La re-traduction surgit de la nécessité non certes de supprimer, mais au moins de réduire la défaillance originelle".
"Every translation is deficient, that is to say entropic, whatever its principles. This means that any translation is marked by some "non-translation". And first translations are those which are most affected by non-translation. It is as though the anti-translating forces which cause deficiency were in that case most powerful. [...]. Retranslation is a result of the need, not to suppress entirely, but at least to reduce previous deficiency." (My translation).

21 *Assises* 90, 50-51: "When you translate a text at the time of its publication, it is always difficult to know how it will evolve, especially if it is to become an important work. There are parameters that cannot be considered when translating starts whilst the ST is still being written. [...] I think that retranslation is then like a 'cold' process. The first translation is working on a 'hot' ST, the next on a 'cold' one, benefitting from the hindsight and distance that 20 or 30 years make possible, and also from progress in translation theory." (My translation). This is also analysed in David Bellos' unpublished paper "Some Like it Hot: Hot and Cold Translations" presented at the Burns Conference in 1994.
22 Matthew Ward, Translator's note to *The Stranger*, New York: Vintage, 1989, vi.
23 An analysis of translators' introductions is beyond the scope of this article, but for more information see for example Tancock's prefaces or essays or more generally translator's introductions of classics.
24 Faber and Faber, 1998. The translation was commissioned and first performed in London in September 1998.
25 Demanuelli, *Assises* 90, 50: "Je crois aussi qu'on a tendance, dans une première traduction, à asservir le texte-source à la langue-cible pour que précisément ce texte soit plus accessible à un public qui ne connaît pas encore l'œuvre". "I also think that there is a tendency to make the ST subservient to the demands of the TL in a first translation, so that the TT becomes more accessible to a readership who does not yet know the literary work." (My translation).
26 "La retraduction comme espace de la traduction", 5. In "La Retraduction, retour et détour", *Méta*, Vol. 39, 3, 1994, 413-417, Yves Gambier also discusses this evolution in detail.
27 *Ibid.*, 6: "A un moment donné il devient «enfin» possible de traduire une œuvre. [...] Il devient possible d'inscrire la signifiance d'une œuvre dans notre espace langagier". "At a given time it becomes possible 'at last' to translate a literary work. [...] It is at last possible to convey all the work's meaning into our own language space". (My translation).
28 "La retraduction comme espace de la traduction", 5: "It is a special type of abundance: rich language, extensively or intensively, rich relationship with the ST, textual richness, rich meaning ..." (My translation).
29 *Ibid.*, 3: "They represent an event in the TL; they are extremely systematic; they are the meeting point between the language of the translator and that of the original; they create an intense link with the original; they constitute a precedent; they are all retranslations". (My translation).
Berman's examples include St Jerome's *Vulgate*, Luther's *Bible*, Galland's *Mille et Une Nuits*, Schlegel's Shakespeare, and he has made some detailed analyses of texts that he considers to be great translations, for example Chateaubriand's translation of Milton's *Paradise Lost*, in *La traduction et la lettre*, 109.

30 Roger Huss, "Translating Flaubert" *TLS*, 22 October 1993, 24.
31 Peter France, "Love on a Tight Rein", *TLS*, 1 January 1993, 20.
32 *S/Z*, Paris: Seuil, 1970, 22-23. Trans. Richard Miller, London: Blackwell, 1974, 15-16: "But for those of us trying to establish a plural, we cannot stop this plural at the gates of reading; the reading must also be plural, that is without order of entrance [...]. [T]here is no *first* reading, even if the text is concerned to give us that illusion by several operations of *suspense* [...]. If then, a deliberate contradiction in terms, we *immediately* reread the text, it is in order to obtain [...] not the *real* text, but a plural text: the same and new".
See also the chapter "La lecture plurielle" in J.B. Fages, *Comprendre Roland Barthes*, Toulouse: Privat, 1979, 159-170.
33 *Assises* 90, 24: "There are several ways to read a text and it is possible to offer different translations which are as valid although very different. If translation constitutes one possible reading amongst others, we could then relate translation theory to the theory of plural reading such as Valery sees it, and hence to a form of reception theory". (My translation).

## 2.
## IN SEARCH OF THE FOREIGN:
## A STUDY OF THE THREE ENGLISH TRANSLATIONS OF
## CAMUS'S *L'ÉTRANGER*

This paper originated from a number of factors. *L'Étranger* appeared in 1942[1], and its first translation, by Stuart Gilbert, was published in 1946.[2] The second translation, by Joseph Laredo, came out in 1982,[3] and the third, performed by Matthew Ward, came out in 1988.[4] According to J.M. Cohen, "Every great book demands to be re-translated once in a century, to suit the change in standards and taste of new generations, which will differ radically from those of the past".[5] Cohen may be seen as being a little pessimistic as regards the frequency of retranslation, but nevertheless it is pretty rare for a contemporary novel to be translated three times within the forty years following its publication. As I wondered what motivated the retranslations, I was reminded of Goethe's famous statement on retranslation:

> There are three kinds of translations. The first acquaints us with the foreign country on our own terms; [...]. A second epoch follows, in which the translator attempts to place himself into the foreign situation but actually only appropriates the foreign idea and represents it as his own. [...] The third epoch of translation [...] is the final and highest of the three. In this, the goal of the translation is to achieve perfect identity with the original, [...]. The reason why we call the third epoch the final one can be explained in a few words. A translation that attempts to identify itself with the original ultimately comes close to an interlinear version and greatly facilitates our understanding of the original.[6]

It was tempting to put the grand old man's declaration to the test and see whether the three successive translations of *L'Étranger* conformed to the ideal of an increasingly close reproduction of the original and especially of its foreign flavour. Hence my choice of title for this article, generated with the existence in French, of a pun on the title of the novel itself "L'Étranger" and Goethe's ideal of "the foreign flavour".

Viewed from the perspectives of contemporary translation and translation studies, retranslations are interesting for historical and ontological reasons. One could question the validity of Goethe's statement by stressing that it belongs to another age, and that literal translation, or translation which emphasizes formal equivalence, is no longer in fashion. The general trend nowadays is for "communicative translation", that is translations which are freed from the fetters of linguistic form and are turned or tuned to the public's tastes and expectations. But, on the other hand, any kind of generalisation has to be qualified by a look at reality. Goethe's views on translation have survived and have been revisited in recent years in literary circles, by Berman[7] in France, and more recently by Venuti in the United States. Rather than speaking of a triadic cycle, these modern theoreticians appear to favour a binary opposition which might well serve our purpose. I quote Venuti:

> A translator [can] choose the now traditional domesticating method, an ethnocentric reduction of the foreign text to dominant cultural values in English; or a translator [can] choose a foreignizing method, an ethnodeviant pressure on those values to register the linguistic and cultural differences of the foreign text.[8]

I wished, then, to see whether Goethe's theorem, which has to some extent been revisited by modern theoreticians, could be verified with the test of a concrete case of retranslation, and I decided to organize my study along the two main lines which are suggested by Venuti's statement. The first of these is what might roughly be termed the cultural paradigm, and the second the linguistic and stylistic paradigm.

## The Cultural Paradigm

Within the cultural paradigm I have attempted to identify four categories in which the degree of domestication or preservation of the foreign text could be measured. The first two of these categories are connected with the designation of individuals, that is the translation of proper names and titles, whilst the third and fourth of my categories are connected with objects and institutions, i.e. the translation of units of measurement and of cultural referents.

## Proper names

These could be described as the translated text's ultimate link with the original because, as a rule, they are not translated. Their preservation is a concession to the foreign language and culture, contributing to the local colour and general foreign flavour of the text, if only through their phonetic or graphic strangeness. All of the three translations preserve names, and even such a simple and apparently obvious practice as this is, calls for a number of remarks concerning its effects. Initially I shall explore this by using one of the first sentences in the novel as an example:

> L'asile de vieillards est à Marengo, à quatre-vingts kilomètres d'Alger. (Camus 1942/1957:7)

> The Home for Aged Persons is at Marengo, some fifty miles from Algiers. (Gilbert 1946:13)

The above provides an instance of different treatments of signifiers of proper names: "Marengo" is not translated, whereas the town named "Alger" in French has an equivalent English spelling, so the term does not sound so foreign as "Marengo", even if it is more exotic in its connotations. As for the signified, it can be said to operate at two levels: denotation and connotation. At the level of denotation, those names are markers indicating that the action takes place in Algeria. As regards connotation, the meaning, images, or associations will vary according to the reader, quite independently from the translator's action.

The name "Marengo" may not mean much to the average English speaker, but for many French people it is connected with classroom memories of a victorious campaign in Italy by Napoleon, or even more commonly perhaps with "veau Marengo", a type of veal casserole in tomato sauce, a dish created on the day of that battle. These associations really belong to the collective unconscious and they cannot be conveyed by straight transposition at an individual word level. This indicates that proper names can carry a great deal of hidden meaning. The simultaneous presence of those two names in the same sentence symbolises the dual nature of the Algeria of those days, when there was an indigenous element which was expressed in native names such as Algiers, and a French element was superimposed, visible in that imported name assigned to the town, thus flagging up French history.

It is indicative of the cultural importance of proper names (and of their degree of foreignness) that after the departure of the French the town of Marengo was renamed "Hadjout".

The name "Algiers" will possibly only evoke a more or less exotic Arab country in North Africa to the Anglo-Saxon or European reader, whereas to the French reader it is likely to carry with it the connotations of past conflict and of a time when the country was considered part of France. For Camus himself, however, Algeria was his home, his native country and connected with memories of childhood and youth, mixed with the deep love of the countryside and atmosphere of the place which transpires in his descriptions in *Noces* and *L'Été*. It is unclear whether that Algeria was exotic to him, even if he regarded it as a kind of paradise. It is significant that the editor of the first translation, Cyril Connolly, felt the need to give a description of Camus as an Algerian in his introduction:

> What is an Algerian? He is not a French colonial, but a citizen of France domiciled in North Africa, a man of the Mediterranean, an *homme du midi* yet one who hardly partakes of the traditional Mediterranean culture, unlike Valéry whose roots spread from Sète by way of Montpellier to Genoa; for him there is no eighteenth century, no baroque, no Renaissance, no crusades or troubadours in the past of the Barbary Coast; nothing but the Roman Empire, decaying dynasties of Turk and Moor, the French Conquest and the imposition of the laws and commerce of the Third Republic on the ruins of Islam.[9]

The image of Algeria conveyed by Camus in *L'Étranger* is Mediterranean in a generic and disembodied way, hardly connected with the native Arab element and only loosely connected with southern France. This break with the traditional cultural outlook of the home country contributes to Camus being perceived as something of a stranger himself, and we shall see that it has significant connections with the style he adopted for this novel.

The first conclusion to be drawn regarding the translation of proper names is that the three translators follow common practice, achieving the usual effect of the conveyance of local colour. On the other hand, one is confronted with an irremediable, if variable, loss on the side of the foreign readers due to their relative unfamiliarity with the cultural referent of those names. This raises the question of notes and paratexts in connection with translation, and in this respect only the first Penguin edition, with Connolly's introduction, provides some general information for the new readership.

*Titles and designators*

In the first line of the novel, the word "Maman" is used. This is normally translated by "mother", and this is the solution which is adopted by both Gilbert and Laredo. None of the translators uses "mum" or "mummy", but Ward goes against linguistic tradition by using the borrowed word: "maman" in his translation. Later the warden says to Meursault: "Mme Meursault est entrée ici il y a trois ans" (Camus:9). This is a case of the use of a designator in conjunction with a proper name, and it is treated rather differently by the three translators, who are not always coherent in their own general policy in this respect. Laredo, who is normally something of a literalist, uses the English form: "Mrs Meursault came here three years ago." (Laredo:10), whilst Gilbert, who usually tends to anglicize the text, retains and even develops the French form of address: "Madame Meursault entered the Home three years ago." (Gilbert:14). Ward acts in the same way, indulging once again his tendency to integrate French: "Madame Meursault came to us three years ago." (Ward:4).

The "concierge" is a stock character of French realistic or humouristic literature, and is usually connected with the idea of nosiness. A possible equivalent in English culture could be the landlady.[10] Of course, this form of transfer is not possible here, and Gilbert uses "door-porter" whilst Laredo and Ward both choose "caretaker". None of the three translations retains the French word. In fact "concierge" does not appear in the Oxford *Advanced Learner's Dictionary* but it does in Longman's *Dictionary of Contemporary English* and it is also used in a textbook edited by Monica Charlot,[11] indicating that its use could be a possibility.

"Le directeur" of the Home becomes "the warden" in both Gilbert and Laredo, but Ward uses the Latin originate "director". In direct speech, French speakers use the title as a form of address: "J'ai dit: «Oui, monsieur le Directeur»" (Camus:9-10), whereas English usage favours the more hyperonymic "sir", as does each of the three translators. In the court-room, when he is examined by the judge, Meursault replies: "Oui, monsieur le Président" (Camus:129). Gilbert chooses the neutral form "Yes, sir" whereas both Laredo and Ward use the domesticating form "Yes, Your Honour" (Laredo:85, and Ward:87). Once again in the court-room the narrator Meursault says he follows "les instructions de mon avocat" (Camus:129), and the three translators employ the term "lawyer". Even Ward does not go so far as a more precise word such as "barrister" or "advocate".

A conclusion that can be drawn about the translation of designators is that it evinces Ward's attempt to preserve the foreign flavour of the text, either through borrowing ("maman", "madame"), or by the use of a word of latin origin ("Director"), but at the same time one must acknowledge that the translators' policies here are not entirely homogeneous. Ward misses or refuses a number of opportunities.

*Units of measurement*

These are subjected to contrasting treatments: Gilbert and Laredo favour conversion, with the aim of naturalization and the translation of meaning:

> L'asile de vieillards est à Marengo, à quatre-vingts kilomètres d'Alger. (Camus 1942/1957:7)

> The Home for Aged Persons is at Marengo, some fifty miles from Algiers. (Gilbert 1946:13)

> The old people's home is at Marengo, fifty miles from Algiers. (Laredo:9)

Ward opts for preservation with the aim of foreignization: "eighty kilometers".

*Cultural referents*

The warden of the home is described as "un petit vieux, avec la Légion d'honneur." (Camus:9), and Laredo gives the most literal translation: "a small, elderly man with the Legion of Honour" (Laredo:10). Gilbert and Ward both use expanded translations which convey annotative descriptions:

> The Warden was a very small man, with grey hair and a Legion of Honour rosette in his buttonhole. (Gilbert:14)

He was a little old man with the ribbon of the Legion of Honor in his lapel. (Ward:4)

Both additions are very visual and efficiently convey the image present in the mind of French people when that decoration is mentioned. This is a case when simply borrowing the term is perhaps not sufficient for the average reader of a translation.

## The Linguistic and Stylistic Paradigms

*Paragraphs and general layout*

According to Vinay and Darbelnet:

> Since punctuation differs from language to language, we can readily accept that two languages do not have the same conventions about layout of text either. [...] A simple count of paragraphs in bilingual Canadian or European documents shows that for the same text English uses fewer paragraphs than French and that paragraph borders do not always coincide.[12]

This statement has to be qualified with regard to translation by bearing in mind the options of the translators, particularly in their tendency to clarify the text at both visual and intellectual levels. This technique is particularly visible in Gilbert's work. The second paragraph of the first chapter of *L'Étranger* is comparatively long, and Gilbert divides it into two in his own text, the unity of his third paragraph being made up of the hero's reflections following his apologies to his employer. In contrast to this, the other two translators preserve the paragraph format of the source. Gilbert's propensity to air, or expand, the text appears in another form with his translation of the fourth paragraph of the novel. The French text here contains both narrative and dialogue, interspersed with reflections. Both Laredo and Ward retain this layout, whilst Gilbert creates distinct paragraphs for the dialogue and the interior monologue.

*Latin words*

One way of communicating the flavour of the French original is to use a Latin word, despite the fact that an English alternative may exist, or, if possible, to use a calque of the word found in the source text. These are techniques which Laredo uses frequently. For instance when Meursault says: "J'ai cru qu'il me reprochait quelque chose [...]". (Camus:9). Laredo translates: "I felt as if he was reproaching me for something." (Laredo:10), whereas Gilbert writes: "I had a feeling he was blaming me for something." (Gilbert:14), whilst Ward uses: "I thought he was criticizing me for something." (Ward:5).

Here are two more examples:

Mais il m'a interrompu. (Camus:9)
But he interrupted me. (Laredo:10)
But he cut me short. (Gilbert:14)
But he cut me off. (Ward:4)

Vous n'avez pas à vous justifier. (Camus:9)
You've no need to justify yourself. (Laredo:10)
There's no need to excuse yourself. (Gilbert:14)
You don't have to justify yourself. (Ward:5)

Gilbert even resorts at times to the technique of modulation in order not to use an equivalent of Latin origin:

Deux d'entre eux [chevalets], au centre, supportaient une bière recouverte de son couvercle. (Camus:12)

Two of the latter stood open in the centre of the room and the coffin rested on them. (Gilbert:16)

whilst both Laredo and Ward simply translate this with:

Two of these, in the centre of the room, were supporting a coffin. (Laredo:12)

Two of them, in the middle of the room, were supporting a closed casket. (Ward:6)

*Idioms*

These culture-specific fixed expressions "often carry meanings which cannot be deduced from their individual components",[13] and moreover they "cannot generally be translated literally into another language and preserve [their] meaning".[14] They stand at the frontier of literal translation and could appear as constituting a limitation on the possibility of preserving the foreign flavour of the text. However, as we shall see, idioms are not as impassable a barrier as one might imagine.

There are relatively few idioms in *L'Étranger*, perhaps as a consequence of Camus's attempt to achieve a style which is, like his hero, devoid of ornamentation. Idiomatic phrases in dialogues and in narratives concerned with Meursault's life in Algiers can be found. Take for example, the scene when Meursault and Emmanuel run after a lorry:

> J'ai pris appui le premier et j'ai sauté au vol. Puis j'ai aidé Emmanuel à s'asseoir. Nous étions hors de souffle, le camion sautait sur les pavés inégaux du quai, au milieu de la poussière et du soleil. Emmanuel riait à perdre haleine. Nous sommes arrivés en nage chez Céleste. (Camus:40)

Gilbert, as is his want, tampers with the text (additions are underlined and omissions are put between square brackets in the text below). The other two translators are relatively successful in rendering idiomatic phrases, and do not work against set equivalences in order to reach a calque. This, with all due respect to literalists, would be meaningless when idioms are involved, as for instance in the case of "arriver en nage":

> I was the first <u>to catch up with the truck</u>. I took a flying jump, <u>landed safely</u>, and helped Emmanuel to scramble in beside me. We were both out of breath and the bumps of the truck on the roughly laid cobbles made things worse [au milieu de la poussière et du soleil]. Emmanuel chuckled, <u>and panted in my ear, 'We've made it!'</u>
>
> By the time we reached Céleste's restaurant we were dripping with sweat. (Gilbert:33-34)

Laredo is more sober and sticks to the text:

> I caught hold first and took a flying leap. Then I helped Emmanuel up. We were both out of breath and the lorry was jumping about in the sun and the dust on the rough cobbles of the quayside. Emmanuel was laughing so much he could hardly breathe.
>
> We arrived at Céleste's dripping with sweat. (Laredo:30)

Ward is fairly literal too:

> I was the first to grab hold and take a flying leap. Then I reached out and helped Emmanuel scramble up. We were out of breath; the truck was bumping around on the uneven cobblestones of the quay in a cloud of dust and sun. Emmanuel was laughing so hard he could hardly breathe.
>
> We arrived at Céleste's dripping with sweat. (Ward:26)

All three translators experience rather more difficulty in providing a close or literal rendering of spoken speech, particularly when Camus transcribes the French dialect spoken by the popular classes of Algiers. This can be seen when Meursault relates a conversation that he had with his neighbour, the pimp Raymond Sintès:

> «Vous comprenez, monsieur Meursault, m'a-t-il dit, c'est pas que je suis méchant, mais je suis vif. L'autre, il m'a dit: «Descend du tram si tu es un homme.» Je lui ai dit: « Allez, reste tranquille.» Il m'a dit que je n'étais pas un homme. Alors je suis descendu et je lui ai dit: «Assez, ça vaut mieux, ou je vais te mûrir.» (Camus:44-45)

The register is made up of specific constructions and idiomatic phrases of the figurative type. Once again Gilbert's translation, though not entirely inaccurate, does not attempt to render the foreign flavour even if it is a realistic possibility:

> 'I'm not one who looks for trouble', he explained, 'only I'm a bit short-tempered'. That fellow said to me, challenging, like, 'Come down off that tram, if you're a man', I says, 'You keep quiet, I ain't done nothing to you.' Then he said I hadn't any guts. Well, that settled it. I got down off the tram and said to him, 'you better keep your mouth shut, or I'll shut it for you.' (Gilbert:36)

> 'You see, Meursault', he said, 'it's not that I'm a troublemaker, but I'm no coward'. This bloke, he said to me, 'Get down off that tram, if you're a man.' I said to him, 'Just calm down, okay.' Then he said I wasn't a man. So I got down and said to him, 'All right, that's enough, or you'll get flattened.' (Laredo:32)

> 'You see, Monsieur Meursault,' he said, 'it's not that I'm a bad guy, but I have a short fuse'. This guy says to me, 'If you're man enough you'll get down off that streetcar.' I said, 'C'mon, take it easy.' Then he said, 'You're yellow.' So I got off and said to him, I think you better stop right there or I'm gonna have to teach you a lesson.' (Ward:29)

The phatic introduction, which is so characteristic of the beginnings of conversations in French, is deleted by Gilbert: "Vous comprenez, monsieur Meursault", whereas both Laredo and Ward retain this form; Ward is even more literal than Laredo for: "c'est pas que je suis méchant", translating it with "It's not that I'm a bad guy". Ward tends to overidiomatize certain renderings, as for instance in the case of "je suis vif", which he renders by "I have a short fuse". Gilbert translates this in a quite classical way, with "quick-tempered". Of the three translators Laredo is the only one to keep the repetition of "if you're a man", the other two prefer to use an idiomatized item as anaphoric: "he said I hadn't any guts" (Gilbert), and "You're yellow" (Ward). The typical French segmented structure: "L'autre, il m'a dit" is treated with a form of domesticating compensation by Gilbert: "That fellow said to me, challenging, like." (Gilbert). On the other hand Laredo attempts to preserve something of the original with, "This bloke, he said to me" (Laredo). For his part Ward literally flattens it out by saying: "This guy says to me" (Ward).

None of the three translators is able to overcome the obstacle of an etymological translation of "je vais te mûrir". Laredo's "or you'll get flattened" is something of an undertranslation. The phrase used by Camus does not belong to standard French slang and seems to be typical of former Algerian French residents. It can be understood in two, not dissimilar ways; either it may mean: "I'll punch your face till it looks like an overripe fruit" or "till it is the colour of a blackberry". From that point of view a suitable rendering might be something like "I'll beat/punch your face black and blue", but whether or not this is a suitable collocation is debatable.

*Contrastive linguistics and style*

In the *Routledge Encyclopedia of Translation Studies*, Michael Hoey and Diane Houghton define contrastive linguistics as "a linguistic study of two languages, aiming to identify differences between them in general or in selected areas."[15] For instance, the study of contrastive linguistics can identify language tendencies such as the more extensive use of the passive voice in English. Linguists and translation studies scholars have distinguished discourse tendencies:

> French, at least in its literary, philosophical, scientific and legal discourse, cultivates these structural markers and finds it difficult to manage without the connections they can bring to the presentation of thought. English, on the other hand, even in its traditional written forms, is much less dependent on these explicit connectors and instead relies on the juxtaposition, or parataxis, of

the elements of the utterance, leaving it to the readers to provide for themselves the necessary connections.[16]

Delisle's statement "Il est admis que l'anglais manifeste une certaine prédilection pour la juxtaposition et la coordination alors que le français préfère l'articulation et la subordination."[17] is exemplified and supported by quotations from French linguists, and the translations of *L'Étranger* confirm, at least in part, the truth of this remark on French and English discourse.

> Puis il m'a serré la main qu'il a gardée si longtemps que je ne savais trop comment la retirer. (Camus:9)

> Then we shook hands, and he held mine so long that I began to feel embarrassed. (Gilbert:14)

> Then he shook my hand and held it for so long that I didn't quite know how to take it back again. (Laredo:10)

> Then he shook my hand and held it so long I didn't know how to get it loose. (Ward:4)

As a matter of fact, in this case, each of the three translators has turned the relative clause into a coordinate clause and they seem to conform to linguistic conventions.

When I examined connectors in *Relations Discursives* I noted that the importance of subjectivity had been underestimated.[18] For instance translators, for all sorts of reasons, do not necessarily follow the same tendencies when dealing with discourse. If we consider the following example:

> J'ai dormi pendant presque tout le trajet. Et quand je me suis réveillé, j'étais tassé contre un militaire qui m'a souri et qui m'a demandé si je venais de loin. (Camus:8-9)

> Anyhow, I slept most of the way. When I woke I was leaning up against a soldier; he grinned, and asked me if I'd come from a long way of, and I just nodded, to cut things short. (Gilbert:14)

> And when I woke up, I found myself cramped up against a soldier who smiled at me and asked me if I'd come far. (Laredo:10)

> And when I woke up, I was slumped against a soldier who smiled at me and asked if I'd been traveling long. (Ward:4)

The French text contains two relative clauses, which are replaced by an independent clause in Gilbert. In this he follows the patterns of correspondence revealed by contrastive analysis, and, as such, could be described as a translator who listens to his own language, whereas Laredo and Ward both seem to be more receptive to the foreign language and to attempt to replicate the form of the original. But this pattern is comparatively limited because there are few subordinate clauses in *L'Étranger*. Atypically as regards French, this novel contains a large number of coordinate clauses, which however are common in English discourse.

The study of *L'Étranger* and its translations is particularly interesting from this point of view as it can show the limitations of certain generalisations which have been developed from contrastive linguistics, when these do not take into account the fact that a text is not just made up of abstract or standard language, but rather a text is a language which has been turned into a style. Barthes situates Camus as among: "ces écritures neutres, appelées ici «le degré zéro de l'écriture»",[19] which he describes in the following terms:

> L'écriture blanche, celle de Camus, celle de Blanchot ou de Cayrol par exemple, ou l'écriture parlée de Queneau, c'est le dernier épisode d'une Passion de l'écriture, qui suit pas à pas le déchirement de la conscience bourgeoise.[20]

Camus's style is seen as a historical event, something of a landmark, in the evolution of French prose:

> L'écriture neutre est un fait tardif, elle ne sera inventée que bien après le réalisme, par des auteurs comme Camus, moins sous l'effet d'une esthétique du refuge que par la recherche d'une esthétique enfin innocente. L'écriture réaliste est loin d'être neutre, elle est au contraire chargée des signes les plus spectaculaires de la fabrication.[21]

Barthes continues in more detail:

> La nouvelle écriture neutre[...]; c'est plutôt une écriture innocente. Il s'agit de dépasser ici la littérature en se confiant à une sorte de langue basique, également éloignée des langages vivants et du langage littéraire proprement dit. Cette parole transparente, inaugurée par *L'Étranger* de Camus, accomplit un style de l'absence

> qui est presque une absence idéale du style; l'écriture se réduit alors à une sorte de mode négatif dans lequel les caractères sociaux ou mythiques d'un langage s'abolissent au profit d'un état neutre et inerte de la forme; [...].²²

The apparent simplicity of Camus's style, as to a degree with that of Queneau, is actually a deliberate attempt to break away from classical French models, partly through the use of patterns derived from oral language. Moreover, in *L'Étranger* this coincides with an effort to create a style which reflects a rather naïve (or innocent) and disconnected perception of the world. This quality is achieved through two main stylistic devices: the use of short sentences and the unwonted use of coordination. Generally speaking, sentences are very short in *L'Étranger*, the shortest kind being the simple sentence (subject — verb — object — adverbial) sometimes barely a line long. These short sentences convey the image of the unsophisticated hero who comprehends the world around him in small touches, at a level of immediacy which precludes elaborate thought.

Gilbert does not hesitate to go against this pattern, merging two sentences into one, generally by using coordination:

> J'ai lu le dossier de votre mère. Vous ne pouviez subvenir à ses besoins. (Camus:9)

> I've looked up the record and obviously you weren't in a position to see that she was properly cared for. (Gilbert:14)

The other translators retain the separate sentences:

> I've read your mother's file. You weren't able to look after her properly. (Laredo:10)

> I've read your mother's file. You weren't able to provide for her properly. (Ward:4)

I quote another example:

> Un jour [...] un gardien est entré et m'a dit que j'avais une visite. J'ai pensé que c'était Marie. C'était bien elle. (Camus:107)

> One day [...] a warder entered and said I had a visitor. I thought it must be Marie, and so it was. (Gilbert:76)

> One day [...], a warder came in and told me that I had a visitor. I thought it must be Marie. It was. (Laredo:72)

> One day [...] a guard came in and told me I had a visitor. I thought it must be Marie. It was. (Ward:73)

Another device used by Camus in order to increase the number of short sentences is to use the stylistic full stop: instead of having a form of complex sentence with two coordinated clauses, he separates them with a full stop before the conjunction. In the case of the famous beginning: "Aujourd'hui, maman est morte. Ou peut-être hier, je ne sais pas." (Camus:7), the three translators follow the original:

> Mother died today. Or, maybe, yesterday; I can't be sure. (Gilbert:13)

> Mother died today. Or maybe yesterday, I don't know. (Laredo:9)

> Mother died today. Or yesterday maybe, I don't know. (Ward:3)

Sometimes Gilbert breaks this pattern by creating longer sentences:

> J'ai voulu voir maman tout de suite. Mais le concierge m'a dit qu'il fallait que je rencontre le directeur. (Camus:9)

> I asked to be allowed to see Mother at once, but the door-porter told me I must see the Warden first. (Gilbert:14)

> I wanted to see mother straight away. But the caretaker told me I had to meet the Warden. (Laredo:11)

The short sentences which are so characteristic of *L'Étranger*, particularly in the first part of the novel which has few syntactic connectors, are the grammatical or stylistic expression of the absence of logic or causality as perceived by Meursault. The narrative constitutes a record of actions, punctuated by the monotonous repetition of "je" at the beginning of sentences:

> L'asile de vieillards est à Marengo, à quatre-vingts kilomètres d'Alger. Je prendrai l'autobus à deux heures et j'arriverai dans l'après-midi. Ainsi, je pourrai veiller et je rentrerai demain soir. J'ai demandé deux jours de congé à mon patron et il ne pouvait pas me les refuser avec une excuse pareille. Mais il n'avait pas l'air content. Je lui ai même dit « Ce n'est pas de ma faute. » Il n'a pas répondu. J'ai pensé alors que je n'aurais pas dû lui dire cela. En somme, je n'avais pas à m'excuser. C'était plutôt à lui de me présenter ses condoléances. (Camus:7-8)

The nine instances of "je", the first person singular, of the above passage are reduced to seven in Gilbert's translation:

> The Home for Aged Persons is at Marengo, some fifty miles from Algiers. With the two-o'clock bus I should get there well before nightfall. Then I can spend the night there, keeping the usual vigil beside the body, and be back here by tomorrow evening. I have fixed up with my employer for two day's leave; obviously, under the circumstances, he couldn't refuse. Still, I had an idea he looked annoyed, and I said, without thinking: 'Sorry, sir, but it's not my fault, you know.'
>
> Afterwards it struck me I needn't have said that. I had no reason to excuse myself; it was up to him to express his sympathy and so forth. (Gilbert:13)

Finally there are a number of boundaries, especially with regard to word order and constructions, which translators seem wary of overstepping. For instance, the French tend more frequently to place adverbials at the beginning of sentences: "Aujourd'hui, maman est morte." (Camus:7). This is not an impossibility in English and yet in the present example none of the translators goes against the conventional English word order: "Mother died today."

Thematisation is another typical French construction. An element is taken up in the main body of the sentence as an object or adverbial phrase in the form of a pronoun:

> J'ai couru pour ne pas manquer le départ. Cette hâte, cette course, c'est à cause de tout cela sans doute, ajouté aux cahots, à l'odeur d'essence, à la réverbération de la route et du ciel, que je me suis assoupi. (Camus 1942:8)

The three translators all reduce the string of thematised nominal juxtapositions and the pronoun, to a single phrase: "my hurrying like that" (Gilbert), "all this dashing about" (Laredo), "all the rushing about" (Ward), leading to slight stylistic loss, as Camus uses the apparent simplicity and the rhythm of Meursault's speech to produce something close to the canons of classical verse. But it must be acknowledged that they all attempt to make up for the loss by inserting extra coordinations which recreate something of the rhythm of the original. This use of a stylistic device which is typical of the receptor language is a fine example of transposition, but it does not result in the preservation of the foreign touch:

> I had to run to catch the bus. I suppose it was my hurrying like that, what with the glare off the road and from the sky, the reek of petrol and the jolts, that made me feel so drowsy. (Gilbert:14)

> I had to run for the bus. It was probably all this dashing about and then the jolting and the smell of petrol and the glare of the sky reflecting off the road that made me doze off. (Laredo:10)

> I ran so as not to miss the bus. It was probably because of all the rushing around, and on top of that the bumpy ride, the smell of gasoline, and the glare of the sky and the road, that I dozed off. (Ward:4)

## Conclusion

This study focuses on various issues concerning the status and nature of translation. In the first instance, the desire to expose the reader to a foreign culture raises questions of both the preservation and the reception of cultural elements. This presupposes a certain degree of openness and curiosity on the part of the reader, but it is not enough for the translator merely to preserve traces of foreign culture. Rather he should aim to clarify matters through the use of a preface and of notes, whilst attempting to avoid the excess of an overscholarly edition. A translation need not look like an original, in terms of layout it ought to assert its specificity. If translation lays claim to the introduction of foreign culture to a mass public, then it should make the foreign culture accessible, otherwise translation may become no more than an almost meaningless rendition of local colour. The introduction to the first Penguin edition was particularly welcome regarding this point.

Secondly, whilst assessing the linguistic dimension of the operation of transfer, I noted how frequently translation deals with paradoxes. Of course it is tempting to take particular translations as a basis for generalizations on language, but the study of texts rapidly reveals that they are as much the product of a linguistic system, as they are the product of the individual use of that system, turned into a style. The linguistic paradox of *L'Étranger* is that the novel epitomizes a moment in the history of French stylistics: when Camus and others were bringing their style closer to an Anglo-Saxon way of writing, embodied to an extent by the contemporary American novel, as typified in Hemingway's prose. Theoretically, Camus's style in *L'Étranger* should translate easily into English, sounding hardly foreign at all. I hope that I have managed to convey already, that there are at least two limitations to this. These are the translator's action, as exemplified by Stuart Gilbert, and more generally speaking, a resistance on the part of language in which it seems to reach an irreducible otherness, as in the case of certain constructions, idioms, and specific flavours of spoken jargon or register.

Finally I return to one of the preliminaries of my introduction, the validity of theorisation and its relation to the reality of translation. The translations of *L'Étranger* are to some extent a fairly good illustration of the validity of Goethe's statement, particularly insofar as Gilbert and Laredo are concerned. Ward's translation is a mixed case of the acceptance of the foreign, with the voluntary or involuntary introduction of domestic or personal touches. Reality is never so clear as generalisation: translation is rarely pure and homogeneous. Rather than describing translation as a natural ethical movement towards the fuller acceptance of foreign elements, I would see it to be a cyclic movement in which theoreticians and critics, as well as translators themselves are agents. I would argue that Gilbert's translation recalls the *belles infidèles*, with the tendency it displays for censorship and the alteration of cultural elements, with its loose re-creation and recourse to paraphrase. Laredo's work is a good example of scrupulous translation; and Ward's, also carefully performed, is proof that the translator does not easily relinquish his idiosyncrasies. A fitting way to describe translation is perhaps to say that it constitutes negotiation in a quest for the foreign.

Michel Ballard

## Notes

1 Albert Camus, *L'Étranger* (1942), Paris: Gallimard (Livre de Poche), 1957.
2 Albert Camus, *The Outsider*, trans. S. Gilbert (1946), Harmondsworth: Penguin, 1966.
3 Albert Camus, *The Outsider*, trans. J. Laredo (1982), Harmondsworth: Penguin, 1985.
4 Albert Camus, *The Stranger*, trans. M. Ward (1988), New York: Vintage Books, 1989.
5 J.M. Cohen, *English Translators and Translations*, London: Longmans, ("Writers and their Work"), 1962, 9.
6 Goethe in Rainer Schulte and John Biguenet, *Theories of Translation. An anthology of Essays from Dryden to Derrida*, Chicago and London: The University of Chicago Press, 1992, 60-63.
7 Antoine Berman, "La traduction et la lettre" in A. Berman et al., *Les tours de Babel, essais sur la traduction*, Mauvezin: Trans-Europ-Repress, 1985, 31-150.
8 Lawrence Venuti, *The Translator's Invisibility. A History of Translation*, London and New York: Routledge ("Translation Studies"), 1995, 81.
9 Cyril Connolly, "Introduction" to Stuart Gilbert's translation of *L'Étranger, The Outsider (1946)*, Harmondsworth: Penguin, 1966, 5.
10 This is a stand taken by Donald Watson in his translation of Ionesco's *Le nouveau locataire*, a statement made by himself in Donald Watson, "Bon esprit, bon sens ou bons mots?", *Palimpsestes*, n°1, 1987, 116.
11 Monica Charlot et al., *Pratique du thème anglais,* Paris: A. Colin, 1982, 60-61.
12 Jean-Paul Vinay and Jean Darbelnet, *Comparative Stylistics of French and English. A Methodology for Translation*, translated and edited by Juan C. Sager and M.-J. Hamel, Amsterdam/Philadelphia: John Benjamins, 1995, 244-245.
13 Mona Baker, *In other Words. A Coursebook on Translation* (1992), London and New York: Routledge, 1995, 63.
14 John O.E. Clark, *Word Wise. A Dictionary of English Idioms*, London: Harrap, 1988, 1 of a non-paginated preface.
15 Michael Hoey and Diane Houghton, "Contrastive analysis and translation" in Mona Baker (ed.), *Encyclopedia of Translation*, London and New York: Routledge, 1998, 46.
16 *Comparative Stylistics of French and English,* 234.
17 Jean Delisle, *L'analyse du discours comme méthode de traduction*, (1980) Ottawa, Presses de l'Université, 1982, 198. "English shows a tendency to highlight co-ordination and juxtaposition, whilst French emphasises articulation and subordination." (My translation).

18 Michel Ballard, "La traduction de *and* en français" in M. Ballard (ed.), *Relations discursives et traduction*, Lille: Presses de l'Université, 1995, 285-289.
19 Roland Barthes, *Le degré zéro de l'écriture suivi de Nouveaux essais critiques*, Paris: Seuil, 1972, 9.
20 *Ibid.*, 10.
21 *Ibid.*, 49.
22 *Ibid.*, 56.

## 3.
## THE TRANSLATOR'S INTERVENTION: DIALOGUE IN *STRAIT IS THE GATE*

Dialogue in fiction can sometimes appear "une encombrante convention" (a cumbersome convention), as argued by Nathalie Sarraute in *Conversation et sous-conversation.*[1] But dialogue can represent complex interaction and fulfill a number of poetic functions, as described by Marmontel in *Éléments de littérature,*[2] where the locutors "s'abandonnent aux mouvements de leur âme" (surrender to the moods of their souls), communicate secrets, strive to persuade, or else it can function dialectically, and express conflicting views and feelings. However, whereas the function of dialogue in narration and characterisation has been widely discussed in terms of literary technique, the issues raised by the translation of dialogue have received less attention. Statements such as Maurice-Edgar Coindreau's "On juge un traducteur à ses dialogues" (A translator is judged on her dialogues)[3] may signal the awareness of the practitioners, but this has to be weighed against the relative paucity of theoretical accounts. One possible explanation for the lack of visibility of dialogue as a translation issue could be the fact that most of its characteristics, such as greater orality, and the use of discourse markers, are already discussed, often in the context of translation-oriented contrastive linguistics, under the broader headings of register or dialect, and connectors, or regarding theatrical performativity. For instance, interesting studies on the translation of dialect have implicitly focused on its use within dialogue through exemplification. The question that arises here is whether dialect, as a social, temporal and geographical variation of language, is the only aspect of dialogue which would lead to a notable "shift of expression" in Popovič's sense, when "the relationship between the wording of the original and that of the translation"[4] is examined and shows visible intervention by the translator. More subtle changes can be due to the way connectors, phatic and others, fare in the translation, how pronouns of address are dealt with, and how cultural references which are embedded in the dialogue are handled by the translator.

Language variation is one of the main difficulties which the translator faces with dialogue. The available translation options — the choice of either neutralisation or of cultural transposition — come with more than a fair share of consequences, which risk disrupting the flow of the narrative. Nevertheless it is not the only aspect of dialogue that the translator must contend with, and with this consideration in mind I will look at dialogue as it appears in *Strait is the Gate*, the English translation of André Gide's novel *La porte étroite*.[5]

## Dialogue in *La porte étroite*

It has been suggested that *La porte étroite* set a standard for the short novel in French in the twentieth century. The book consists largely of a series of "scenes" in which the principal characters, Jérôme and his cousin Alissa, interact between themselves, and with others. The story is recounted by Jérôme in the first person, and his narrative is interwoven with extracts from a series of letters and Alissa's diary. The overall effect is the creation of a "mosaic of quotations", to borrow from Julia Kristeva's discussion of Bakhtin[6].

Dialogue plays a large part in Gide's novel, occuring frequently in the scenes where Alissa and Jérôme appear together, and featuring in many others. In addition, it can be said that instances of dialogue are provided by both the correspondence that Alissa and Jérôme exchange, and Alissa's diary, although addressed to God, positions Jérôme as the implied reader. Alissa declares "Je ne l'avais jamais écrit que pour lui" (172) (I only wrote it for him) (124). The use of the first person in the narrative tends to blur any formal distinction between the "récit" and the "dialogue" which is incorporated within it. In the same way Alissa's presence in the novel is realized not only through her conversations with Jérôme and others, but also by means of her letters and, posthumously, her diary and the misgivings which it reveals. This has led to the suggestion that there are two possible readings of *La porte étroite*, one through Jérôme's eyes, and one through Alissa's.[7] Moreover, dialogue between Alissa and Jérôme, the lovers who inhabit "un espace de séparation" (a space of separation),[8] assumes particular importance due to its relative scarcity: the number of scenes which feature the main characters together are outweighed by the number of those in which either Alissa or Jérôme interacts with the other characters in the book.

## Strait is the Gate

At a first glance, Dorothy Bussy's translation of *La porte étroite* can be viewed as an example of "transparency", if the term is taken to suggest the lack of the visibility of the translator and the attempt to assimilate the foreign text. Her name does not even appear on the front cover, at least in the 1977 Penguin Edition, and it can only be found in the small print which details translation copyright. Nor is there any translator's foreword or preface, and there is only one translator's footnote. However, to infer from these features that this is a "fluent" translation, to use Venuti's terminology,[9] would be misleading, as Bussy's version does not consistently anglicise and obliterate the source, as is shown by her treatment of verse quotations. These, almost always, are left in French in the text and there is no recourse to translator's notes. The strategy applied to literary references is particularly relevant to our discussion, as they occur mostly within passages of dialogue or correspondence.

Bakhtin speaks of the novel as a literary genre which encompasses a diversity of discursive modes ("hétérologie"), a diversity of languages ("hétéroglossie"), and a diversity of voices ("hétérophonie").[10] The first and third of these categories can be said to feature in *La porte étroite*, the narrative of which is based on correspondence, diary entries, recounted dialogues, as well as Jérôme's "récit". But the second category, the diversity of languages, is virtually non-existent, as the dialogues draw little on the vernacular, which adds to the narrative and thematic continuity of the novel, and this is reflected in the English translation. To some extent, this uniformity of language promotes the invisibility of the translator. The more marked dialogues are, in terms of register,[11] in relation to the rest of the text, the more visible will the intervention of the translator be, whether the choice is that of neutralisation or, as seems to be more often the case, equivalent markedness in the target language with its associated risk of over-colloqualisation, or simply over-idiomaticity. As Michel Volkovitch states "on rêvait d'être fidèle, neutre, transparent, et voilà que l'absence d'équivalent exact vous accule à choisir, à vous déclarer implicitement pour telle ou telle école de traduction."[12] In the following examples the translator opts for naturalness.

"Que Monsieur descende vite, la pauvre Madame est en train de mourir!" (15)
"Sir, sir, come quick! My poor lady is dying." (16)

"Ne montez pas Monsieur Jérôme! Ne montez pas: Madame a une crise." (17)
"Don't go up, Master Jerome. Don't go up! Mistress is having an attack." (18)

In the first instance the translator substituted the more direct imperative form for the one used in the source text, which was the more formal third person. In addition she emphasised the distinction that exists in formality of tone between "la pauvre Madame" and straightforward use of the term "Madame". The target text's "My poor lady" conveys less conventionality than the use of "Mistress" would have done.

*Connectors*

Other instances of Bussy's quest for naturalness are provided by the manipulation of the connector "mais" in conversational patterns. In an article identifying different levels of language transformation, referred to as "syntactic constraints", "collective stylistics", and "subjective choices", Jacqueline Guillemin-Flescher specifically examines the translation of "mais"[13] in passages of dialogue in *La porte étroite*, arguing, from the viewpoint of contrastive linguistics, that specific linguistic constraints were at play. Compare thus these extracts from *La porte étroite* and its English version as regards the treatment of "mais":

« Tout ce que je serai plus tard, c'est pour toi que je le veux être.
— Mais, Jérôme, moi aussi je peux te quitter.» (30)

"Whatever I hope to become later is for you."
"But Jerome, I may leave you too." (26)

« N'es-tu pas assez fort pour marcher seul? C'est tout seul que chacun de nous doit gagner Dieu.
— Mais c'est toi qui me montres la route. (30)

"Aren't you strong enough to walk alone? We must each of us find God by ourselves."
"But you must show me the way." (26)

with the following:

> «Est-ce que tu crois qu'il deviendra quelqu'un de remarquable?»
> «Mais, mon enfant, je voudrais d'abord savoir ce que tu entends par ce mot: remarquable! Mais on peut être très remarquable sans qu'il y paraisse [...]. (28)
>
> "Do you think he will become a remarkable man?"
> "First, my dear, I should like to understand what you mean by "remarkable". One can be very remarkable without its showing [...]." (24)
>
> — Qu'est-ce qu'il faut encore?
> — Mais, mon enfant, que veux-tu que je te dises? Il faut de la confiance, du soutien, de l'amour... (28)
>
> "What more must there be?"
> "Oh, my child! I can hardly tell. There must be confidence, support, love —". (25)
>
> « Alors, qu'est-ce que vous attendez pour vous fiancer? Pourquoi est-ce que vous ne vous fiancez pas tout de suite?
> — Mais pourquoi nous fiancerions-nous? (43)
>
> "Then, what are you waiting for? Why don't you get engaged at once?"
> "Why should we get engaged? (35)
>
> « Mais, Jérôme, cela ne se peut pas. Mais elle ne l'aime pas! Mais elle me l'a dit ce matin même. Tâche de l'empêcher, Jérôme! Oh! qu'est-ce qu'elle va devenir?...» (79)
>
> "Oh Jerome! It mustn't be. She doesn't love him! Why, she told me so only this very morning! Try to prevent it, Jerome! Oh! what will become of her?" (59)
>
> « Mais non! mais non! [...] mais non! ce ne sera rien. C'est l'émotion; une simple crise de nerfs. [...] (80)
>
> "No, it's nothing. The effect of emotion. Just a nervous attack. [...] (60).

Whilst in the first two of the above examples "mais" can be said to point to an asserted relationship, which explains why it is given an equivalent connector in the translation, in the latter examples this connector indicates a hypothetical relationship, hence there was no attempt to reproduce it in English. Guillemin-Flescher's explanation, which highlights the role of stylistic norms in translation as opposed to overt syntactic constraints, can be used to illustrate the intervention of the translator and the motivated nature of translation choices, which corresponds to "the inscription of domestic values in the foreign text".[14]

*Pronouns of address*

When dialogues alternate in the use of the "tu" and "vous" forms, as occurs in *La porte étroite*, it is clear that the translator is faced with linguistic constraints which prevent her from conveying in English the shift which has taken place, in the following case from familiarity to greater distance, and back to the use of the "tutoiement", in an expression of Jérôme's despair.

> — Hélas! je ne l'invente pas. Elle était mon amie. Je la rappelle. Alissa! Alissa! vous étiez celle que j'aimais. Qu'avez-vous fait de vous? Que vous êtes-vous fait devenir?"
> [...]
> — Jérome, pourquoi ne pas avouer tout simplement que tu m'aimes moins?
> — Parce que ce n'est pas vrai! Parce que ce n'est pas vrai!" [...]; parce que je ne t'ai jamais plus aimée." (135)

"Alas! I am not inventing. She was once my friend. I call upon her. Alissa! Alissa! it was you I loved. What have you done with yourself? What have you made yourself become?"
[...]
"Jerome, why don't you simply admit that you love me less?"
"Because its not true! Because its not true!" [...] "because I never loved you more." (97)

This is not an isolated case of a translation problem due to lack of formal equivalence between the two languages. This also holds true for one of Jérôme's monologues, which uses the "vous" form when addressing Alissa:

> Non, même alors je ne vous accusai pas, Alissa! mais pleurai désespérément de ne vous reconnaître. A présent que je mesure la force de votre amour à la ruse de son silence et à sa cruelle industrie, dois-je vous aimer d'autant plus que vous m'aurez plus atrocement désolé? (126-27)

> No! Even then, Alissa, I did not accuse you, but wept despairingly that I could recognize you no longer. Now that I can gauge the

strength of your love by the cunning of its silence and by its cruel workings, must I love you all the more, the more agonizingly you bereft me? (90-91)

The "vouvoiement" here is marked in relation to the form of address Jérôme normally uses with Alissa. This is neutralised in the English text, although it could perhaps be argued that the stiffness of the English compensates for the neutralisation of effect and creates a formal distance.

*Literary references*

A translator's intervention is felt not only at the level of individual instances of direct discourse, but also in the way these instances fit together. An interesting change of translational strategy can be noted between the overall interweaving of dialogues with the narrative, which, as we have suggested, indicates a definite attempt at "naturalness", and the treatment bestowed upon the literary references within dialogues.

Literary and religious quotations, references, and allusions abound in *La porte étroite*, and mainly, though not exclusively, they are interwoven with Alissa and Jérôme's conversations and letters. In terms of the narrative itself, these references reinforce the sense of intellectual and spiritual closeness that Jérôme and Alissa share through their common familiarity with the "classics", French and otherwise.

Religious references, mostly taken from the gospels of Luke and Matthew, are translated throughout, and the selection of accepted phrases in English can be seen as an attempt towards naturalness. This is in line with the approach applied by the translator to the main narrative. This also applies to literary references in prose, which are translated, whether or not the quotes or references are attributed:

In a conversation which he recounts, Jérôme quotes Goethe who was referring to Madame de Stein: "Il serait beau de voir se réfléchir le monde dans cette âme." (38) This is translated as "It would be beautiful to see the world reflected in that soul" (31). Much later, in her diary, Alissa quotes La Bruyère "Il y a quelquefois dans le cours de la vie, de si chers plaisirs et de si tendres engagements que l'on nous défend, qu'il est naturel de désirer du moins qu'ils fussent permis : de si grands charmes ne peuvent être surpassés que par celui de savoir y renoncer par vertu." (160). This is again translated: "In the course of this life one sometimes meets with pleasures so dear, promises so tender, which are yet forbidden us, that it is natural to desire at least that they might be permitted; charms so great can be surpassed only when virtue teaches us to renounce them." (114).

In Alissa's final diary, Pascal is mentioned and quoted: « Tout ce qui n'est pas Dieu ne peut pas remplir mon attente » (171), translated as "Whatever is not God cannot satisfy my longing" (124), and further on, this time with no reference in *La porte étroite* to Pascal: « Joie, joie, joie, pleurs de joie... » (172), translated as: "Joy, joy, joy, tears of joy..." (124), followed by the only translator's note found in the book, which indicates that this quotation is from Pascal.

By contrast, all extracts of verse are left in French (or in Italian as in the case of a Dante's verse on pages 61 and 47 of the original and its translation respectively). It can be argued that the reasons which underlie the choice of strategies made by the translator may be related to publishers' norms as much as to Bussy's own subjectivity, but the effect of the seemingly transparent translation (transparent here in the sense that the original "shines through") is not negligible. In the dialogues where this occurs and when the French quote is inserted in the English text, the internal cohesion is disrupted and the reference is somehow distanced from the locutor. In a conversation with Juliette, Jérôme refers to, and quotes Baudelaire:

« Bientôt nous plongerons dans les froides ténèbres; (42)

and Juliette continues:

— Adieu, vive clarté de nos étés trop courts! (42)

The verses are not translated in Bussy's version (34).

Another example is provided by verse by Sully-Prudhomme which is quoted by Abel, Jérôme's friend:

Le meilleur moment des amours
N'est pas quand on a dit: Je t'aime (60)

In contrast to Baudelaire's verse, no mention is made of the poet in the French text. The origin of the quotation could, I would argue, have merited a translator's note.

The following extract occurs twice in Alissa's correspondence, first in a letter to her aunt Plantier, where Alissa describes the reference as being a religious paraphrase of Corneille's, and the second time in a letter to Jérôme, when Alissa realizes that the verse is in fact taken from Racine's *IV Cantique spirituel:*

> Quel charme vainqueur du monde
> Vers Dieu m'élève aujourd'hui?
> Malheureux l'homme qui fonde
> Sur les hommes son appui (86, 89)

Once more, the verse is kept in French in the English translation (64 and 66).

The distancing effect created by the translator's intervention shows that choosing not to translate is not neutral and that the transparency thus created vis-à-vis the source text is not without consequences. This is particularly obvious in the following example which is a parody of one of Néron's lines in Racine's *Brittanicus*. Abel declares his love for Juliette:

> J'aime, que dis-je aimer, j'idolâtre Juliette (59)

The "foreignising" effect of the lack of an English translation is compounded by the fact that this is not a straight quotation, but a literary allusion which is integrated into the French dialogue (there is no reference made to Racine).

The distinction made between verse and prose in terms of translation strategies proves again disruptive in the following example provided by an encounter between Jérôme and Juliette; Jérôme asks:

> — Partout! la vie tout entière m'apparaît comme un long voyage —
> avec elle, à travers les livres, les hommes, les pays... Songes-tu à ce
> que signifient ces mots: lever l'ancre? (45)

Given that earlier in the same encounter, both Jérôme and Juliette had recited Baudelaire, "lever l'ancre" can be identified as an explicit allusion to *Le Voyage*[15], but, in the English text, the literary sub-text is neutralised as the phrase is distanced from the previous Baudelairean quotations:

> "Yes, everywhere! All life seems to me like a long journey — with
> her, through books and people and countries. Have you ever
> thought of the meaning of the words "weighing anchor"?" (36)

## Conclusion

This evaluation of Bussy's translation of dialogues in *La porte étroite* may well have revealed several instances of loss which are due to a combination of formal features and linguistic constraints (such as the use of the "tu" and "vous" forms) and of translational choices (for instance, the treatment of literary references). But any evaluation will also have to be made in the light of its wider publishing context. As Berman so convincingly puts it:

> Analyser une traduction sans remonter au système de normes qui l'a modelée, puis la «juger» sur cette base, est donc une opération absurde, et injuste, puisqu'elle ne *pouvait* pas être autrement, et qu'elle n'avait sens comme acte de traduction que comme opération assujettie à ces normes.[16]

To speculate on the factors which motivated Bussy's choices could prove futile, however tempting it might to project one's conceptualisation onto past practice. A historical reading of translation practice, and indeed associated discourse, shows only too well the complexity of factors which bear upon the translator's work — not only translation norms but also publishing constraints, as well as personal preferences. Last, but not least, one could add the unavoidable linguistic changes, which mean that a translation tends to be judged against the standards of contemporary language, whilst the classics, or "canonical" texts are not subjected to the same evaluation.

James Holmes stated that in their work contemporary literary translators "show a marked tendency towards modernization and naturalization of the linguistic context, paired with a similar but less clear tendency in the same direction with regard to the literary intertext, but an opposing tendency towards exoticizing and historicizing in the socio-cultural situation."[17] A similar conflict of tendencies can be found in *Strait is the Gate*, which goes some way to explain the apparent contradictions, in terms of translational strategies.

Dorothy Bussy may have emphasised naturalness of form in her version of *La porte étroite*, but she has also chosen transparency with regard to the original as far as literary references are concerned. By choosing to alternate between masking the source text, and then unveiling it, the translator has made her intervention quite visible, demonstrating how dialogues can constitute a critical area of intervention and translational decision-making.

Myriam Salama-Carr

### Notes

1 Nathalie Sarraute, "Conversation et sous-conversation", *La Nouvelle Revue Française*, 37, Jan/Feb 1956, 234. Translated by Maria Jolas, "Conversation and sub-conversation" in *Tropisms and the Age of Suspicion*, London: Calder, 1963, 97-120.
2 Marmontel, "Éléments de littérature" (1787), in *Oeuvres Complètes de Marmontel*, Tome XIII, vol. 2, Paris: Verdière, 1819, 147-149.
3 Quoted by Michel Gresset in "La traduction du dialogue" in *"Traduire le dialogue"*, *Palimpsestes*, vol. 1, Paris: Université de la Sorbonne Nouvelle (Paris III), 1987, 10.
4 Anton Popovič, "The Concept Shift of Expression" in J.S. Holmes (ed.), *The Nature of Translation*, Paris: Mouton, 1970, 78-87.
5 André Gide (1909) *La Porte étroite*, Paris: Mercure de France, 1959. Trans. Dorothy Bussy (1924) *Strait is the Gate*, London: Penguin, 1977.
6 Julia Kristeva, "Word, Dialogue and the Novel" in *Desire in Language: A Semiotic Approach to Literature and Art*. Trans. T. Gora, A. Jardine and L. Roudiez, New York: Columbia University Press, 1980.
7 See Zvi H. Levy's discussion in *Jérome Agonistes — Les structures dramatiques et les procédures narratives de **La porte étroite***, Paris: Nizet, 1984.
8 *Ibid.*, 14.
9 Lawrence Venuti, *The Translator's Invisibility*, London & New York: Routledge, 1995.
10 Mikhaïl Bakhtine, *Le Principe dialogique*, Paris: Seuil, 1982.
11 Register is used as "The set of features which distinguishes one stretch of language from another in terms of variation in context to do with the language user (geographical dialect, ideolect, etc.) and/or language use (field or subject matter, tenor or level of formality and mode of speaking versus writing)." Basil Hatim and Ian Mason, *The Translator as Communicator*, London: Routledge, 1996, 222-23.
12 Michel Volkovitch, in *Actes des deuxièmes assises de la traduction littéraire*, Arles: Actes Sud, 1985, 144. "You dream of being truthful, neutral, transparent, and yet the lack of an exact equivalent obliges you to choose, to

implicitly declare your allegiance to one school of translation or another." (My translation).

13 Jacqueline Guillemin-Flescher "Langage, culture et traduction" in *Des théories de la traduction*, Actes du colloque CETL-ISTI, Équivalences, Revue de l'ISTI de Bruxelles, vol. 24/1, 1994, 37-54.

14 Lawrence Venuti, *The Scandals of Translation — Towards an Ethics of difference*, London & New York: Routledge, 1998, 27.

15 Charles Baudelaire, "Le Voyage" (1857), in *Les Fleurs du mal et autres poèmes*, Paris: Garnier-Flammarion, 1964. "Mort, vieux capitaine, il est temps! levons l'ancre! Ce pays nous ennuie, ô Mort! Appareillons!" (155).

16 Antoine Berman, *Pour une critique des traductions: John Donne*, Paris: Gallimard, 1995, 53. "To analyse a translation without returning to the system of norms which modelled it, and to 'judge' it on any other basis, is therefore absurd and unjust, given that the translation *could* not be otherwise, and that it had no *meaning* as a translation act but as an operation subject to those norms." (My translation).

17 James S. Holmes, *Translated! Papers on Literary Translation and Translation Studies*, Amsterdam: Rodopi, 1988, 48.

**4.**
# WHEN IS LOSING FINDING?
# TRANSLATING SURREALISM

Let me start by recounting a dream which I had whilst I was thinking about this paper. It gave me more than I could have imagined. Verlaine has translated Verlaine, and it has become interesting. I am delighted. I say to him: "That is what translation is." Perhaps that is indeed it: translating a language into its sameness, differently.

This leads me to Mallarmé, and to Breton's outburst:

> The others, the die-hards of the Mallarmean school, are now sinking in the sand of God only knows what mental Easter Island, their mouths, for the most part, level with oblivion.

I do not think this refers to Mallarmé, but rather to his emulators, his schoolfollowers, as it were. No matter what they did, they were never translating a language into its inner self, rather into the imitation of someone else, that of their leader.

The point, I think, about translating surrealism is an inside point. Not to be part of a school, but part of an idea. And that idea includes within itself the necessary mistakes, in language and in interpretation. Interpretation, we know, is the most interesting — probably the only valid — form of translation. Every good translation, which is not simply mimetic, is an interpretation, and in the case of the great ones, deserved by the great texts, the union of text and interpretation produces, according to Derrida, a lasting thing — a child. He says that the amphora of translation inscribes in itself already the "différance", that is, language's inevitable slippage from itself. The amphora which Derrida invokes is like the urn, traditional in the *ars poetica*: "one with itself though opening itself to the outside — and this openness opens the unity, renders it possible, and forbids its totality. Its openness allows receiving and giving". The translation contract that Derrida sees as being set up is one in which "two adjoined fragments complete each other, form a larger tongue that changes them both".[1] The internal quarrel *between* the substance and style of the text speaks aloud:

> "For it is necessary to be faithful to the violent love-hate relation between letter and spirit, which is already a problem of translation with the *original* text."²

There is a warning here, issued by Barbara Johnson after Lautréamont, about the bridge of translation, the bringing-over: it "releases within each text the subversive forces of its own foreignness, thus reinscribing those forces in the tensile strength of a new neighbourhood of otherness. [...]." [Here is] the sign that Lautréamont sets up: "Vous, qui passez sur ce pont, n'y allez pas." "You who are crossing over this bridge, don't get to the other side."³ It is all impossible.

What happens, of course, is that our (often mistaken) text covers over the other. Richard Sieburth puts this perfectly:

> Anyone who has engaged in translation has probably experienced that particular phase of the process (it is one of the stages in what George Steiner terms 'the hermeneutic motion') in which one's translation seems to have more or less completely 'covered' the original. I use the term 'cover' here in a number of senses, all involving various implications of protection, concealment, and Mastery. One displays one's mastery of a subject or field by covering it. Stallion covers mare. Text covers text in a palimpsest. A book in turn may or may not be told by its cover.⁴

I want to put it under the aegis of an act of poetry, taking as my lead here what Ruben Brower says in the Introduction to his *Mirror on Mirror: Translation, Imitation, Parody*.⁵ Within the broad range of acts of the imagination that we call "poetry", there is a scale of varying but related activities that we call "translation". He says a better term would be: "version" because the foreign languages have taken over "translation" with an overtone of literalism.

This article is centered around the certainty of losing in translation what one was aiming at, unless — as I will maintain is the case — what one is actually aiming at is precisely that loss. I will apply this to surrealism, having spent a good deal of my time (and other people's) in attempts at translating surrealist or once-surrealist authors, specifically including René Char, the Dada Tristan Tzara, and — popish, if brilliant André Breton.

Here is the ground of my thought: André Breton marvels at Tristan Tzara's not having the words to ask for cigarettes in a "tabac", declares how you can perfectly well say "Adieu" to your beloved, whom you are delighted to be greeting, and laments how he speaks least well of what he loves the most. For me, these are the most moving parts of his reflection upon surrealist language. I want to examine how these losses and misprisions contribute to the strength of the surrealist entreprise as I conceive it, care about it, and translate the parts of it which I most want to share. For if the very being of its most intimate poetics is based on paradox is not our best response likely to be — in fact, fated and chosen to be — a paradoxical, even an oxymoronic one? Might one not find, both the entreprise and oneself precisely through an essential first step of losing? Is not this kind of incapacity a strange capacity here, in this place of surrealist poetry and poetics? This seems to me to be the promise surrealism holds out. I am counting on the hope that this sort of entreprise, so easily seen as deconstructionist, can be also creative and constructionist at the same time.

The interest lies, of course, in what happens in the translation of what we think of as hard or complicated texts (complication bearing within itself that Mallarméan pleat or "pli", like *ex*-plication, the unfolding of the pleat). These pressure points, as Barbara Johnson puts it, are where both the problem and the attendant delight may lie. "Language", in fact, she says, "can only exist in the space of its own foreignness to itself."[6]

From the other point of view these pressure points can be seen as so many breaks. Here let me quote Antoine Berman, defining "the finding and seeking of the break in the rule (the unruly, *le non-normé*) in the maternal language, so as to insert there the foreign language and its pattern of speech (son dire)".[7]

These breaks in logic, and in our capacity, are the moments where we are conscious of having to do more, to worry more, our anxiety points. There are some big deals, like titles, and some other deals, like the beginnings and endings of poems. I will take my examples mostly from surrealism, but given my present obsession with Mallarmé, a little of his own textual complication may come in.

Mark Polizzotti and I have been translating Breton's *Point du jour*, over which title we have already had one of the usual hesitations that titles bring about: *The Break of Day* having finally given way to *Daybreak*.[8] But take also the title of *Les Vases communicants* that

Geoffrey Harris and I translated together: were we to simply put *Communicating Vessels*, or to add the article "the"?[9] I also remember my anxiety over the title: *L'Amour fou* — would this be understandable in English, as *Mad Love*, or was the French essence part of the entire concept? In fact, the English prevailed, and *Mad Love* sold, in large part, no doubt, because of its title. Like all of Breton's writing the text is both lyric and stilted, romantic and classical — notably difficult, impassioned far beyond ordinary love-writing and writing about love. Here I shall quote from my own preface to that translation.

> The Translation may be seen turning like the sunflower (tournesol, celebrated poem), its emblematic incarnation, toward the captivating and terrible illumination of Breton's prose and yet placing itself in doubt in relation to the original effect of the French text, totally unlike other texts as it is. This is, it seems to me, the only original worth <u>going after</u>, the one we sense behind what we read; to go after it is not to chase a prey for complete capture, but to believe in an interior and impulsive correspondence with one of the truest surrealist texts.

To translate such a classic in the sure knowledge of failure is — perhaps — to make an impossible gesture of gratitude to a work and an author of primary significance for us all. It is really a gesture, all these years later, of our own mad love.[10]

Now what is it that makes one want to make a public admission of failure? I have begun to believe that it must be difficulty that plunges us into this. And so believing, I have started reading others on translation, a luxury I thought I should forbid myself until I had really done enough to merit that break. George Steiner, in *After Babel*, praises Pierre Leyris's translations of Gerard Manley Hopkins, surely one of the most impossible authors anywhere to render in any case, referring no doubt, although he does not say so, to Hopkins' notion of "inscape". "The achievement of 'inscape' (*Einfühlung*) is both a linguistic and an emotive act."[11] I have come to adapt Hopkins' concept, regarding it as the interior landscape we have, or feel, or find, within a text. And I am especially tuned into Steiner's quotation from Theodore Adorno: "The only true thoughts are those who do not grasp their own meaning."[12] That kind of necessary slippage within the text seems to me what I am aiming at here: how useful it is to us as translators precisely to realize that the authors themselves may not grasp the meaning, as if a whole congeries of uncertainties were to spring up and crowd around the very idea of translation.

And certain authors lead us there, signaling the difficulty in their openings. To return a moment to Breton's *L'Amour fou*, where the very first word is "boys", the English word, with the meaning of nameless actors. The word could not be altered: "boys" remained, signaling straight off the difficulty of the entire act. It is saying: Come, I dare you to do anything with me.

It is, I think, like a few other things I have translated in full knowledge of imminent and certain failure, in one sense, like "rien" which is at the beginning of Mallarmé's *Salut* — itself a nest of problems, containing at once a toast and a salvation — or like "Yeux", of *Pitre châtié*, an equally impossible beginning for a poem: "Eyes"? This poem was given a far simpler, more indirect first version, showing the difficulty to be a deliberate choice. Here is the first stanza of the final version:

> Yeux, lacs avec ma simple ivresse de renaître
> Autre que l'histrion qui du geste évoquais
> Comme plume la suie ignoble des quinquets,
> J'ai troué dans le mur de toile une fenêtre.

> Eyes, lakes with my simple passion to be reborn
> Other than the actor, evoking with gestures
> For feathers the ugly soot of stage lights,
> I have pierced a window in the canvas wall.[13]

Breton's poem "Vigilance", is yet another almost impossible case, containing the wonderful lines:

> Je vois les arêtes du soleil
> A travers l'aubépine de la pluie

for which I tentatively gave:

> I see the ridges of the sun
> Through the hawthorn of the rain[14]

Of course there was no way of getting those "arêtes", or fish bones, up to the sun, no way of having them sparkle on the hawthorn, no way — at least I did not find one — of evoking Proust who had been responsible in the first place for the hawthorns. The poem ends:

> Je ne touche plus que le coeur des choses je tiens le fil
>
> I touch nothing now but the heart of things I hold the thread.[15]

and somehow that upbeat ending gave me courage. I published the translation with no further worry. But the reassurance had to come from within, which made me think of the notorious concept of internal translation, which is about the slippage that already exists between the original text and its own meaning.

Another Bretonian impossibility, a famous one this time, is that of "L'Union libre", probably Breton's most celebrated poem. I found it impossible to bring over into English, for its first line begins: "Ma femme à". I see now that one cannot say "my woman" or "woman of mine", as we tried to do. I think it must be, after all, "beloved", so that possession is included in the term, rather than jutting out with "ma".

Translating surrealism can be fun; like trying to play the writer's variety of word games (sometimes love games if we follow Breton: words are no longer playing, they are making love). Robert Desnos is another wonderful example of this, as in his parody of the Lord's Prayer:

> O toi quiète aux yeux...

One of the easiest is Bretonian word play, oddly, because his serious texts are far harder. In his superb prose poem "Le Verbe être" the expression "la mer à boire" turns into "un verre à boire". But what is a success in French does not always prove to be so in English.

My own obsession with translating Breton has to do with what I call his "totalizing figures", arising as they do at the completion of the poem. For example, "L'Air de l'eau", which begins:

> On me dit que là-bas les plages sont noires
> De la lave allée à la mer...
>
> They tell me that over there the beaches are black
> With the lava run off to the sea

and ends:

> Tout le pommier en fleur de la mer
>
> The whole flowering apple tree of the sea.

The ending itself serves to rescue whatever entirety might still be available, after all the dismembering into parts of *L'Union libre* and other texts. Finally, these summits are the most translatable things, because our entire imagination is involved in their condensation, and our entire hope in their use.

Mary Ann Caws

### Notes

1 Jacques Derrida, "Des Tours de Babel", in Joseph F. Graham (ed.), *Difference in Translation*, Ithaca: Cornell University Press, 1985, 191.
2 Barbara Johnson, "Taking Fidelity Philosophically", in *Difference in Translation*, 147.
3 *Ibid.*, 148.
4 Richard Sieburth, "Second Thoughts on Translating Holderlin," in *The Art of Translation: voices from the Field*, ed. Rosanna Warren, Boston: Northeastern University Press, 1989, 239.
5 Ruben Brower, *Mirror on Mirror: Translation, Imitation, Parody*, Cambridge: Harvard University Press, 1974, 1.
6 In *Difference in Translation*, 146.
7 Quoted by Rosanna Warren, in her preface to *The Art of Translation: voices from the Field*, 5.
8 André Breton, *Daybreak*, trans. Mary Ann Caws and Mark Polizzotti, Lincoln and London: University of Nebraska Press, 1999.
9 *Communicating Vessels*, trans. Mary Ann Caws and Geoffrey Harris, Lincoln and London: University of Nebraska Press, 1990.
10 Preface to André Breton *Mad Love*, Lincoln: University of Nebraska Press, 1987.
11 George Steiner, *After Babel*, London and New York: Oxford University Press, 1975, 409.
12 *Ibid.*, 229.
13 Stéphane Mallarmé, *Selected Poems and Prose*, New York: New Directions, 1983, 5-6.
14 André Breton, *Selected Poems*, trans. Jean-Pierre Cauvin and Mary Ann Caws, Austin: University of Texas Press, 1982, 78-79.
15 *Loc.cit.*

## 5.
## TACTICS AND NON-TACTICS:
## THE EXPERIENCE OF A TRANSLATOR OF MODERN POETRY

This is not intended to be what Michel Deguy calls a "self-story", a narcissistic exposition of my experience of translating either fragments or relatively large swathes of the work of poets of the past two centuries, from Lamartine and Desbordes-Valmore to Prévert, Frénaud, Char, Noël and, above all, twenty-eight contemporary French women poets and, more recently, much work of the fine Franco-Lebanese poet, Salah Stétié. But it is an honest account of the factors involved in such work as I have lived and spontaneously meditated them. And, if I stress the spontaneity of this meditation of my own act of translation, it is to make fully clear from the outset that the translator, whilst having certain global "tactics" guiding his or her process and production, equally is bound — or, if you prefer, freed, liberated — by a host of impulsive, pulsional, unsystematisable factors which, in all straightforwardness, faced as he or she constantly is with this or that word or set of words, give rise to the consciousness of the fragility, the relativity, the unknowing, unguided, tactic-less course upon which translation embarks one. What Peter Newmark, in his useful book *About Translation*, refers to as our "generalisations" about the translating process, is thus, not just for him, as critic, analyst, but for the translator too, in a constant tussle with what he terms "translation examples".[1] Translation, for the translator, is not really theory; it is practice, a creative act of what Derrida calls "transformation" that, as it were, he theorises *sur place*, in situ, textually. The poetics of translation as creative transformation — "all art is in a sense a process of translation", Burton Raffel tells us in *The Forked Tongue*[2] — the poetics of translation arguably mutates dramatically when it becomes a poetics of what Haskell Block terms "literary endeavor".[3] And certainly those who have thought with subtlety and ease and even humour about translation concur that the translator must be — to quote from Willis Barnstone's lively *Poetics of Translation* — a "creative person", albeit at the risk of becoming occasionally an "erroneous slob".[4] The freedom from pure theory and the creativity liberty the translator is thus born to, do not for Barnstone imply any freedom to make errors. Of course, for the translator, everything turns about the definition of error, and therefore truth — or does it, if all is "transformation", thus defying what Edmond Cary speaks of as the "optical illusion [of] the printed text's immobility"?[5]

The observations that follow then, centre upon what for me have proved to be points about which the translation of poetry commonly revolves. I shall speak, succinctly, of questions of motivation; selection of material; the nature of the edition; issues of coherence and obscurity, cultural and other reduction, and faithful honouring of complexity; structural modification; sound performance; critical assessment by other readers of one's translations; issues of gender; critical paraphernalia that may accompany translation; pagination, visual presentation; the need to satisfy the self. A quasi-conclusion only will result.

*Motivation.* Why a given poet? Why this poet now? For what audience is the translator translating, for what culture? These and related questions may touch in varying measure the conscious mind of the translator who may or may not quite share Rossetti's prescriptive view that "the only true motive for putting poetry into a fresh language must be to endow a fresh nation, as far as possible, with one more possession of beauty".[6] If Rossetti's argument may appear overly aestheticising, somewhat ideally Mallarméan, it nevertheless probably remains at the root of much poetic translation. It is difficult to disagree with the opening gambit of Barnstone's at once witty and perspicacious "ART of *revelation*".[7] Revelation, that is, of beauty, originality, individual genius (in the simplest, least elitist sense of this term), revelation of difference, aesthetic, psychological, philosophical, cultural, etc., and, of course, linguistic. My own translation of contemporary French women poets may be thought of as a political act of revelation, but it is equally urgent at the strictly human, personal, and what one might term "spiritual" level (in the broadest sense of the term) an exchange of minds, psyches, with women I know and respect, and not just via their poetry, and this, moreover, in the context of my own growing consciousness of complex issues of womanhood. Barnstone is undoubtedly right to stress that poetic translation fosters a "FRIENDSHIP between poets".[8] The difficulty and the difference of friendship, of joining/separation, of this betweenness that is the precarious locus of translation's revelations. André Lefevere's global position expressed in *Translating Poetry*[9] that translation enriches, at once universalising and differentiating, that it helps us understand what is at stake in poetics, deconstructing literary assumptions, and that it thus opens up the act of teaching — is a position which I am inclined to espouse as linked very much to my personal motivations. Nevertheless, I prefer to shift the ground under the latter, feeling, with Willis Barnstone, that, somewhere, somehow, "a good translation is a good JOKE"[10] — but to this J of his ABC, I should add, a joyous, jubilant joke, a smiling shared pleasure in the unpretentious yet vital act of transformation.

*Selection.* Clearly, I do not mean here, again, motivation as just discussed. Rather, the question of selection addresses what it is materially possible to translate if limitations are imposed by space or time or some other factor of feasibility. To publish a fully translated collection by a given author or even the complete works naturally circumvents the issues that interest us here. The selection of a small sampling for publication in a journal, magazine or anthology can, however, be quite tricky. My own approach here has been to make a larger choice, whittling it down impulsively to respect needed limits, but according to certain criteria: deciding which are the best results and the best reflections of an individual poet's genius and specificity; ideally making a selection to reveal equally the range of such specificity, modally, tonally, thematically. This, for example, I sought to accomplish — but it is extremely difficult in five or six pages — in *Women's Poetry in France, 1965-1995*.[11] The translations of the poetry of Salah Stétié, for Bloodaxe Books, offer a much wider range. Even so, broad selection still poses questions of continuity and coherence and one must be able to make informed, unanguished judgements, respecting the "atmosphere" of original collections thus cannibalised just as Hilaire Belloc would have us respect, at the micro-level of translation (a different sort of selection) what he calls the "atmosphere of the word".[12] Discussion of selection with colleagues, friends, even the poets themselves may assist. But, as with final translated text, selection of material remains something for the translator to assume. It is part of Barnstone's "art of revelation". Carefully plodding, logical thinking can take one just so far. Choosing 100 or 200 poems is no easier than choosing five, moreover.

*The edition.* Again, if we are not to slip into the considerations just reflected on, the main issue here is whether the edition (or group of poems translated) will appear with or without the original texts. Putting aside the very real questions of available space and thus cost, things turn about use, audience, desire, perceived need. And, of course, more or less flagrant accountability. The monolingual publication — most translation emerges without the original, though poetry tends in the opposite direction — could tempt the translator to overly subscribe to Dr. Jowett's observation in the preface to his own *Translation of Plato* that "the first requirement of an English translation is that it be English".[13] Thus, with the best will in the world, and utterly benignly, the translator may drift, freed definitively from all trace of the original, towards an ethnic mutation deemed to be the ultimate in beauty, but a beauty quite rejected by Browning, who argues (it is John Addington Symonds who quotes him) that "only [an absolutely literal] translation [with exact rendering of words, and words placed in the order of the original] gives any real insight into the original".[14] To be or not to be pure Englishness, pure otherness... All kinds of brews are possible in the monolingual edition, but, as Marilyn Gaddis Rose writes in *Translation Spectrum*, "if the match of translation to reader has been made appropriately, then the readers will not be obliged, even quasi-consciously, to consider as problems any of the issues raised by translation types and conventions".[15] As so often with such generalisations, much can be picked apart, most pickily if we are so inclined. But, I am not. Suffice it to say that the bilingual edition — assuming non-unilinguist readers — imposes heightened, more palpable responsibility, and shows that, if the translated poem, as Barnstone says, "aspires to INDEPENDENCE"[16], it does so conscious of the latter's impossibility, at best contingency, conditionality, provisionality.

*Clarity, obscurity.* What we have just heard Jowett and Browning argue, is, of course, at the centre of what is for many the central question of, on the one hand the desirability of literalness, conservation of original obscurity, a certain *illisibilité* or "unreadable" authenticity, and on the other hand the virtues of clarity, coherence, unforeignness and the consequent delights of what Georges Mounin terms in his book so titled, "les belles infidèles"[17]: unfaithful beauties, beauteous infidelities — it is so simple, but, as you will agree, too tricky to translate, but you catch my meaning... Derrida tells us that "a good translation is always destined to abuse" (*abuser:* to make ill use of, to take advantage of, to deceive, delude, to overstep the mark — necessarily, of course, translation must carry over, journey away, from its liminal marks). Translation may thus slip from Dr. Jowett's action of obligatory "compensation".[18] It is all very well for Hilaire Belloc to tell us "never embellish".[19] Has he not just told us also to "transmute boldly" and "render idiom by idiom"?[20] Distinctions here there certainly are, but they are fine and, probably, hopelessly too abstracted from practical contexts grappled with. Moreover, such boldness erasing original idiomaticity can push us ever closer to that supremely coherent Englishness, that familiar clarity that Julien Green is rightly, in my view, concerned with, lest it tip the scales, colonialising the other, taming expression and, with it, meaning (Mounin, 74).[21]

In effect, as Mounin argues, "le mot à mot trahit aussi sûrement le texte que les infidélités les plus désinvoltes" (word for word translation betrays the text as surely as the most off-handed infidelities).[22] Are we then to settle for that wonderfully French position, *le juste milieu*? As the 1885 editor of London's *Journal of Education* reminds us, "'free' and 'literal' [in reference to translation] are relative terms, and it is impossible to give a categorical reply [to the person inquiring as to which is better] without ascertaining first the subjective standard of the querist". He adds, smilingly, "it is like asking, Do you prefer a hot or cold room — strong tea or weak?".[23] Certainly, in theorising, Belloc runs through a fair gamut of issues in translation and one can appreciate his caution as to the paradoxical danger in over-literal translation of "diluting and marring each [language] with the properties of the other"[24] — a danger ironically stemming from, he feels, too intimate an acquaintance with both. Decidedly, translation is a dodgy *métier*! But surely, we are not to abandon our competence any more than we are to resolve the question at hand by surrendering to some pure, unfettered subjectivity. Fine judgements are constantly called for in the literary, especially poetic context, but I admit to being inclined to Walter Benjamin's view that "a true or real translation is transparent to the extent that it exhibits the *literal difference of language* in translation".[25]

*Structural modification*. What I have in mind here is not merely — though it is a significant factor for any translator — the matter of preservation or alteration of sentence structure (involving say, inversion, omission-plus-compensation, the use of present participles instead of finite verbs, two words instead of one, and so on — the list is endless, and endlessly pertinent). I am also thinking of punctuation, whose codes may differ intrinsically in radical ways from language to language; of the matter, in the selection of a limited number of numbered poems, of retaining or dropping such signs. This is not to mention how to deal with titles: do we give them where none exist in the original?; and with capitalisation (especially of titles in English, where virtually no capitalisation may exist in the French); and so on. Are we to acquiesce in Hilaire Belloc's view that "nearly always must a translation be of greater length than the original"[26], a view clearly implying that paraphrasing is fundamental to translation. André Lefevere argues, no doubt rightly, but a little tiresomely if one thinks about it, that both compression and expansion constitute distortion and falsification.[27] To translate "arbre" by "tree" or "the" by "la" is indeed to distort, but we may as well give up if we cannot accept that transformation cannot be identification at either the macro- or micro- levels. As for myself, some of the elements involving structural modification I have found fascinating, as well as recurrent and central are: 1. the need to think in terms of using prepositions to convey verbal structure in moving from French to English; 2. the use or possible over-use of the present participle mentioned earlier; 3. the often subtle matter of translation of the French definite article; 4. the related issue of translation of French demonstrative adjectives. These seemingly elementary issues can give a translation dramatically differing effects according to their resolution. I shall not speak of structural modification involved in the fragile transposition of metre and rhythm. Here, language can be almost unrecognisably altered. Witness Mathew Arnold's various endeavours, or André du Bouchet's translation of the epilogue to Shakespeare's *Tempest*.

*Sound performance*. Of course, comparing overall sound qualities of original and translation is not so much a thankless task, but, whilst essential, incapable of anything other than low approximation. If tone and sound are two of Robert Bly's "eight stages of translation"[28], real resolution of a problem cannot be what is at stake. Better not even to see the matter as a problem, but rather, remembering the translator's inherently creative stance, to pursue, *tant bien que mal*, some equipollency in the realm of sound and sound's rhythmic dimensions that will capture something in relation to what Hilaire Belloc calls — one cannot but be in sympathy with him here — the "magic", the "thrill", the "poignancy proper to the original".[29] My experience here has led me sometimes to the preparation of cassette tapes of translated poems, now for my own increased sense of the translation's value, now with the intention of showing others (students, editors, other readers prior to publication or other use) not just how a poem sounds, but also how its rhythms of meaning may deploy themselves, offering thereby a fusion of elements coherent and discontinuous, revealed and withdrawing.

*Assessment by other readers.* If it is true up to a point, as Burton Raffel suggests, that only a bilingual person can judge a translation[30], it remains equally true, in my experience, that a unilingual or only half-competent bilingual reader who yet is drawn to the poetic, can be of immense assistance to the translator in raising questions that the translator — and the translator only — must finally resolve. Of course, truly bilingual readers can be invaluable also. My experience here is that it is good to have one's work looked at by readers with *and* without the original, and that feedback from readers listening to one's taped translations can be equally most instructive.

*Issues of gender.* I cannot say that I was nervous in translating the many women poets for the Wake Forest University Press bilingual anthology, any more than I was nervous about the critical work I have devoted in recent years to these and other women writers. The generosity, the moral support, the instinctive view of all the poets I have worked with — and a view that, instinctively, I also had from the outset — that there was nothing problematic in the exchange undertaken: all these factors rendered, and still render, both translation and criticism by a male of a woman's writing relatively easeful. Nevertheless, there is much to be alert to. Duras writes (in translation), "when women write, they translate their darkness... The writing of women is really translated from the unknown".[31] It might thus be deemed presumptuous and doubly distorting to translate such translation. And, quite simply, there are *many* factors, physiological, psychological, socio-political and so on, one may not, as a male translator, be sufficiently sensitive to, able, as it were, to live, to truly live viscerally, spiritually. And then there are, going from French to English, linguistic issues that carry great weight: how to translate "l'homme" in many contexts, how to convey the feminine markers the poem may generate, how to translate the language of the female body with adequacy, etc. The challenge of moving between feminine voice and masculine voice is, however, not unlike translation's "mov[ement] BETWEEN tongues, [it] acquires difference"[32], as Willis Barnstone puts it. And this acquisition or maintenance of difference, in effect, is good, good to experience and to rejoice in. Barnstone can deem it to be a "dwell[ing] in exile"[33], but I have always experienced it as a force that urges respect of difference and tends to disallow that universalising, flattening effect that translation can risk bringing to the voice of the other. "A poet translator", Barnstone writes — he's up to X in his ABC! — "is a XENOPHILIAC"[34]. And indeed the translator's high-wire performance demands a most delicate act of balancing intersubjectivity and maintenance of absolute alterity. At all events, my own politico-spiritual project did not count for nothing in all of this. Translation of women poets in bilingual format provides access to much work hard to find in bookstores or even bibliographies, for students, many being women, colleagues, and even for a wider public. Translating the work of Salah Stétié, nominated for the Nobel, may not have raised gender issues, but the issues of cultural difference parallel those I have just discussed.

*Critical paraphernalia.* The translated text, accompanied or not by the original, functions inevitably as the primary place of revelation. However, just as the translator should ideally understand the pertinence and value of the poems he or she has chosen to "transform" (as Derrida would have us see it), so may one see certain critical accompaniments — preface, notes and so on — as of especial utility. This will be all the more so if the work translated is either relatively unavailable, new even, or intrinsically complex. Such paraphernalia need not be long and, it is my view, are as apt to please in a magazine context as in a full-blown translated collection. They can situate, concentrate the mind, alert to difficulties in translation as well as the original. They are not necessarily scholarly, they would aim to caress the text as it lodges itself in the reader's mind and body. They would demonstrate that if the translator is a writer, he is one who knows *why* he is writing. Many types of critical contextualising are, of course, feasible. The choice made may vary according to the readership. But it will always risk showing that both the original and the translation have urgency, life, and always exist here and now, for this reader reading.

*Pagination, visual presentation.* It may seem a little fatuous to turn attention to apparently banal factors such as pagination and visual presentation in translation. For many poets, however, such matters are of great significance. I recall conversations or correspondence with poets such as Anne-Marie Albiach, Yves Bonnefoy, Silvia Baron Supervielle, Salah Stétié and various others over these matters. By and large, respect of original pagination seems desirable, though it may conflict with format or, naturally, economics. One wonders, with the American-French poet David Mus, why Mallarmé's *Coup de dés* gets today the added space its original edition did not provide. Many issues can arise in these matters: does one paginate a collection originally unpaginated? Does one modify typeset significantly? Does one even know for sure how the typographical orchestration works in the original, whether lines are in "verse" or prose? Does one accumulate poems on the same page, or one after the other, when they are widely separated in the original, perhaps published in different books? And so on. And, needless to say, visual presentation includes a host of issues from the design of front and back covers to the nature of initial pages before translation begins. If the poet is living, consultation is always called for to avoid, above all, unwitting *gaffes*. Final adjudication is, largely, with translator and publisher. However, I have seen good translations spoiled through inattention to final material detail.

*Satisfying the self.* Not to seek such a satisfaction would no doubt be a contradiction in any field of endeavour. The translation, however, must attain to a fine and passionately wise balance between knowledge that translation, as Barnstone puts it, "dwells in imperfection"[35] (266), and that other "important knowledge"[36], as Raffel terms it, coming from sensing that this is the best one can do. The translator cannot be one to anguish: he or she is a doer, a creator who reaches decisions, neither in a spirit of self-adulation nor with a sense of real failure. What Dryden says of the poetry critic may be said, in all simplicity, of the translator-poet: "True judgment in poetry, like that in painting, takes a view of the whole together, whether it be good or not; and where the beauties are more than the faults, concludes for the poet against the little judge".[37]

Is there any coherent conclusion to be drawn from all of this? Certainly not a formal ABC of Translation, serious or tongue-in-cheek. It is, however, reasonable to venture a few generalisations, leaving two short "translation examples" to speak for themselves, the shadow of these remarks at least cast across them. It is difficult to disagree with Dr. Jowett's conclusion that translating (poetry in particular) is an "art which in our judgment cannot be imparted by any formal rules or precepts".[38] This is no doubt true of any art, were we even to have night and day at our beck and call the finest of masters or mistresses. That translation is destined always to "betray", as Mounin and others insist, seems to me a quite unnecessary psychologisation of the inherent difference it performs. Nor do I see any absolute need to draw lines between translating *ut interpres* and writing-translating *ut orator*, as, again Mounin would have us do.[39] All knowledge is, implacably, as Heidegger has reminded us, interpretation and one cannot but agree with David Ross when he writes that "translation is hermeneutical, bridging different times and worlds. There can be no definitive, objective translation".[40] For the translator to become absolute *orator*, however, beyond the bounds accepted by the *interpres*, is to risk either that "taming" of language and meaning that Julien Green would have us avoid, or a certain hubristic independency from the original which bilingual editions tend to hold, happily I believe, in check. To translate poetry, however — though it is true of all translation — certainly can remind us that, as Edmond Cary put it, "c'est du vivant que nous pesons" (we are involved in weighing up something live and living).[41] To go back to Baudelaire or Rimbaud is, like translating contemporaries such as Denise Le Dantec or Esther Tellermann, to realise that all remains possible, newly readable, thinkable, transformable, and that, as observed by Walter Benjamin, translation could — and should — contribute significantly to something like a theory of meaning for language.[42] Translators tend, I believe, to recognise this instinctively, but prefer to live the excitements and enchantments of practice rather than devote their time to pure conceptualisation. If we can share Michel Deguy's feeling when he says "un certain athéorisme me déplaît" (I don't find to

Tactics and Non-Tactics: The Experience of a Translator of Modern Poetry    69

my liking a certain lack of theorising one's act), the translator increases his or her knowledge largely through *exercising* that Derridean "transformation". Exercising it, moreover, ideally in joy, seeking an unegotistical satisfaction of self, and with a full consciousness of the provisionality of his or her production. Relaxation and unpresumptuous exuberance can allow us to smile with some approval at Barnstone's final flourish, the Z of his ABC: "translation is a ZOO and a heavenly ZION". Salah Stétié, I know, would smile too.

    Heather Dohollau

    "Comment perdre..."
    Comment perdre ce qui est toujours là
    Le vrai incroyable
    La présence d'un feu, un lit, un jardin
    L'ombre en tête d'oiseau de la plume
    N'est pas plus fidèle
    Que ces lieux où nous vivons
    Par la caution des choses

    La table, les chaises, les fleurs
    Dans l'eau des heures
    L'espace partagé
    Où en tendant la main
    Nous poussons la porte du présent
    Et le regard s'arrondit comme un fruit

    "How can we lose..."
    How can we lose what is ever there
    The incredibly true
    The presence of a fire, a bed, a garden
    The bird-headed shadow of the pen
    Is not more faithful
    Than these places wherein we live
    By the surety of things

    The table, the chairs, the flowers
    In the water of hours
    Shared space
    Where our hand proffered
    We push open the door of the present
    And our gaze fills out like fruit

Salah Stétié

"Le texte est..."
Le texte est de croissant sur des brisures
De cicatrices sur ces cristaux aigus
Qu'un ciel couvre de ciels arrachés ou figures
Jusqu'à l'obscur oeillet qui respire

Paysage à la destruction de l'épaule
A ce bois contenu par la lune
Quand cela bat dans l'arbre et s'embrouille avec colère
Et d'aile, d'un éclat, fait la mer trop grande

— Où allons-nous, doux époux?

Alors vient la femme avec étoiles ici et jambes
et vraie menthe
Et lignes pour le vent l'assoupir avec plis
dans ses beaux linges
Allume un ongle de miroir à la nuit où ses doigts
s'éteignent
Afin que l'oiseau casse et tombe dans les chambres
du monde

"The text is..."
The text is crescent-like over scarry
Cracks over sharp crystals
That a sky covers with skies torn free or figures
Down to the obscure carnation that breathes

Landscape of shoulder's destruction
Of this wood contained by moon
When things flap in the tree and confuse in anger
And a-wing, with a flash, have the sea racing

— Where are we going, gentle husband?

Then comes the woman with stars here and legs
and real mint
And lines for the wind lulling it with folds
in her fine linens
Lights a mirroring nail to the night in which her
fingers die away
So that the bird snaps and falls into the rooms
of the world

Michael Bishop

## Notes

1. Peter Newmark, *About Translation*, Clevedon/Philadelphia: Multilingual Matters, 1991, 5.
2. Burton Raffel, *The Forked Tongue*, The Hague: Mouton, 1971, 103.
3. Marilyn Gaddis Rose (ed.), *Translation Spectrum*, Albany: SUNY, 1981, 125.
4. Willis Barnstone, *The Poetics of Translation*, Yale U.P., 1993, 117.
5. Edmond Cary, *Les Grands Traducteurs français*, Paris: Librairie de l'Université, 1963, 130.
6. Paul Selver, *The Art of Translating Poetry*, London: John Baker, 1966, 21.
7. *The Poetics of Translation*, 265. My italics.
8. *Ibid.*, 266.
9. Lefevere, André. *Translating Poetry*. Amsterdam: Van Gorcum, 1975.
10. *The Poetics of Translation*, 268.
11. Michael Bishop, *Women's Poetry in France, 1965-1995*, Winston-Salem: Wake Forest University Press, 1997.
12. Hilaire Belloc, *On Translation*, Oxford: Clarendon Press, 1931, 17.
13. *Essays in Translation*, London: Journal of Education, 1885, vii.
14. *The Art of Translating Poetry*, 26.
15. *Translation Spectrum*, 39.
16. *The Poetics of Translation*, 267.
17. Georges Mounin, *Les Belles Infidèles*, Marseille: Cahiers du Sud, 1955.
18. *Essays*, vii.
19. *On Translation*, 35.
20. *Ibid.*, 34, 27.
21. *Les Belles Infidèles*, 74.
22. *Ibid.*, 77.
23. *Essays*, vi.
24. *On Translation*, 20.
25. Joseph Graham (ed.), *Difference in Translation*. Cornell U.P., 1985, 25.
26. *On Translation*, 23.
27. *Translating Poetry*, 95.
28. Robert Bly, *The Eight Stages of Translation*. Boston: Ally Press and Rowan Tree Press, 1986.
29. *On Translation*, 36.
30. *The Forked Tongue*, 104.
31. Luise von Flotow, *Translation and Gender*, Manchester: St. Jerome Publishing/Ottawa University Press, 1997, 12.
32. *The Poetics of Translation*, 265.
33. *Ibid.*, 266.
34. *Ibid.*, 271.

35 *Ibid.*, 266.
36 *The Forked Tongue*, 176.
37 *Ibid.*, 14.
38 *Essays,* vii.
39 *Les Belles Infidèles*, 77.
40 *Translation Spectrum*, 11.
41 *Les Grands Traducteurs français,* 130.
42 *Difference in Translation*, 24.

# 6.
# RHYME'S WRONGS: DEALING WITH VERLAINE'S RHYMES IN ENGLISH

The problems of translation are generally the same for whatever kind of poetry. According to Claire Malroux, the French translator of Douglas Dunn, they are about the search for equivalent sounds, about preserving rhythm, and, as far as possible, about maintaining rhyme.[1] This is uncontroversial, no doubt, but a potential trap is flagged by the concession of "as far as possible". No question but that the translator must find equivalent sounds, and must place a weight of responsibility on rhythm. Most translators would surely agree, even if "equivalent" invites development and discussion. But rhyme, it is surely implied, can be the weakest link in the translator's already stressed poetic and semantic chain.

Of course, Malroux's concern is translation from English into French, and French poetry, historically, has relied substantially on rhyme, for reasons which need not be taken up again here. It may be that a translator working into French feels significantly more constrained by the exigencies of rhyme than does one working into English. With its strong traditions of unrhymed poetry, does English prosody not sanction relative liberty in the domain of rhyme? Cannot something other than perfect end-rhyme legitimately be substituted? The predictability of end-rhyme can be upset by internal rhyme, cross rhyme, initial rhyme, random rhyme, while the insistent grip of perfect rhyme can be relaxed with the various kinds of near-rhyme available: imperfect rhyme, half-rhyme, dissonant rhyme, unaccented rhyme, and, of course, their close relatives assonance and alliteration. Besides these, modernist English poetics offers the end-stressed rising line and the front-stressed falling line, both of which can enhance the fluidity of a stanza or a group of lines by downgrading the importance of end-rhymed, end-stopped lines, so prevalent in the French poetic tradition. But, in the last analysis, should the translator into English not consider jettisoning rhyme altogether when confronting the over-predictable orthodoxies of French prosody? For it seems that too often the use of rhyme manages only the paradoxical result of making worse a translation which would have been better off without. Thanks to the tortuous and all-too-frequently infelicitous re-jigging of syntax which the demands of rhyme can impose, rhyme becomes the prehensile tail which wags the translation. And perfect rhyme, especially when used in conjunction with crude and insistent metre, all too frequently can sound comical in English when no humour is intended.

These matters take on particular importance in the case of one major poet who has been translated into English only spasmodically and rather randomly, Paul Verlaine. At the front of my mind are two controlling stanzas in "Art poétique" (*Jadis et Naguère*, 1884), in which Verlaine, unshackling himself from the old prosodic dogmas, inveighs against rhyme:

> Tu feras bien, en train d'énergie,
> De rendre un peu la Rime assagie.
> Si l'on n'y veille, elle ira jusqu'où?
>
> O qui dira les torts de la Rime?
> Quel enfant sourd ou quel nègre fou
> Nous a forgé ce bijou d'un sou
> Qui sonne creux et faux sous la lime?[2]

Such English translations of Verlaine as have been readily available in the UK are often mediocre or downright bad, for two main reasons: one, the translators' perceived need to use out-of-date and quaint expression; the other, insistence on rhyme. Indeed, the impression is sometimes given that the translator has first worked at the rhyme, then "justified" the artifice of it by building up the lines with pseudo-poetic expression. Perhaps this style is a little more acceptable in the translations made, very roughly, around Verlaine's time and shortly after, such as those by Ernest Dowson, William Robertson, Agnes Drey and Arthur Symons. But, on the often-proposed principle that every generation needs its own translations, it seems odd that Verlaine's more recent translators have not used the lexical, syntactical and prosodic apparatus of their own times. The impression too frequently given by, for example, Muriel Kittel, Vernon Watkins, Kate Flores and Joanna Richardson, modern translators for whom rhyme seems to be almost sacrosanct, is of distortion and discomfort, as if their target texts somehow remained outside their linguistic expression.

# Rhyme's Wrongs: Dealing with Verlaine's Rhymes in English

If this sounds harsh, let me add that occasionally all the translators named achieve some lovely results; perhaps not entire poems, but certainly individual moments and particular lines. Also, I must add that one or two new translations of selected Verlaine poems have been published recently in the USA, which I have not yet seen.

The translator's main problem lies perhaps in Verlaine's famed music, those subtle effects which harmonise with wonderful choices of word and phrase, and blended so often into the measures of very short lines. A subtle and complex music indeed, but I want to suggest that, within this complexity, rhyme can be isolated, and altered or removed by the translator in a bid to maintain Verlaine's heart-beat.

I offer now some reflections on three published English translations, each of two poems by Verlaine. The French originals have been chosen because they are among the most often translated of Verlaine's output; the translations, made at various points in the last one hundred years, should (theoretically) offer evidence of different ideologies of translation. The following reflections, which are made from the viewpoint of a notional translator facing tricky choices and decisions, naturally are subjective.

First, the celebrated "Chanson d'automne", from *Poèmes saturniens*:

Les sanglots longs
Des violons
De l'automne
Blessent mon cœur
D'une langueur
Monotone.
Tout suffocant
Et blême quand
Sonne l'heure,
Je me souviens
Des jours anciens
Et je pleure;
Et je m'en vais
Au vent mauvais
Qui m'emporte
Deçà, delà,
Pareil à la
Feuille morte.[3]

This light, vanishing poem of course is technically so finely tuned that it poses the severest of tests to the translator. It is one of those webs from which the removal of a single thread risks collapsing the whole structure.

William Robertson renders it thus in his 1895 translation:

An Autumn Song

The long-drawn sighs,
Like violin-cries,
Of autumn wailing,
Lull in my soul
The languorous shoal
Of thoughts assailing.

Wan, as whom knells
Of funeral bells
Bemoan and banish,
I weep upon
Days dead and gone
With dreams that vanish;

Then helpless swing
On the wind's wing;
Tossed hither and thither
As winter sweeps
From swirling heaps
Worn leaves that wither.[4]

This is surely a perfectly acceptable translation within the conventions of its times. But the reversal of noun and participle in ll. 3 and 6 sounds infelicitous to the modern ear. It smacks of "Poetry". Then, in l.7, the literary, truncated construction surely nowadays would have to be expanded to include a personal object pronoun to which to relate "whom" ("him", "her", "they"). Lexically, "bemoan", "upon", just possibly "wan" sound quaint. None the less, Robertson's translation is reasonably unobtrusive; nothing much glares... Except the liberties he has taken, in order to obtain rhyme, by expanding what Verlaine has written. Lines 3 and 6, already mentioned, add elements which are not there in the beautifully simple lines of Verlaine. Clearly, this is to get the rhyme, and a cheap and easy one it is too. The corresponding short lines in the remaining stanzas (ll. 9, 12, 15, 18) have received similar treatment. The exquisitely wrought trisyllabic line has been inflated disproportionately in all cases. Indeed, they now become longer than the lines around them, reversing Verlaine's pattern. While such re-arrangement need not necessarily be a sin, here surely it is artistically invalid to stand Verlaine's system so glaringly on its head. Unless, of course, as must be Robertson's position, you believe that rhyme must prevail to the detriment of everything else. But this exigency has painted Robertson into quite a corner. When "coeur" becomes "soul", the "shoal of thought" has to be conjured up from nowhere. And, perhaps sensing grave difficulties with "monotone", Robertson has given it token recognition in "lull", and has avoided the rhyme. Then, the total reversal of order of lines 7-9, with their greatly expanded elements (the implied comparison of "as whom"; "funeral", "bemoan and banish", none of which is stated in Verlaine's elliptical lines) surely is over-interpretative for a poem of such insubstantiality. Further, the marvellous fragility of Verlaine's single, final, floating leaf is crushed by the weight and aggression of Robertson's plural leaves in his last three lines. And where Verlaine concludes on three syllables about death, Robertson brings the leaf back to life twice ("worn", "wither"). Here is Agnes Drey's 1911 translation:

An Autumn Song

The sobbing sighs
And long-drawn cries
Of Autumn's wane
Fill my dull ear
With bodings drear
And languid pain.

When pale leaves fly
Dejected by
On the cold blast,
Dead memories stir
In the wild air;
My tears fall fast.

As the leaves swirl
In the wind's whirl,
And then decay,
Sere, worn and dry
I hurry by
And pass away.[5]

This account, like Robertson's, clearly proceeds on the basis that full rhyme must be maintained, although once a near-rhyme is used (lines 10-11). It seems to me that Drey combines rhyme and rhythm in a more successful way than does Robertson. She has used a short, consistent line, very close to Verlaine's pattern, and within those constraints has managed to sustain schematic rhyme. But — and it is a very big but — this has been bought at the expense of a considerable re-arrangement of the original. (Admittedly, the volume in which Drey published "An Autumn Song" indicates that her translations are *after* various poets). In the first stanza, line 3 regrettably is expanded, as is line 6. Verlaine's "coeur" becomes an ear, the uncomplicated "monotone" fussily becomes "bodings drear", with its ponderous reversal of noun and adjective. The rhyme and rhythm patterns are tight, no doubt, but at a cost. However, the real problems start in the second stanza. Lines 7-9 seem merely to be pre-echoes of the final stanza, and, as such, are repetitious and redundant. They also traduce Verlaine. The whole of the ominous section about choking, blanching and ringing has been jettisoned. Lines 10-12 bring us back recognisably to what Verlaine has written, though the detail of Drey's choices is unconvincing (the gentleness of "anciens" becomes "wild", used presumably because it is a convenient monosyllable). I begin to wonder if what came first to Drey as she attacked this stanza were tears falling "fast", back from which she worked hard to establish rhythm and rhyme.

Drey's final stanza ties itself more closely to Verlaine but still manages to expand the original. Verlaine does not make his single leaf become a swirling plurality, nor is the plain fact of death elaborated into decay plus three uneconomical adjectives. Then, the understated but eloquent "je m'en vais", by saying less says more than do "hurry by", and, worse, "pass away", the second with its unnecessary and even inaccurate allusion to the poet-persona's own death.

Drey's poem surely is exemplary of the pitfalls of an approach which favours technical correctness over the poem's truth. Of course, one can appreciate and sympathise with this translator's predicament. Her reasoning quite possibly would have been that to lose the form of Verlaine's little poem was a graver sin than to de-restrict its content. And we might agree that, read independently of the original French, Drey's lines read and sound well enough.

Let me turn to a much more recent rendering of "Chanson d'automne", Joanna Richardson's, of 1974:

Autumn Song

The long sobbing
Of violins
On autumn days
My heart doth wound
And I despond
Unbearably.

All words are gone.
Sallow and wan,
When the moment nears
I then recall
Time's funeral
And I shed tears:

It is my end,
And the rough wind
Bears me, in grief,
This way and that,
Precipitate,
Like a dead leaf.[6]

Richardson's pattern approximates closely to that of Drey. Both have opted for a tetrasyllabic line, consistently maintained except for line 10 of Drey, although convention might allow "mem'ries"; and except for line 9 of Richardson, although again, at a stretch, the "e" in "the" might be elided. But this very elision highlights what I find unsatisfactory about Richardson's strategy. Her whole approach is archaic. To my mind, a translator working as recently as the 1970s cannot indulge in artifice of the sort found in lines 4-5. Perhaps this is the least successful individual moment in Richardson's poem, but the rest of it certainly reads stiffly and formally. It seems that she has conceded that Verlaine's poem is so difficult that the only strategy is to abandon attempts to get an English translation for her times, and instead to re-create a late-Victorian imitation. This seems all the more a pity because Richardson does seem to have escaped the tyranny of rhyme, to the considerable benefit of her translation. Lines 1-2 are refreshingly assonantal, lines 4-5 and lines 13-14 alliterative, and there is some near-rhyme too, catching the reader perhaps a little by surprise but still capturing the essence of Verlaine's form. Thus, lines 10-11, lines 16-17. Respect is still paid to exact rhyme in lines 7-8, lines 9 and 12, lines 15 and 18. Note, too, that there is no coincidence of sounds between lines 3 and 6, unlike the corresponding sections of the second and final stanzas. The question is: does this freedom destroy or impair Verlaine's sense, or is it a neutral matter, or indeed, can it be considered wholly justified, even successful? My own feeling is that it works by being unremarkable, and that Richardson's relaxed use of rhyme is the single most successful aspect of her translation. I can't help but wonder why, having adopted such a relaxed and *modern* attitude to that one element, she did not apply it to all her strategy, and offer the 1970s a translation for their times. Surely she would not even have had to vary her tetrasyllabic line in the search for a more modern idiom than she has chosen?

The second poem of Verlaine's, for which I also want to consider three published translations, is "Colloque sentimental", from *Fêtes galantes*, of 1869. Almost as celebrated as "Chanson d'automne", it has always been a favourite choice of translators.

> Dans le vieux parc solitaire et glacé,
> Deux formes ont tout à l'heure passé.
>
> Leurs yeux sont morts et leurs lèvres sont molles,
> Et l'on entend à peine leurs paroles.
> Dans le vieux parc solitaire et glacé,
> Deux spectres ont évoqué le passé.
>
> — Te souvient-il de notre extase ancienne?
> — Pourquoi voulez-vous donc qu'il m'en souvienne?
>
> — Ton cœur bat-il toujours à mon seul nom?
> Toujours vois-tu mon âme en rêve? — Non.
>
> — Ah! les beaux jours de bonheur indicible
> Où nous joignions nos bouches! — C'est possible.
>
> — Qu'il était bleu, le ciel, et grand, l'espoir!
> — L'espoir a fui, vaincu, vers le ciel noir.
>
> Tels ils marchaient dans les avoines folles,
> Et la nuit seule entendit leurs paroles.[7]

# Rhyme's Wrongs: Dealing with Verlaine's Rhymes in English

Perhaps not quite as evanescent as "Chanson d'automne", and certainly kinder to the translator by virtue of its meatier lines, "Colloque sentimental" nevertheless is full of temptations to give precious and archaic translations.

Of the three translations I shall look at — by Ernest Dowson, Joanna Richardson and Alistair Elliot — two reveal an absolute fidelity to rhyme, while the approach of the third is akin to Richardson's in her "Autumn Song".

This is Dowson's version, published in 1905:

Colloque sentimental

Into the lonely park all frozen fast,
A while ago there were two forms who passed.

Lo, are their lips fallen and their eyes dead,
Hardly shall a man hear the words they said.

Into the lonely park all frozen fast,
There came two shadows who recall the past.

"Dost thou remember our old ecstasy?" —
"Wherefore should I possess that memory?" —

"Doth thine heart beat at my sole name alway?
Still dost thou see my soul in visions?" "Nay!" —

"They were fair days of joy unspeakable,
Whereon our lips were joined?" - "I cannot tell." —

"Were not the heavens blue, was not hope high?" —
"Hope has fled vanquished down the darkling sky." —

So through the barren oats they wanderèd,
And the night only heard the words they said.[8]

Judging by this translation, and indeed the others to be considered, "Colloque sentimental" is relatively easy to rhyme in English. Adverbial "fast" in line 1 is not strictly necessary but it is inoffensive. It scarcely constitutes translation enhancement. The second couplet offers a very obvious rhyme, on condition that the two clauses in its first line are reversed. Again, that may seem a slight (and quite conventional) liberty. Similarly, the fourth couplet suggests an easy rhyme. The fifth, however, is more strained, using, as it does, pseudo-poetic language from the Poetaster's almanac. The rhyming words surely must have jarred at the beginning of the 20th century, if not as much as they do now. The sixth couplet has partially defeated Dowson, who can offer only a near-rhyme. The penultimate couplet is unexceptionable, while the final couplet gets its rhyme in the way the fifth does, by recourse to a cheap device deemed to befit poetry.

But the virtue of Dowson's piece, it seems to me, is that it has remained almost completely loyal to Verlaine's vocabulary and phrasing. Not only that, but Dowson has opted to copy Verlaine's decasyllabic line all through. Allowing, then, for certain archaic touches ("Lo", "Dost thou", "whereon", "darkling"), this version can be considered a genuine translation, sober but fairly sophisticated, in which the unostentatious rhymes play their part. All the more interesting, then, that Dowson describes his translation as "*after* Paul Verlaine".

The second translation of "Colloque sentimental" is by Joanna Richardson, again from her edition for Penguin:

Sentimental Conversation

In the old lonely park, across the snow,
Two figures passed a little while ago.

Their eyes were lifeless and their lips were dead,
And one could hardly hear the words they said.

In the old lonely park, across the snow,
Two ghosts recalled the days of long ago.

"Do you remember our old ecstasy?"
"Why do you think it should occur to me?"

"Love, does your heart still beat my name to know?
Do you still dream about my spirit?" "No."

"Oh the fine days of wordless ecstasy
When we kissed one another!" "Possibly."

"How blue the heavens were, how hopes ran high!"
"Hope fled, defeated, to a sombre sky."

And so, through the wild oats, they walked ahead,
And only darkness heard the words they said.[9]

To juxtapose this text with Dowson's is instructive. Here, in 1974, is a translator who has adopted virtually the same strategy as her turn-of-the-century predecessor. In theory, there should be nothing wrong in that; why not stick to the decasyllable, why not match Verlaine's rhyming couplets? The trouble is, surely, that Richardson's result was dated even on its publication, and not simply because of her curious decision to phrase language anachronistically (the fifth couplet, notably, but elsewhere too). There is something quaint, bordering on the comical, about such slavish adherence to metre and rhyme. Individually, the rhymes are about as "quiet" as Dowson's. Indeed, in the final couplet Richardson gives a neat solution to what could have been a problem. (In the first couplet, though, the rhyme has been bought at the expense of accuracy). But I would suggest that there is something about the combination of rhyme, metre and phrasing which undermines this translation. I would also suggest that, were just one of those elements to be discarded, this translation could become more consonant with modern English poetic styles, making it more appropriate to its age.

This brings me to my final example, Alistair Elliot's 1991 account of "Colloque sentimental", which, from the title onwards, appears at least to accept an implicit challenge to do a translation for our times:

An Exchange of Feelings

In the old park, deserted in the frost,
A while ago two shapes came drifting past.

Their eyes have died, their lips become so weak
That you can hardly hear a word they speak.

In the old park, deserted in the frost,
A ghost was reminiscing to a ghost.

— Can you recall our ecstasy of long ago?
— Why stir the memory? Why do you want to know?

— Does your heart beat at just my name, as ever?
Do you still see my spirit in your dreams? — No. Never.

— O lovely days of speechless happiness
When our mouths met! — Speechless? Perhaps it was.

— How blue the sky was and what hopes we had!
— Hope ran away to the black sky, defeated.

> So they walk on in the self-seeding grass
> With only night to hear them as they pass.[10]

If there is accuracy in Elliot's title, the very first line has a freedom which suggests that he is going to put strictness of form before fidelity to Verlaine's words. While the two are close, of course, "frost" is not quite the same as "glacé". The second line confirms that Elliot is plotting a syllabic metre, for both are decasyllables. Instead of rhyme, though, he has close alliteration, which, to my ear, is well judged. It appears, therefore, that a pattern is being set, and indeed the whole of the poem shows that this is so — more or less. For the decasyllable yields twice to hendecasyllables (lines 9 and 14), twice to dodecasyllables (lines 7-8), and once to a thirteen syllable line (line 10). These are brief excursions, but, set against the rigidity of Richardson's metre, they help to liven up the translation, as do Elliot's occasional digressions from rhyme. His strategy, if strategy it was rather than pragmatism, seems to have been to opt for exact rhyme in half of the couplets, and for types of near-rhyme in the rest. All of the latter are particularly close — "frost" and "ghost", "happiness" and "was", "had" and "defeated". The virtues of these line-endings make me wish that he had abandoned rhyme altogether in favour of sustained alliteration. Elliot, more than the other translators, brings into my mind Verlaine's strictures about rhyme. It is not that Elliot's rhymes are bad, not at all. It is just — and this is entirely subjective, of course — that consideration of all the six versions I have chosen to discuss steers me tentatively to conclude that, for the contemporary translator certainly, to rhyme Verlaine systematically is the wrong thing to do. If Elliot's first line takes dubious risks in order to establish metre and rhyme, and gets away with it, then his penultimate line, working towards the same objective, surely does not. Yes, oats are classified as a grass; yes, they are self-seeding. But the sheer unsuitability of a scientific register in a poem of this kind is not compensated by the achievement of a dodecasyllabic line whose rhyming component allows Elliot to use "pass" in the final line, and thereby avoid the sort of clumsy ending offered by Dowson.

Better, surely, that the English-language translator confronting Verlaine today take to heart the lessons of "Art poétique". Of course, it is true that some of Verlaine's poems derive their effect essentially from rhyme ("Il patinait..." from the Lucien Létinois cycle in *Amour*, to name but one admirable example). Such a poem probably will need careful and consistent English rhyme to do it justice. This is not the case with all of Verlaine, though. In fact, I would contend that it is true of only a minority of his very considerable output. Take the case of the two poems offered for consideration in this chapter. If the metre were very controlled, compact and harmonious, would it matter at all that a translation of "Chanson d'automne" dispensed with rhyme? Would a translation of "Colloque sentimental" not read better in which carefully stressed metre were favoured over syllabics, and assonance, alliteration and even no coincidence of sound at all were favoured over rhyme? Why not a blanker kind of verse, or at least one in which the subtleties of, for example, end stress and front stress compensated for perfect rhyme? Verlaine's first, therefore arguably key, statement in "Art poétique" — "De la musique avant toute chose" — surely demands highly accomplished metres. On balance, the awe in which translators have held Verlaine's rhymes — I think the six examples discussed represent the broad picture — has done his poetry a disservice. Is it not time that translators of Verlaine into English loosened the grip of rhyme, let it go altogether, so that the music might be heard?

Let me close by laying out, without commentary, my own translation of a much-anthologised sonnet of Verlaine's, "Mon rêve familier", from *Poèmes saturniens*. I offer it with an open mind, moderately happy (leaving aside all other considerations, technical and poetic) that it has not suffered from the rejection of end-rhyme, and modestly hopeful that it may have gained by it. First, Verlaine:

Je fais souvent ce rêve étrange et pénétrant
D'une femme inconnue, et que j'aime, et qui m'aime
Et qui n'est, chaque fois, ni tout à fait la même
Ni tout à fait une autre, et m'aime et me comprend.

Car elle me comprend, et mon cœur, transparent
Pour elle seule, hélas! cesse d'être un problème
Pour elle seule, et les moiteurs de mon front blême,
Elle seule les sait rafraîchir, en pleurant.

Est-elle brune, blonde ou rousse? — Je l'ignore.
Son nom? Je me souviens qu'il est doux et sonore
Comme ceux des aimés que la Vie exila.

Son regard est pareil au regard des statues,
Et, pour sa voix, lointaine, et calme, et grave, elle a
L'inflexion des voix chères qui se sont tues.

My recurring dream

I often have a strange and searing dream
About an unknown woman whom I love
And who loves me; never quite the same
Nor someone else, she loves, she understands me.

Yes, she understands; the pity is
For her alone my heart is obvious,
Simple for her alone who brings to life
My dead face running with her tears.

Is she dark, auburn, blond? I don't know.
Her name? It echoes softly
Like names of loved ones gone for good.
Her gaze is like a statue's gaze,

And in her calm and grave and distant voice
Are modulations of loved voices gone to earth.

Martin Sorrell

## Notes

1  Claire Malroux, "Translating Douglas Dunn into French, or How to Steer Between the Prosaic and the Lyrical" in Ian Higgins (ed.), *Forum for Modern Language Studies*, University of St Andrews and OUP, XXXIII, January 1997, 21-6.
2  "Art poétique", in *Oeuvres poétiques complètes*, Paris: Gallimard, Bibliothèque de la Pléiade, 1962, 326-327.
3  *Ibid.*, 72-73.
4  William Robertson, *French Verse: Being biographical and critical notices of thirty-three French poets of the Nineteenth Century with experimental translations of their poems.* London: A.D. Innes & Co., 1895, 91.

5   Agnes D. Drey, *Poems after Verlaine, Maeterlinck, Leconte de Lisle and others*. London: St Catherine's Press, 1911, 10.
6   Joanna Richardson, *Verlaine: Selected Poems*. Harmondsworth: Penguin Books Ltd, 1974, 45.
7   *Oeuvres poétiques complètes*, 121.
8   Ernest Dowson, *The Poems of Ernest Dowson*, London: John Lane, The Bodley Head, 1905, 136-137.
9   *Verlaine: Selected Poems*, 79.
10  *French Love Poems*, trans. Alistair Elliot, Newcastle-upon-Tyne: Bloodaxe Books, 1991, 87.

# 7.
## EQUIVALENCE AND ADEQUACY IN TRANSLATION: ARE THEY EQUIVALENT? ARE THEY ADEQUATE?

The aim of translation, according to Marge E. Landsberg, is "to reproduce in the TL, as faithfully as possible (i.e. at all levels: morphological, phonological, syntactic, lexical, semantic — and even stylistic) all the linguistic features of which the SL is composed".[1] In order to render all these features into the TL, the translator, as we know, would have to bear in mind the concept of equivalence all the time. However, when it comes to defining what equivalence really means, it seems that it is one of the most controversial concepts in the whole field of Translation Studies — in Peter Fawcett's words "a concept that has probably cost the lives of more trees than any other in translation studies"[2] — and this, needless to say, is due to the tendency either to speak about translation in general terms or to try to apply a sort of mathematical definition that can not be reversed. And it becomes even more difficult to establish a clear definition of this key term when we find it related to the term "adequacy" because sometimes they are both treated as synonyms and at other times they are not clearly differentiated.

Most definitions of translation mention the concept of equivalence as a key factor in the process of rendering a text from one language into another. Let us take, as an example, a small sample of the definitions given of translation. According to Hartman and Stork, translation is "the replacement of a representation of a text in one language by the representation of an equivalent text in a second language".[3] Catford, for his part, defines translation as "the replacement of textual material in one language (SL) by equivalent textual material in another language (TL)".[4] Another definition of translation is that given by Nida and Taber: "Translating consists in reproducing in the receptor language the closest natural equivalent of the source-language message, first in terms of meaning and secondly in terms of style".[5] Now, it is noticeable that these definitions are all focused on one particular goal: the obtaining of equivalence from language or textual material A to language or textual material B. But one has to wonder to what extent, when translation theorists talk about the concept of equivalence, they all mean the same.

In order to try and clarify the meaning of equivalence and, at the same time, adequacy, it will be necessary to define as unambiguously as possible what is understood by both terms and to establish a clear distinction between them.

Equivalence is a term that has often been used not only in the field of Translation Studies but in other fields as well. But, if we quote a simple definition, such as the one given by the *Collins Dictionary of the English Language*, we are confronted, from the very start, with problems. The term "equivalence" is defined as 'the state of being "equal or interchangeable in value, quantity, significance, etc" or "having the same or a similar effect or meaning".[6] Two ideas can be inferred from this definition: a) words like "equal", "interchangeable", "same", "similar" can mean equivalence (i.e. "the state of being..." etc.); b) equivalence always takes place in a pair where some form of relationship between two elements can exist. Thus, there are problems in defining this concept which, sometimes, can go even further than the strictly linguistic point of view. As Sandra Halverson says: "The concept of equivalence touches on several fundamental philosophical problems, most notably the possibility/necessity of comparison and the nature of sameness. These problems underlie much of the debate on the overall relevance or utility of the equivalence concept for translation studies. [...] The contentious nature of the concept thus lies in both the philosophical questions it implies, i.e. comparison and sameness, and in the complexity of its definition and application. Philosophical questions aside, the most problematic questions remain: *what* entities are/can be equivalent, *how alike/similar/equal* are they and *how do we define "alike/similar/equal"*, and in *which feature* are they equivalent?"[7] In trying to answer these questions, and in trying to define the concept of equivalence, it is crucial for the translator to state in a very precise way the type of equivalence s/he wants to achieve in the rendering of a text, as the notion of equivalence is, in itself, and, as we have seen, very broad and vague and "it is determined on the one hand by the historical-cultural conditions under which texts (original as much as secondary ones) are produced and received in the target culture, and on the other hand by a range of sometimes contradictory and scarcely reconcilable linguistic-textual and extralinguistic factors and conditions".[8]

We could even add a third factor in respect of the "equivalence approach", depending on whether the translator directs the ST towards the readership or the readership towards the ST. Statements which are made by translators sometimes indicate that they strive for both equivalence and adequacy. When interviewed about his translation of Mallarmé's *Tombeau d'Anatole*,[9] Paul Auster claims "Mon seul objectif était de faire quelque chose qui ressemble vraiment à l'original. Quelque chose qui fonctionne parfaitement en anglais et qui ne sente jamais la traduction. D'un autre côté, il faut je crois être très fidèle aux intentions de l'auteur; le traducteur n'a pas le droit de changer quoi que soit au texte qu'il traduit."[10] These are three of the many approaches that can determine the analysis of equivalence. In another article, Koller, focusing on the linguistic-oriented approach, distinguishes five factors which play an important role when specifying equivalence types — or equivalence perspectives, as some refer to them: "1. The *extralinguistic content* transmitted by a text". Koller defines this type of equivalence as *denotative equivalence*. This type is determined by the links between two languages, together with the textual factors which result in the choice of a specific equivalent in each specific case. "2. The *connotations* transmitted by means of the word choice [...], with respect to the level of style (register), the social and geographical dimension, frequency, etc". He defines this type of equivalence as *connotative equivalence*. This type takes the denotative meaning of words in each language further; analysing the connotative dimension of each language, looking at different levels such as the speech level, different types of register, the medium used and relating them to the connotative dimensions of the target language. "3. The *text and language norms* (usage norms) for given text types". This is called *text-normative equivalence*. It aims at following the norms and patterns required by each text or by each language in a variety of communicative situations in the target language. Thus, creating parallel texts in both languages. "4. The *receiver* (reader) to whom the translation is directed [...] and to whom the translation is "tuned" in order e.g. to achieve a given effect". This is the *pragmatic equivalence* which aims at the translation of a text for a particular readership. "5. Certain formal-aesthetic features of the SL text, including word play, metalinguistic aspects, individual stylistic features". Koller defines this kind of equivalence as *formal equivalence* which aims at creating in the translation a similarity in form, making use of the possibilities of the target language in relation to its forms or even creating new ones when it is necessary, taking account of the aesthetic features of the source language.[11] Although this can be fraught with difficulties as the translator may be taken to task for overdoing it: "And Scott-Moncrieff, an exquisite translator was very tempted to elaborate, and to use a precious word when a plainer one would serve".[12]

Another factor which can determine the concept of equivalence is the historical-cultural one. According to Sandra Halverson, the scholars who follow the historical-descriptive approach "maintain that the most important translational phenomena are those which cannot be accounted for within a strictly linguistic approach. They have chosen, instead, to focus on features of the target culture and the effects these features have on the translation process and/or product".[13] So that followers of this kind of approach are target oriented in the sense that they are more interested in the various aspects of the target culture and their influence in the act of translating and the translation, than in the linguistic relationship between the source text and the target text, which, in this case, does not play a major role. Apart from being target oriented, these scholars give much importance to translation norms. They see the act of translation as governed by norms which have been created under the assumption that translation is the type of action which is regulated by norms stated as a result of a very careful study of the relevant culture. The consequence of having a theory of translation based on norms is that this historical approach will be ruled by regularities, and the situational/cultural features will be explained by these regularities or norms. Many of the existing translations owe their existence to this approach as it considers the characteristics of both systems (the original and the system towards which the translation is directed); characteristics such as the author, the reader and the text, and also the historical/situational and cultural features which influence their form.

A third factor determining the analysis of equivalence is the one that refers to the approach adopted by the translator, namely whether the translator tries to convey the ST to the readership or to direct the readership towards the ST. One comes across endless quotations — from Dryden to Nida — from theorists who have seen the term of equivalence as a scale ranging from faithfulness to the author — resulting in a closer correspondence — to kindness to the reader — resulting in what has to be called a freer rendering. "Nida distinguishes two types of equivalence, *formal* and *dynamic*, where formal equivalence "focuses attention on the message itself, in both form and content". In such a translation one is concerned with such correspondences as poetry to poetry, sentence to sentence, and concept to concept. [...] *Dynamic equivalence* is based on the principle of *equivalent effect*, i.e. that the relationship between receiver and message should aim at being the same as that between the original receivers and the SL message".[14] Dryden, for his part, had already said that the perfect equivalence is to be found in a target-text that combines the author's intentions with the reader's pattern of understanding. "For, after all, a translator is to make his author appear as charming as possibly he can, provided he maintains his character and makes him not unlike himself."[15] In both cases, it can be seen that both scholars regard the concept of equivalence in a rather general way: equivalence could be found in the author's message or by reproducing as much as possible the effect the text has had on the readership.

Having looked at three of the many approaches from which equivalence can be studied, one has to come mainly to two conclusions in order to understand a little more the concept of equivalence and what we have to look for when aiming at equivalence: 1. Equivalence can be analysed from different points of view. None of them should be considered as more correct than the others; on the contrary, they should be considered equally satisfactory, their use depending on the kind of equivalence one wants to apply, but, above all, depending on the translator's notion of which approach can fulfil his/her initial purpose better. This can vary from text to text. 2. Equivalence in translation studies should not be thought of as a search for sameness. As Susan Bassnett says: "sameness cannot even exist between two TL versions of the same text, let alone between the SL and the TL version".[16] In order to talk about "successful equivalence" we can adopt María Calzada's words: "The success of the conveyance of such equivalence is measured by the gap between the translator's initial purpose and the final result. The smaller the gap, the more successful the equivalence proves to be".[17]

Let us now go on to defining the concept of adequacy, not forgetting that we are also faced with problems when trying to differentiate between equivalence and adequacy because sometimes they are used interchangeably. *The Concise Oxford Dictionary* defines something that possesses adequacy as being "sufficient, satisfactory (often with the implication of being barely so), or proportionate or barely sufficient".[18] As we saw earlier, the *Collins Dictionary* defines equivalence as "the state of being "equal or interchangeable in value, quantity, significance, etc.", or having the same or a similar effect or meaning". There seems to be a difference between these two definitions; the former refers to concepts like "sufficient", "satisfactory", "barely sufficient", whereas the latter refers to concepts like equality, sameness, similarity. Both establish the relationship between, on the one hand, being satisfactory in relation to something else, and, on the other hand, being similar, if not equal, to another element. It seems to me that it is quite clear that in practical terms, there is a difference between the two concepts but, when they are used in Translation Studies the difference does not seem to be so clear. According to Katharina Reiss: "Adequacy is simply appropriateness. Appropriateness is nothing in itself: it has to be seen in relation to an action. You do something appropriate in relation to the purpose of what is done. Every time a translator takes a decision, the dominant factor is the purpose of the translation, so translational decisions must be appropriate for this purpose. Adequacy is thus a relation between means and purpose, and is thereby process-oriented".[19] Reiss defines equivalence as "a relation between two products, the source and the receptor texts" (*ibidem*). She sees one term as the decisive factor in the translation process (adequacy) and the other term as the relationship between the source and the target texts which have similar communicative functions in different cultures (equivalence). In a work written by the same author and Hans J. Vermeer, the relationship between adequacy and equivalence is described as a relation between two things which are different. As they see it, "the term equivalence embraces relationships not just between separate units but also between whole texts. Equivalence on the level of units does not necessarily imply equivalence on the level of texts, and vice versa. Besides, the equivalence of texts goes beyond their linguistic manifestation into the cultural dimension. Adequacy, on the other hand, refers to the correspondence of linguistic units in the source text with linguistic units in the target text, and is therefore taken to be the basic parameter of the translation process".[20] They see equivalence as the term which embraces linguistic units and whole texts, not only in their linguistic aspects but in their cultural ones. Adequacy is considered as the basic parameter on which the translation process is based, as it establishes the correspondences between the linguistic units of both texts, these units being the basic elements for the translation process to take place. Komissarov treats the two concepts as different but closely related. He defines "equivalent translation" as "the correspondence of two linguistic units that can be equated with one another" and "adequate translation" as: "the broader term of the two, and it is often used as a synonym for "good translation", a translation that has achieved the required optimal level of interlanguage communication under certain given conditions".[21] In this respect, adequacy is taken as being the broader term of the two although it looks at the process of translation in a limited way. As Shveitser says in his own article: "In Komissarov's formulation adequacy embraces only the relationship between linguistic units, not between whole texts".[22]

These two categories, especially equivalence, should be used to evaluate the translation process in different grades: when the communicative relationship between two texts includes the semantic and the pragmatic level apart from the functions applied to each text, we can talk about full equivalence; when the communicative relationship between the two texts includes just one of the levels, then we could talk about partial equivalence. Full equivalence has to be considered as an idealized type of equivalence although it does not mean that it does not exist at all. In a text, the concept of equivalence should answer the question "does the target text correspond to the source text?", whereas the concept of adequacy should relate to the conditions which make the communication between languages possible and to the strategies used for an appropriate communicative situation. According to Shveitser, one important difference between the notions of equivalence and adequacy is that "full equivalence presupposes an exhaustive rendering of the source text's "communicative-functional invariant". In other words, it is the highest possible requirements that can be addressed to the quality of a translation. Adequacy, on the other hand, [...] is rooted in the real practice of translating, and that practice often allows for a less exhaustive rendering of the overall communicative-functional contents of the original. Adequacy allows for the assumption that decisions taken by translators not infrequently involve some kind of compromise, that translation requires sacrifices [...]. Moreover, the very purpose of communication not infrequently undergoes some changes in the process of secondary communication, and this inevitably causes some retreat from the ideal of full equivalence between source text and target text".[23]

So, in plain language one could say that these two terms are closely related to each other, but that at the same time there is a difference between the two. An adequate translation should always meet certain requirements in order to be considered adequate; within an adequate translation, equivalence can take place either in full or in just one of its levels. So, these two concepts are not opposed. On the contrary they are related to each other. Adequacy is the generic term which refers to the communicative purpose sought in a translation, while equivalence is connected to the transferring of the source text's communicative effect to the target text as it had been determined by the initial communicative situation and its components. Adequacy can be considered the broader term of the two in which the concept of equivalence is included. The proximity between the two words in terms of their respective meaning has often led the translation theorist to treat both of them as equals — or perhaps we ought to say to treat both of them in similar terms, with the result that the reader is never quite sure what the writer really means by "equivalence" and by "adequacy".

María Sánchez-Ortiz

### Notes

1. Marge E. Landsberg, "Translation Theory: An Appraisal of Some General Problems", *Meta*, vol.21, 1976, 235.
2. Peter Fawcett, *Translation and Language*, Manchester: St Jerome Publishing, 1997, 53.
3. R.R.K. Hartman & F.C. Stork, *Dictionary of Language & Linguistics*, London: Longman, 1972, 173.
4. J.C. Catford, *A Linguistic Theory of Translation*, London: OUP, 1965, 20.
5. Eugene A. Nida & Charles Taber, *The Theory of Translation*, Leiden: The Bible Societies, 1974, 12.
6. Collins Dictionary of English Language, Glasgow: Harper Collins, 1991, s.v. "equivalence".
7. Sandra Halverson, "The concept of Equivalence in Translation Studies: Much

Equivalence and Adequacy in Translation:
Are They Equivalent? Are They Adequate?

Ado About Something", *Target*, vol. 9: 2, 1997, 210.
8   Werner Koller, "The Concept of Equivalence and the Object of Translation Studies", *Target*, vol. 7:2, 1995, 196.
9   "Pour un Tombeau d'Anatole" [A Tomb for Anatole], 1980 in *Paris Review*, éditions du Seuil, Paris.
10  "Paul Auster traducteur de Mallarmé", Gérard de Cortanze in *Magazine littéraire*, no. 368, September 1998, 34-35. "My sole aim was to produce something which, whilst looking good in the target language and closely resembling the original, sat perfectly in English without a trace of it being a translation. On the other hand, I believe, one has to be totally faithful to the author's intentions; the translator does not have the right to alter whatever he likes in the text which he translates." (My translation).
11  Werner Koller, "Equivalence in translation theory", 1979; in Andrew Chesterman (ed.), *Readings in Translation Theory*, Finland: Oy Finn Lectura Ab, 1989, 100-101.
12  Robyn Marsack in "Translation-Transformation?", *La Liberté en traduction*, Actes du Colloque International, E.S.I.T. 7-9 June 1990, M. Lederer and F. Israel (eds), Paris: Didier, 1991, 46.
13  Sandra Halverson, "The concept of Equivalence in Translation Studies: Much Ado About Something", *Target*, vol. 9:2, 1997, 214.
14  Susan Bassnett, *Translation Studies*, London: Routledge, 1991, 26.
15  Reiner Schulte and John Biguenet, *Theories of Translation. An Anthology of Essays from Dryden to Derrida*, Chicago: University of Chicago Press, 1992, 23.
16  Susan Bassnett, *ibid*, 29.
17  María Calzada Pérez, "Trusting the Translator", *Babel*, vol. 39:3, 1992, 171.
18  *The Concise Oxford Dictionary*, Oxford: OUP, 1990, s.v. "adequate".
19  Katharina Reiss, "Adequacy and Equivalence in Translation", *The Bible Translator*, vol. 34:3, 1983, 301
20  Katharina Reiss & Hans J. Vermeer, *The Foundation of a General Theory of Translation*, 1984; quoted in Alexander Shveitser, "Equivalence and Adequacy", in Palma Zlateva (ed.), *Translation as Social Action*, London, Routledge, 1993, 48.
21  V. Komissarov, *The Linguistics of Translation*, 1980; quoted in Alexander Shveitser, *ibid*.
22  Alexander Shveitser, *ibid*.
23  Alexander Shveitser, *ibid*, 51-52.

## 8.
## TRANSLATING THE PAST: *BEFORE THE WAR*, THE ENGLISH VERSION OF ROBERT BRASILLACH'S MEMOIRS *NOTRE AVANT-GUERRE*

This article examines some of the problems involved in translating Brasillach's memoirs, *Notre avant-guerre*, into English and of confronting troubled times as depicted by a controversial author, who had no particular interest in, or indeed liking for, the English-speaking world. Some considerations of an appropriate style for the translation are outlined here, as are those which involve the narration of the past, with specific reference to the use of tenses. Finally, I investigate the autobiographer's perspective with regard to a mid-twentieth-century political ideology and the way in which it may affect the translation and transposition of the work to modern times.

### Translating a Difficult Past

All translations have to confront and come to terms with the past in one way or another. However, the translation of Robert Brasillach's *Notre avant-guerre* involves an era of French history that is particularly problematic and riven with controversy, namely the latter part of the inter-war period beginning in 1925 and ending with the Germans' defeat of the French in June 1940. The venture is hazardous, in the sense that translating the memoirs of a French fascist might easily be perceived as yet another attempt at historical *revisionism*, endeavouring to render more digestible, albeit to a different readership, that "passé qui ne passe pas", to coin a famous phrase.[1]

Two related observations should be made on this count: one, that the period in question is largely the inter-war or pre-war era, not the period that is referred to by Conan and Rousso in their study of the Vichy regime and German-occupied France. The memoirs constitute a genuine, rich, varied, and wide-ranging documentation of France before the Second World War, in the 1920s and 1930s. Secondly, *Notre avant-guerre* offers a panorama of the main events, personalities, and movements of the era, with little ideological bias in the first part of the autobiography. It may be regrettable, or even objectionable, to some readers that the second half of the memoirs displays strong political bias, to the point of transforming itself in places into an apology of French fascism, or at least of Brasillach's own version of it. Yet, as a record of the past, the work has an immediacy, a readability, and a certain poetic style, that make it well worth producing an English version. This is indeed one of the problems confronting the translator: namely, how to render Brasillach's fluid, readable style into a language which in many ways was alien to his culture. As a fundamentally "Mediterranean" writer, he himself rarely displayed any sympathy for the Anglo-Saxon world, except in the relatively circumscribed domain of literature. Ideologically steeped in the "culture" of the French Empire as inherited from the nineteenth century, Brasillach regarded the English as the hereditary enemy. One wonders, then, whether he would have approved of English translations of any of his books. This may be an irrelevant question, since it would seem that the majority of translators do not, and often cannot, normally request the permission of an author to translate his/her work. Nevertheless, it is worth bearing in mind, as Jacques Derrida makes clear, that the act of translating inevitably involves a certain violation of the original, if not a violation of the author's own personal and cultural identity.[2]

The cultural gap between author and potential readers raises a general question concerning readership. For whom is this translation destined? The issues, events, and people who figure in the memoirs are important enough to interest a wider public than simply academics who research and write about this period. Almost sixty years after its composition, and more than sixty years after the period recalled, the ideological mindset of potential readers of the memoirs, whether in French or in English, has changed. As it approaches the milestone of the millennium, at some distance now from the times depicted in the memoirs, our contemporary era will no doubt regard this evocation of the roaring twenties and the turbulent thirties in Paris as essentially social history. But it is also a personal and literary account of a particular group of youngsters who belonged to what has been dubbed the "génération dans l'orage" ("the generation in the storm"), or alternatively "la génération perdue" ("the lost generation"), a phrase which echoes a description of the earlier pre-war generation of Charles Péguy, Henri Alain-Fournier, and Ernest Psichari.[3]

Indeed, the title, *Notre avant-guerre*, with its intriguing and ambiguous possessive adjective "notre", invoking, as it is intended to do, Péguy's account of pre-Great War days entitled *Notre Jeunesse* (1910), provides its own particular dilemma in its translation into English. It might appear to readers that Brasillach's own use of the possessive "notre" indicates the appropriation of an entire generation for his personal ideological purposes. And, to a degree, this is precisely what the memoirs do. But there is so much more in them. Indeed, the "nous" of the title (and the text) is Protean: without going into all its avatars, it begins by describing a small group of students at the École Normale Supérieure in Paris (initially a Parisian "gang of four"), and ends by designating the team of right-wing journalists who contributed to *Je suis partout*, the newspaper of which Brasillach was editor from 1937 to 1943. It is also loosely used, often by implication only, to indicate the French nation.[4] The English title that I have chosen, *Before the War*, with its assonance but also its loss of the possessive adjective "notre", does not constitute an attempt to "sanitize" the work or recuperate it for a modern audience, but rather to encourage interest in a vivid, lively and entertaining picture of an era of crisis in twentieth-century French history which, despite its relative brevity, is of the utmost importance in contributing to a deeper understanding and a greater appreciation of the issues of that time.[5]

Having translated into English two other works by Brasillach, I am convinced that *Notre avant-guerre* is his principal literary achievement, and that it is one of those works that will endure.[6] It evokes an era, the pre-World-War-II era, that is not chronologically so very far from us, and yet it is a world that has disappeared for ever. Even in 1939/40, Brasillach felt strongly that this old world would not return, that it was definitively lost, and that he and his generation stood on the threshold of a new era. Hence, his sense of urgent mission to compose the memoirs, before the memories faded. As a soldier on the Maginot Line from September 1939 to May 1940, Brasillach spent much of his time compiling material for these memoirs, and writing *Notre avant-guerre*.

## Style

A further problem involves the time-lag of sixty or so years between the original and the translation. Since authenticity of reproduction is an important issue for consideration in translation, the dilemma arises, as it must in the majority of these cases, as to what kind of language should be used, that of the period in question or the language of today. In either case, it will be a literary language on the whole, to match that of the original, rather than vernacular or colloquial English, and it will necessarily seem outdated to modern readers. Decisions have to be made on the lexical and syntactical levels, together with decisions concerning appropriate choices of tenses.[7]

One aid to translating, with this consideration in mind, is to have recourse to comparative literature. English memorialists of approximately the same period do exist, and can be helpful, at the very least, as sounding-boards for the style of Robert Brasillach's *Notre avant-guerre*, transposed in English. The memoirs of Siegfried Sassoon, George Orwell, Robert Graves, and Laurie Lee give some flavour of the corresponding English autobiographical style of the period. Examination of such memorialists is not, of course, designed to enable the translator to imitate the style of any particular writer, nor even to make a stylistic amalgam, but, at the least, to have what Joseph Bédier referred to as "la musique de la pensée" of a particular writer, echoing in the background as one translates.[8] Given the "politically incorrect" nature of Brasillach's memoirs, Siegfried Sassoon's semi-autobiographical *Memoirs of a Fox-Hunting Man* were of some interest as far as content was concerned. Fashions of thought change over the decades, and one major debate involved in this type of exercise must centre around whether the unfashionable, and even on occasion the downright distasteful, can be acceptable to modern readers. However, in terms of style, genre and register, Sassoon's autobiographical work (*The Old Century, The Weald of Youth, and Siegfried's Journey*) was of greater interest, the time of composition being roughly contemporary with Brasillach's work, even if the period described was a little earlier.[9]

In order, therefore, to render the style both authentic and approachable to the modern reader, compromises have to be made. For example, there is the issue of whether to opt for linguistic contractions of words, particularly in the main narrative of past events, or, for example, in Brasillach's informal, almost chatty, declarations in his short Preface to *Notre avant-guerre*, which concern the characteristics of the era that he is about to present:

> [...] Ces traits seront forcément personnels, et je n'ai jamais trop eu le coeur aux généralisations. Je sais des garçons de trente ans qui ont connu autre chose de la vie, de ses plaisirs, de ses espérances, que ce qu'en ont connu mes amis et moi-même. Pourtant, je ne crois pas qu'ils refuseront de retrouver quelques-uns des aspects de ces quinze ans, qui viennent d'être brutalement rejetés dans l'ombre. Il ne s'agit ici à aucun degré de confessions. Je n'ai pas à dire absolument tout ce qui m'a tenu au coeur, je rassemble seulement les images de quelques amis, les uns connus, les autres aussi inconnus que les personnages d'un roman pour qui le commence, et je voudrais justement qu'on pût lire ce livre comme un roman, comme une suite d'éducations sentimentales et intellectuelles. Je voudrais qu'on pût le lire comme une histoire plus vaste que la mienne, encore que je désire m'en tenir à ce que j'ai vu. [...][10]

Even in the main body of the text, it was found that there was a need, in some instances, to telescope the full form of tenses — for example, "I have" to "I've", or "I had" to "I'd" —, or to contract negative statements like "it is not" to "it isn't", and so on. It is particularly important in the opening pages of the memoirs, not least because these are likely to be the pages which encourage (or discourage) readers. Brasillach's own style is a mixture of the literary, often quite formal, with a more informal, occasionally journalistic, register. Such a blend of linguistic registers naturally creates problems for the translator, even if they are an integral part of the act of translating and may be regarded in a positive way as a "bonus", or "remainder", to use Lawrence Venuti's terminology.[11]

### Problems of Temporality in Autobiographical Narrative

In autobiography, there appear to be three main temporal viewpoints:

- — the moment being described — succeeded by the next moment in the continuum of the text

- — the moment of writing/recollection (relatively fixed)

- — the moment (of the reader), which changes (as one is reading, and from reading to reading).

We have, as can be seen above, a "sandwiching" effect, with the moment of writing as the relatively fixed point in an otherwise fluctuating chronological framework. Given that one of the characteristics of these memoirs is the constant changing of tenses, it is often difficult to keep the translated narrative on an "even keel", so to speak, without sacrificing too much of the variety which Brasillach maintains by playing on the different tenses in his narrative of the past.

More specifically, the choice of tense in English may not necessarily always correspond with the tense in French. A frequent problem in this area is that of the French historic present, a tense which Brasillach occasionally employs, and which most translators into English generally render in the preterite, or past tense. Hilaire Belloc's advice on this point, for example, is unambiguous:

> Whole pages of French matter will be written in the historic present which, if they reappear in an English form, should be thrown into the past.[12]

My own view is that this issue is clouded by considerations of tone and register. If the author wishes to convey immediacy of impression and a certain direct freshness in the narrative, then perhaps the English past tense may not be appropriate. As for register, the memoirs clearly move into a different gear, as it were, in certain passages, incorporating a journalistic register which, I believe, encourages the use of the present tense in English, without necessarily producing what Belloc eschews as "an exaggerated effect". One of the clearest examples of this can be found in a passage in Chapter VI of *Notre avant-guerre*, which is a reworking of an interview with the Belgian Rexist leader, Léon Degrelle, held probably at some time in the course of the year 1936, in the latter's car, as it speeds homewards through the night towards Brussels. Brasillach recalls:

> [...] Il [Degrelle] était amusant, violent, vivant et passionné. Je me rappelle sa réplique familière à un garçon qui se plaignait de ne pas avoir dormi de deux nuits:
> — Vous vous reposerez quand vous serez mort. [...]
> Et dans la nuit, tandis que l'auto rapide nous ramène à Bruxelles,

il continue alors de parler, pour moi, pour lui. Je ne vois pas son visage. J'entends seulement sa voix dans l'ombre. Je ne sais pas à ce moment-là ce que sera le rexisme, je ne sais pas ce que sera Léon Degrelle: tout est possible dans l'univers, même l'échec après la victoire. Mais je sais que je ne pourrai jamais oublier cette promenade dans la nuit, et ces mots magiques qui montaient d'un jeune homme mis en présence de son destin. [...]

Par métier de journaliste, [...] j'ai assisté ces années-là [...] à la campagne électorale de 1937 où Léon Degrelle fut battu par M.Van Zeeland.[...][13]

My English translation has attempted here, as elsewhere, to render the tone of the narrative, as well as the style and content. In most of the examples of verbs given here, the translator has opted for the equivalent tense in English, unless this causes an awkwardness of expression. The choice of tense also has some effect on linguistic contractions (mentioned previously) and vice versa. With respect to the foregoing, therefore, the translator has taken particular care to transmit the quality of the narrative "voice" of the author/narrator.

## Conclusion

The principal concern of the translator of *Notre avant-guerre* has, therefore, been to maintain and transmit the authenticity of the original text, wherever possible. In the two examples dealt with here, namely that of the title of the memoirs and the "tense-rich" Degrelle passage quoted above, manipulation or, in more sophisticated terms, a degree of "interpretive transformation" have been deemed necessary.[14] Nevertheless, since the translator's concern for authenticity remains the principal criterion here, a sustained and lucid consciousness of context has been one of the most important pre-requisites. For of what use or interest is text without context? This approach necessitates not only a thorough understanding of the period, but also an awareness of its paradoxes, together with those inherent in the author's own perspective.

Robert Brasillach's memoirs bristle with paradoxes: for example, that of the ephemerality of the images from the past (as, for example, in the potentially "destabilizing" chronological effect on the reader of the Léon Degrelle passage quoted above) which the author attempts to render permanent in his memoirs, like a photographic developer processing a snapshot.[15] Yet all memoirs necessarily attempt the same feat, in varying degrees, namely that of "fixing" a sequence of fleeting, transient moments, together with some more durable sensations and impressions, in narrative form. Another paradox involves Brasillach's apparently elitist view of his potential readers, only some of whom, according to his opening sentences, will possess "le sens du passé".[16] Does this imply that he discounts the others, who are presumably not fortunate enough to be touched by this form of Proustian "grâce"? How then do we reconcile their exclusion with his apparent attempt to render this period accessible to readers generally by depicting in clear and colourful detail the people, events, and circumstances that fill the pages of this autobiography? The solution to this paradox, I believe, lies in the adverb "apparently" which I use to qualify his elitism: in short, he is simply referring in the Preface to his own role as a sort of conjurer of the past, an enabler, or communicator, for his readers. He is, in a sense, merely presenting his credentials there.

As for the altogether larger problem of translating memoirs which contain an unfashionable, or at least controversial, view of the past, this is clearly not simply confined to concern over possible accusations of "revisionism". The exercise also implies something like a "double exhumation" of the past, once on the part of the memorialist, and then again by the translator. In his Postface to *Notre avant-guerre*, written in May 1940, Brasillach summarises some of the details which appear in the memoirs, and portrays himself as a literary "archaeologist".

> Nos écoles, nos revues, nos maisons, nos voyages, nos plaisirs, n'ont été que les apparences singulières, il me semble, par lesquelles se désignait à nous notre époque. A les décrire dans leur particularisme, j'ai déjà l'impression de diriger des fouilles.[17]

Translating the past involves digging up all sorts of relics, uncovering different archaeological strata, and reviving both pleasant and unpleasant memories. Both author and translator are, moreover, engaged in one sense in a "packaging" exercise and in presenting these relics to an ever-changing public. Whether the kind of packaging, or presentation, of those memories and images that Brasillach undertook to present in 1940 in *Notre avant-guerre* is acceptable to a modern, English-speaking readership is something that only the publication of these memoirs in English will be able to demonstrate.

Peter Tame

## Notes

1. Eric Conan and Henry Rousso, *Vichy, un passé qui ne passe pas*, Paris: Gallimard, 1996 (Folio: Histoire, 71). The phrase encapsulates emblematically the problem of a past, 'un passé', which cannot be properly "digested" by the present (the verb "passe" is in the present tense). *Notre avant-guerre* therefore presents an example of a difficult transition, or "passage", in chronological terms, from past to present, as well as in linguistic terms from French to English.
2. Jacques Derrida, "Des Tours de Babel", in Joseph F. Graham (ed.), *Differences in Translation*, Ithaca and London: Cornell University Press, 209-248, with translation by J.F. Graham, 165-207.
3. "Une génération dans l'orage" is the collective title of Robert Brasillach's *Notre avant-guerre* and its "sequel", *Journal d'un homme occupé*. This work was published by Plon in 1968 (original edition by Les Sept Couleurs, 1956).
4. See Luc Rasson, *Littérature et fascisme: les romans de Robert Brasillach*, Paris: Minard, 1991, 150-153, for a detailed analysis of the 'Protean' function of the personal pronoun "nous" in *Notre avant-guerre*.
5. This "loss and gain" syndrome is, of course, part of the process of compromise and compensation which is normally involved in the activity of translation. See Susan Bassnett, *Translation Studies*, London and New York: Routledge, 30.
6. My other two translations are *The Conqueress* (*La Conquérante*, Plon, 1943) and *Six Hours to Kill* (*Six heures à perdre*, Plon, 1953). Neither translation has yet found a publisher.
7. The current debate surrounding the issue of authenticity in translation is complex, and constitutes a problem that is far from being resolved. See, for example, Lawrence Venuti, *The Scandals of Translation: towards an ethic of difference*, London and New York: Routledge, 1998, 81-87.
8. In *La Chanson de Roland*, publiée et traduite d'après le manuscrit d'Oxford par Joseph Bédier, Paris: Union Générale d'Editions, 1982, Avant-propos, xi, Joseph Bédier identified this "musique", or literary style, as being the most untranslatable element of all: "[...] poésie ou prose, l'art d'écrire réside tout entier dans la convenance de l'idée et du sentiment au rythme et au nombre de la phrase, au son, à la couleur et à la saveur des mots, et ce sont ces

rapports subtils, ces harmonies, que tout traducteur dissocie nécessairement et détruit, puisqu'il est l'esclave de la littéralité et qu'il peut bien rendre enson propre langage la pensée, mais non pas la musique de la pensée, non pas cette petite chose, le style". — "[...] whether it be poetry or prose, the art of writing consists entirely of matching ideas and feelings with the rhythm and structure of the sentence, with the sound, the colour, and the flavour of the words, and it is these subtle relationships and harmonies that the translator is bound to dislocate and destroy, since he is in thrall to 'literalness', and because he can convey the thought in his own language, but not the musicality of the thought, not that little thing that is called style". (My translation).

9 Siegfried Sassoon, *The Old Century and Seven More Years* (1938); *The Weald of Youth*, London: Faber & Faber, 1942; *Siegfried's Journey* 1916-1920, London: Faber & Faber, 1945.

10 Robert Brasillach, *Oeuvres complètes de Robert Brasillach*, vol. VI, Paris: Club de l'Honnête Homme, 1964, 13. My translation of this passage reads as follows: [...] These features are bound to be personal, for I've never been very fond of generalisations. I've met young men of thirty who have experienced life, its pleasures and its hopes in a different way from that experienced by my friends and myself. Nevertheless, I don't believe they'd deny that at least some of the characteristics of the last fifteen years can be found here, however abruptly overshadowed by current events. These aren't in any sense confessions. I don't wish to relate absolutely all my innermost thoughts and feelings; I'm merely collecting together the portraits of a few friends, some of whom will be familiar, others as unfamiliar as the characters at the start of a novel. Indeed, I'd like to think that this book could be read as a novel, as a story of emotional and intellectual experiences. I'd also like to think that this might be read, not just as my own particular story, but as a much broader history, although I intend to confine myself to what I personally have seen. [...] (*Before the War*)

11 *The Scandals of Translation*, London and New York: Routledge, 1998, 10. The term "remainder" was coined by Jean-Jacques Lecercle in his *The Violence of Language*, London and New York: Routledge, 1990.

12 Hilaire Belloc, *On Translation* (The Taylorian Lecture), Oxford: The Clarendon Press, `1931, 28.

13 *Oeuvres complètes de Robert Brasillach*, vol. VI, 238-39. My translation reads as follows: "[..] He was entertaining, violent, lively and passionate. I recall his friendly retort to a young lad who was complaining that he had not slept for two nights:

"You can rest when you're dead." [...]
And, in the night, as the speeding car takes us back to Brussels, he goes on talking for my benefit and for his own. I cannot see his face. I can only hear his voice in the darkness. I do not know then what will become of Rexism, I do not know what will become of Léon Degrelle: everything is possible in this world, even failure after victory. But I know that I shall never be able to forget that night-ride and those magic words emanating from a young man who knew that he had a date with destiny [...]
As a journalist, and out of curiosity for the figures of our time, I attended a few meetings, as did others during those years [...] and [...] I was present at the electoral campaign of 1937 in which Léon Degrelle was beaten by M. Van Zeeland. [...]". (*Before the War*)

14 Lawrence Venuti (ed.), Rethinking Translation: *discourse, subjectivity, ideology*, London and New York: Routledge, 1992, 8.
15 On the topic of permanence and ephemerality in the memoirs, see Peter Tame, "Le paradoxe de l'éphémère et du permanent dans *Notre avant-guerre*", *Cahiers des Amis de Robert Brasillach*, 41, Spring 1996, 65-78.
16 *Oeuvres complètes de Robert Brasillach*, vol. VI, 15.
17 *Ibid.*, 338. 'It seems to me that our schools, our magazines, our houses, our travels, our amusements, were merely the distinctive manifestations by which our era revealed itself to us. Describing them in all their details already makes me feel as though I am conducting an archaeological investigation.'

## 9.
## TRANSLATING SARTRE'S *SITUATIONS, V*

Sartre's *Situations, V: colonialisme et néo-colonialisme*[1] has much to interest researchers in history, political science, cultural theory and postcolonial studies. The absence of a complete translation of the work until now is possibly due to a decline in Sartre's status, eclipsed by the rise of structuralism and post-structuralism. However, his apparently old-fashioned humanism is postmodern in its understanding of reality and subject-positions as constructs, and a revalorization of his work seems to be underway. Another major reason for the increased interest in his work in general, and for the publication of our translation in particular, is the realisation of the importance of its contribution to postcolonial studies. Written from a position of independent Marxism, *Situations, V* critiques French colonialism in Algeria and, through an analysis of Black Africa's liberation (then in full swing), contributes to our understanding of de-colonisation. The preface to *Les Damnés de la Terre* which the book contains draws attention to Sartre's relationship with Fanon, a founding figure of postcolonial theory. As Fanon's writings have impacted notably on the work of Edward Said and Hommi Bhabha, the absence of a translation marks a serious gap in the historiography of postcolonial studies.

Recent writing on translation emphasises that it should be examined in the context of its cultural setting. Sherry Simon, for instance, notes that this "turn to culture" adds an important dimension to translation studies: "instead of asking the traditional question which has preoccupied translation theorists — 'how shall we translate, what is the correct translation?' — the emphasis is placed on a descriptive approach: 'What do translations do, how do they circulate in the world and elicit response?'".[2] Likewise, Susan Bassnett and Harish Trivedi observe that "[t]ranslations are always embedded in cultural and political systems, and in history".[3] Lawrence Venuti addresses the same theme: "The viability of a translation is established by its relationship to the cultural and social conditions under which it is produced and read".[4] A particular aspect of the cultural embeddedness of rewriting that is also much discussed is patronage. Maria Tymoczko, for instance, draws our attention to the fact that "[s]tudies of translation are increasingly alert to the circumstances under which books are chosen for translation and translations are published".[5]

This view of rewriting as embedded in a specific historical and cultural moment encourages translators to plot the co-ordinates of their source text and their own translation. As indicated above, *Situations, V* contains material important for the postcolonial debate, but it should not be considered as a post-colonial text itself. Much of the discussion about the translation of post-colonial writing concerns the problems of transferring texts from subaltern cultures to dominant cultures such as those of the UK and USA.[6] One of the major difficulties with post-colonial writing is that the alien lexis, concepts and practices contained in what Lefevere calls the source texts' "universe of discourse"[7] remain unintelligible to readers at the "centre" (i.e. the dominant culture, often the former metropolitan country). This raises the question as to the best methods for bridging the gap between the two cultures, preferably allowing as much of the source culture as possible to pass over into the receptor culture.[8] Another difficulty is the hierarchical slope between the less prestigious subaltern texts and high-status centre texts. With the rise of multiculturalism and the attainment of canonical status by postcolonial texts such as Rushdie's *Midnight's Children*, the gradient may be in the process of levelling out, but it has far from disappeared. In the light of these remarks, we can see why Sartre's text cannot be classed as a post-colonial one: it was written from the centre (metropolitan France), in a canonical discourse (educated French) by a controversial but nevertheless high-status writer.

Where the gap between the source and receptor culture is great (as is the case with much post-colonial writing and rewriting), the tendency to moderate or even obliterate the otherness of the source text — to "domesticate" it — is strong. The whole question of whether the target text should be "foreignised" or "domesticated" has been a major recent concern of translators and translation theorists. This question is examined at length by Lawrence Venuti who advocates the practice of "resistancy" or "foreignisation". By this he means theory and practice which "eschews a fluent strategy in order to reproduce in the translation whatever features of the foreign text abuse or resist dominant cultural values in the source language".[9] *Fluency* is the opposite of *resistancy* in his scheme: a fluent translation (sanctioned by the current orthodoxy in Anglo-American translation) domesticates the source text. He suggests two main ways to achieve foreignisation: either by translating what is perceived as a canonical work in the target culture with a marginal discourse (such as archaism), or by choosing a foreign text that is perceived as marginal in the target culture and translating it with a canonical discourse (310).

Although generally sympathetic to Venuti's wish to foreignise translations, we are not convinced that either of these two strategies can be applied to Sartre's text. In the first place, the attribution of either canonical or marginal status to *Situations, V* in source and receptor culture is not as straightforward as one might think. Amongst left-wing intellectuals both inside and outside France, it might well enjoy canonical status, but beyond that constituency, canonicity would probably be denied. Venuti's rather undifferentiated description of the position occupied by a text in a given culture needs refinement. More importantly, however, his strategies build a conscious and wilful distortion into the process of rewriting in the service of a political and cultural agenda. It is not altogether clear how the *deliberate* misrepresentation of the status or the discourse of a text can rectify any *involuntary* misrepresentation that inheres in any act of translation. We believe that our text achieves substantial resistancy or foreignisation, but thanks to methods different from those suggested by Venuti, namely by incorporating selected items of French lexis into our text and reproducing in English certain aspects of French style. These foreignising strategies are further enhanced by a critical apparatus.

Resistancy draws attention to the "cultural otherness" of the source text. Venuti draws a parallel with Schleiermacher's pronouncement that "[e]ither the translator leaves the author in peace, as much as possible, and moves the reader towards him; or he leaves the reader in peace, as much as possible, and moves the author towards him" (19-20): the foreignising translation leaves the author in peace and moves the reader. Maria Tymoczko observes that "the greater the prestige of the source culture and the source text, the easier it is to require that the audience come to the text".[10] Given the status of French culture and Sartre's writing amongst our intended audience of English-speaking academics, we felt it appropriate to bring the audience to the text as far as possible. We recognise that if we are to foreignise the text, we need to provide our readers with some assistance in order for them to appreciate it as fully as possible. Our confidence is this approach is reinforced by the fact that they will be accustomed to approaching a challenging text with the help of paratextual devices such as their own critical apparatus. These are the methods referred to by Tymoczko to help readers in the context of post-colonial rewriting: "In the form of introductions, footnotes, critical essays, glossaries, maps, and the like, the translator can embed the translated text in a shell that explains necessary cultural and literary background for the receiving audience and that acts as a running commentary on the translated work".[11]

In the case of this translation this is facilitated by the fact that the distance between the universe of discourse of the earlier readers and that of our intended audience of academics is small compared to the cultural distances that sometimes have to be spanned by some subaltern and central texts. The transfer is from dominant discourse to dominant discourse, from centre to centre. We in fact found that much of the style of the French discourse could be successfully transferred into English (examples of which follow below). It is our belief that the anglophone readership will benefit from signs of the otherness of the source text.

Venuti frequently refers to the domestication of the source text as cultural aggression. He talks of the "violence that resides in the very purpose and activity of translation".[12] He fails to give sufficient emphasis, however, to what might be described as the violence done by translation to the receptor culture. In contrast, André Lefevere gives this aspect appropriate consideration: "translation is a channel opened, often not without a certain reluctance, through which foreign influences can penetrate the native culture, challenge it, and even contribute to subverting it. 'When you offer a translation to a nation,' says Victor Hugo, 'that nation will almost always look on the translation as an act of violence against itself.'"[13] Lefevere links this act of violence to a consciousness of lack in the receptor culture: "why is it necessary to represent a foreign text in one's own culture? Does the very fact of doing that not amount to an admission of the inadequacy of that culture?" (2).

Considering the violence that is done to many texts as a result of Anglo-American cultural dominance, this emphasis on violence is understandable. The rewriting of alien, subaltern cultures has often served the ends of colonialism and imperialism, resulting in the sort of "othering" discourse described by Edward Said in *Orientalism*. Against this background, translation can be seen as at best parasitic, at worst predatory. But Lefevere's recognition of lack in the receptor culture as the reason behind translation gestures towards openness and acceptance, not aggression. Rewriting doesn't always have to be perceived as the destructive ingestion of a source culture, but also as often genuine attempts to embrace the alien and benefit from it. The fact that this form of transcultural communication is always imperfect (as Tymoczko observes, "perfect homology is impossible between translation and source"[14]) should not cause us to lose sight of its positive aspects. Rewriting makes aspects of a foreign culture available to an audience that would otherwise be deprived of them. In view of this, and given the overwhelming preponderance of translations from English into less dominant languages, the decision by a major publisher to commission a translation into English of *Situations, V* should be welcomed as an enrichment of our culture.

At the time of their writing, the pieces gathered as *Situations, V* were regarded in French intellectual circles as controversial but prestigious texts composed in a dominant discourse. The book consists of thirteen self-contained writings published in a variety of places: one as a preface to an album of Cartier-Bresson photographs of China, one as a preface to Frantz Fanon's *Damnés de la Terre*, one as a preface to the speeches of Patrice Lumumba, five in *Les Temps Modernes*, and five in *L'Express* (which was more left-wing then than it is now). The patrons of the source texts were thus varied, but generally located on the left of the political spectrum, in keeping with the protest nature of Sartre's writing. Forty years later the translation is being inserted into a different cultural situation. Our audience will not be interpellated to the same extent or in the same manner as Sartre's original audience: his writing is addressed to an earlier generation in their contemporary cultural space. The original audience had a political and often emotional investment in the texts; our audience will have a purely academic interest. Our translation is published with a reputable academic press (Routledge) for whom the texts are less controversial, owing to the distance created by time and space.

We move now to a more detailed examination of our translation strategies. In such a varied volume of essays, the number of items which are challenging for the translator is inevitably considerable. Among these we have identified as the focus of our commentary a number of elements which occur frequently throughout the work: referencing and annotation; vocabulary; style and register; sentence structure; gender; the use of the pronoun on; use of tenses.

Since de Saussure, we have known that languages map the world differently and furthermore that one-to-one correspondence is elusive[15]: the translator is confronted with culture-bound concepts that are difficult, and in extreme cases, impossible to transfer in any succinct way.[16] Thus one of the most significant challenges in translating this text was how to deal with its dense network of cultural references to the France of the late 1950s and early 1960s. Inevitably, there are a very large number of political and historical references, mainly related to France and the colonies. For example, central to Sartre's statement in 'Nous Sommes tous des Assassins' is the bombing of Sakiet by the French airforce. This is compared to the massacre of the people of Oradour by the Germans at the end of the Second World War. A footnote is certainly desirable in this and similar instances. Not all of Sartre's references to contemporary events are strictly political; many are social and cultural, or refer to locations in France. He refers, for example to: *la 4 CV* (*Situations, V,* 62); *les Editions de Minuit* (75); *les cultivateurs de l'Aveyron* (72). Footnotes, we feel, are a suitable way of explaining these concepts, and have the added benefit of foreignising the translation.

In the area of lexis, too, non-transferable items specific to Francophone culture abound. Most are discreet items, but some can be grouped into categories. For example, some terms relate to the colonial experience: *évolué, indigénat, collabos*. In writing about Algeria, Sartre inevitably uses terms of Arabic origin which had become current in French, such as *les fellagha* and *le fellah*. Similarly there are terms linked to the activities of the French army in Algeria, such as *une ratonnade,* and other words, like *bougnoule*, with racist connotations. English, for obvious reasons, provides no easy equivalent. Furthermore, many political words at first sight offer no resistance to the translator: *République, Référendum, régime gaulliste* and *jacobin*. But *République* and *Référendum* do not connote the same as *republic* and *referendum*, and *Gaullist* and *Jacobin* have a precarious existence in English. In a discussion of elements of the source culture which may prove tricky to translate, Tymoczko argues that one way of dealing with them is to incorporate them unchanged into the target language[17], with positive effects: "translation is one of the activities of a culture in which cultural expansion occurs and in which linguistic options are expanded through the importation of loan transfers, calques, and the like".[18] In some cases (such as, for example, *évolué*), this is our strategy for dealing with such terms (an explanation is footnoted). Here, as in the previous section, these strategies have the added advantage of incorporating the cultural other into the rewritten text.

Sartre's original articles include only a handful of footnotes in the whole volume, and no introduction. As we have indicated, we feel that it is appropriate to provide some additional information on a number of relevant items for the readers of the translation. Our difficulty becomes one of selection. Cultural allusions are notoriously difficult to translate without explanation, as Chuquet and Paillard remind us.[19] For example, when Sartre asks the question "Où sont les impératrices d'antan?" (10) ("Where are the empresses of yesteryear?"), it is easy enough for a French specialist to recognise the play on a quotation from a famous poem, but is it sufficiently important or interesting to merit a footnote? Other examples of this dilemma occur throughout. For example, in the first section, "D'une Chine à l'autre" (originally the preface to a collection of Cartier-Bresson photographs), the text informs the reader that Henri Michaux was the first to show the Chinese as they really are. There is, however, no reference to his works or even to the fact that he was a writer (though the translator could insert "the writer" before Michaux). We are also told that he was the first to portray China "sans lotus ni Loti" (8) ("without Lotus or Loti"), the literal translation of which makes little sense unless the reader knows that Pierre Loti wrote a story called *Madame Chrysanthème* which became Puccini's *Madame Butterfly*. Referring to another writer — Maurice Barrès — , Sartre comments on a photo illustrating the Chinese custom of wrapping up dead infants in a red sheet to be taken away at night by rubbish collectors and buried in the common grave. Sartre criticises Barrès's reaction to this custom ("cette jolie coutume") (16) ("this charming custom"), and his linking the body of the dead child to the warm body of a concubine; he sums up this passage with "Nous y sommes: du sang, de la volupté, de la mort" (16) ("There we have it; blood, voluptuousness, death"). Not too difficult to translate, but though Sartre does not mention it, the second half is also the title of a piece of writing by Barrès.

Such aspects pose difficulties, but the texts' stylistic idiosyncrasies are easier to reproduce. To increase the impact and persuasiveness of his messages, Sartre brings into play a number of rhetorical strategies, the most obvious of which are: addressing the reader directly; a mix of formal and informal lexis and syntax; and lengthy arguments (often in a single paragraph with complex punctuation) contrasted by truncated sentence fragments. The mainly direct, conversational style was intended to suggest to the readers that they were all implicated and to provoke a reaction of outrage. "Le Colonialisme est un Système" was originally a speech, but the other articles read largely in the same way owing to the author's manner of involving the reader: "Je voudrais vous mettre en garde contre" (25) ("I would like to alert you to"); "Nous, Français de la Métropole" (47) ("We, the people of France").

A problematic aspect of his direct style presents itself in "D'une Chine à l'autre", in that it frequently refers directly to some of the photographs: "Mais regardez ce marchand qui vend ses cigarettes sous la protection d'un Tchang Kaï-chek et de deux Sun Yat-sen" (13) ("But look at this peddler who is selling his cigarettes under the protection of a Chiang Kai-shek and two Sun Yat-sens"). It is impossible to understand what this means without seeing the photograph which shows a man selling his product under the protective gaze of pictures of the two illustrious leaders in a shop window. At another point, Sartre refers to a photograph of a eunuch: ("Dans un bocal, il conserve précieusement ses 'précieuses'; (...) ce visage ridé, ciré" (9-10). ("In a jar, he lovingly preserves his 'precious jewels'; (...) that wrinkled, weathered face"). The quality of the original here, with its play on *précieusement* and *précieuses*, is difficult to render in translation. Furthermore, the text alone is not sufficient to convey accurately the image of the old eunuch, and we intend to approach the publisher with a view to including the appropriate photographs in the volume.

The texts are written in a lively, ironic and often informal prose, which, despite the seriousness of content, occasionally borders on the slangy and even vulgar. This forestalls any temptation to archaise the

English text; we use current British English. A blend of the erudite and the racy is a trademark of Sartre's prose, and readers in translation should be allowed to share this. An example: "un pays stratifié, transi de méfiance et de morosité, qui répétait sans cesse et non sans fatuité: 'J'ai rendez-vous avec l'Histoire!' et qui s'est aperçu que l'Histoire lui avait collé un lapin" (127), ("a stratified country that shot through with mistrust and gloom which kept on repeating, not without self-conceit 'I have a date with History!', and which realised that History had stood it up.") Amongst the more surprising items to appear is *foutre* (even the 1994 edition of the Oxford Hachette dictionary describes this as "very informal"). An example: "Qu'est-ce que l'armée vient foutre ici?" (80) ("What the fuck's the army got to do with it?"). This use of strong language should not be normalised; if anything, this verve should be intensified to create the same effect on our audience, accustomed to a more permissive linguistic atmosphere. This can be achieved by opting for what might be considered shocking even for today's readership (for example, the use of the taboo word *fuck* in preference to the milder *hell*). Such considerations can be signalled to the reader in an introduction.

Another aspect of Sartre's style which should not be domesticated is its habit of alternating very long, carefully-punctuated sentences with short — often fragment — sentences. (Similar techniques are used for paragraphs, but space constraints prevent discussion. Compare the relatively long first paragraph on page 129 starting "La vérité" with the following nine short paragraphs on pp.129-30.) For example, in "Les Grenouilles qui demandent un roi", Sartre draws up a lengthy list of changes needed for France to become a great nation (127-8). Each new section is introduced with an infinitive and punctuated with a semicolon (our italics[20]: "*Comprendre* que la grandeur d'une nation ne se mesure pas à la quantité de sang qu'elle fait couler (...); *arrêter* les hostilités sur le champ" etc.) ("We should: understand that the greatness of a nation is not measured by the quantity of blood that it sheds (...); stop the hostilities immediately"). The paragraph continues for 34 lines. The aim is to convince the reader of what needs to be done to make France great. This long paragraph is followed by a sentence whose tight first clause sums up the potential result of such changes: "En dix ans, la physionomie de la France ne sera plus la même" (128) ("In ten years, the face of France would be transformed"). (These dramatic rhetorical crescendos followed by a short sharp shock possibly reveal the playwright in Sartre.) Another example is the longish sentence involving a repetition of "c'est que nous" which is immediately followed by the abrupt "'Oui' c'est le rêve; 'non' c'est le réveil" (144) ("'yes' is a dream; 'no' is an awakening"). Incidentally, repetition — often threefold — is one of Sartre's stocks-in-trade with which he hammers home a point (see, for example, the three "peur" on p.136, or the three "pour" on p.137).

The source text contains numerous sentence fragments without finite verbs. Chuquet and Paillard note that this stylistic feature of French – "la proposition nominale" – seems to be "à niveau de langue équivalent, plus fréquent en français qu'en anglais".[21] Broadly, the effect created is that of a colloquial but well-informed talk: "Bon. Cette description, cent autres l'ont faite" (*Situations, V,* 116); "L'Assemblée? Bah!" (127); "Donc il couvre. Comme Gaillard" (141); "1961. Ecoutez" (169); "Généreux, nous? Et Sétif?" (188) ("OK. All of this has been described many times before"; "The Assembly? Huh!"; "So he covers up. Like Gaillard"; "1961. Listen"; "Us generous? What about Setif?") etc., etc. These fragment sentences serve a number of rhetorical ends depending on context. For example, in the "Grenouilles'" essay, Sartre claims that many people would favour giving Algeria its independence if they dared. He goes on: "Mais justement: ils n'osaient pas. Ils avaient peur. De leurs voisins, des espions, je ne sais trop. Mais surtout d'eux-mêmes" (131) ("But that's just the point: they didn't dare. They were afraid. Afraid of their neighbours, spies, I don't know what. But above all, themselves".) The intention is to convince us that behind the French inertia regarding Algeria lies a simple and basic cause: fear. Sartre uses both these techniques throughout the volume with varying communicative aims. As they are typical of his rhetorical strategy and transfer easily and appropriately into English, they should be retained.

We were faced on many occasions with the problem of how to translate what at first sight appears to be a masculinist text: when talking about men and women inclusively, Sartre invariably employs the word "homme" or other masculine nouns and pronouns (significantly, Chuquet and Paillard do not address the issue). There seems to be no consensus amongst theorists on how to deal with texts that exclude — or appear to exclude — reference to women. For example, in *Gender in Translation* Sherry Simon notes that some feminist Biblical scholars "oppose inclusive language. They feel that this adjustment to contemporary norms in fact softens the harsh and intransigent message of a truly patriarchal document".[22] This is a defensible position. However, Simon, along with other commentators, has come to see translators as active participants in the creation of meaning and believes that they have the right to intervene in such matters: "they can use language as a cultural intervention, as part of an effort to alter expressions of domination whether at the level of concepts, of syntax or of terminology" (9). We largely share this view and, since inclusive language is more usual in English than in French, our own pragmatic solution is to move the translation in the direction of inclusion where the context suggests that this is an appropriate strategy, or where there is ambivalence.

It has been possible in many cases to accurately translate "hommes" by "people" or by "men and women". The following are some examples where it is likely that, in using the word "homme(s)", Sartre meant "people/human beings/men and women", and it is appropriate to translate accordingly: "Les instantanés de Cartier-Bresson attrapent l'*homme* à toute vitesse" (*Situations, V*, 12); "Le colonialisme refuse les droits de l'*homme* à des *hommes* qu'il a soumis par la violence" (52); "puisque tous les *hommes* ont les mêmes droits, on fera de l'Algérien un *sous-homme*" (44); "une idéologie pétrifiée s'applique à considérer des *hommes* comme des bêtes qui parlent"[23] (55). There are occasions when the translator has to make a judgement on what the author's intention was: "Restent des hommes qui se ressemblent en tant qu'*hommes*"[24] (9) — men, people, or men and women?

In contrast, there are many instances where it would be inaccurate to change the masculine form in translation. It is most likely in the following examples that "homme" refers only to the male sex and should be translated by "man": "Et quels sont les 'sacrifices' que l'Etat consent au colon, à cet *homme* chéri des dieux et des exportateurs?" (33); "nul ne peut traiter un *homme* 'comme un chien', s'il ne le tient pas d'abord pour un *homme*" (55); "Car c'est bien l'*homme* qu'on veut détruire, avec toutes ses qualités d'*homme*" (86); "Si j'allais découvrir une complaisance criminelle en l'*homme* qui vient de me serrer la main"[25] (64).

Apart from the word "hommes", the author's use of masculine plural nouns normally presents no difficulty and, when translated, reflects either masculine or *both* masculine *and* feminine: "Ses *Chinois* déconcertent" (9) ("His Chinese are disconcerting"). A different set of problems is presented by masculine singular nouns. They may be translated by a singular and thus serve as masculine *or* feminine in English, but this is not always straightforward: "la propriété du *colon lui* est venue de l'état gratuitement" (30) ("the colonist's property came to him from the State for free"). Here the word "colon" might simply be translated by "colonist", but the presence of the pronoun "lui" effectively rules out the use of the singular to convey both masculine and feminine. In order to represent both male and female colonists, "colon" and "lui" would have to be translated by a plural.

In "Une Victoire", there is a fascinating passage in which the feminine noun "victime" is used, referring to men but also serving to create an image of the male victim, in the sessions of torture, as a woman: "Quand *elle* se tait *la victime* sauve tout; quand *elle* parle, personne n'a le droit de *la* juger, pas même ceux qui n'ont pas parlé". If the sentence were to end here, there would be no difficulty for the translator. The article refers to men who are tortured, so the victim is certainly male. "Elle" is used to match the gender of the noun "victime", and can be translated by "he", and "la" by him. The difficulty arises, however, in the second half of the sentence, with the introduction of the word "femme" and a sexual image: "mais *elle* s'accouple avec son bourreau, c'est sa *femme* et ce couple enlacé s'abîme dans la nuit de l'abjection" (74). Sartre here suggests a perverse, sexual relationship — heterosexual rather than homosexual — between the tortured and the torturer, made possible linguistically through the use of the feminine noun "victime", referring first to a man then to a woman. This complex image is extremely difficult to convey successfully in English:

> When the victim remains silent, all is saved; yet when the victim talks, no one has the right to make a judgement, not even those who did not talk. But the victim is coupled with the tormentor, and becomes his woman; and this entwined couple is plunged into the abyss of a night of debasement.

This is also a striking example of how Sartre observes the way some human beings debase others and attempt to reduce them to a subhuman level — "les ravaler au rang de la bête" (86) ("reduce them to the level of animals") — , by likening them to animals or insects. Whilst some are fairly easy to translate ("Les nègres [...] c'étaient de bons chiens" (8) ("The niggers [...] were good dogs"); "une sauterelle chinoise" (12) ("a Chinese grasshopper"); "le troupeau est là. A quatre pattes" (18) ("The herd is there. On all fours"); "Dompter, dresser, châtier" (86) ("Bring to heel, train, punish")); others are less straightforward. For example, at one point, Sartre refers to "la bête humaine" (77). The absence in English of a direct equivalent of the noun "bête", with its range of meanings, makes an ideal translation difficult; we settled on "the human animal". In some of his numerous references to death and violence, he uses colloquialisms which are evocative and effective in conveying the horror he is observing, as in "des mouches en train de *bouffer* les yeux" (16) ("flies devouring eyes"). The effect of this cannot quite be conveyed in English, as there is no precise equivalent of "bouffer". Similarly, Sartre's use of "crever", more brutal than "mourir", is difficult to render with the same impact: "un môme *crevé*" (16) ("a dead child"); "*crever* comme des rats" (16) ("die like rats"); "ou nous allons *crever*" (58) ("or we're going to die"); "il fallait qu'ils *crèvent* ces sous-hommes" (85) ("these sub-humans had to die").

    We were struck by the number of times Sartre uses the pronoun "on" in these articles and also by the range of meanings it expressed. As Chuquet and Paillard comment, "la très grande fréquence du pronom *on* en français correspond en anglais à une gamme assez étendue de procédés pour renvoyer au générique".[26] They provide a list of possible translations (67-70). Since "on" can be construed in such a variety of ways, this is an area where our ideological and cultural bias may come to bear. As might be expected, the most natural English version was produced by using a passive construction: "*on* a refusé aux Musulmans l'usage de leur propre langage" (*Situations, V,* 39); "*on* a construit des barrages" (41); "les crimes que l'*on* commet en notre nom" (58) ("The Muslims were refused the use of their own language"; "dams were built"; "crimes which are committed in our name"). There are, however, occasions when the use of "they" seems more appropriate, particularly when Sartre is referring to the government and other authorities: "Ensuite, seulement, *on* mettra le système économique en place" (29); "Parce que la propriété tribale était le plus souvent collective et qu'*on* voulait l'émietter" (31); "l'Etat français possède 11 millions d'hectares (...); *on* a laissé 7 millions d'hectares aux Algériens" (32) ("Only then will they put the economic system in place"; "Because tribal property was more often than not collective, and they wanted to break it up"; "the French state possesses 11 million hectares (...); they left 7 million hectares to the Algerians".

The flexibility of "on" is largely due to its having no gender and also to the fact that, although it is a third person subject pronoun, it does not always strictly refer to the third person. The following are examples where we preferred to translate by "we" or "you": "Rien ne montre mieux la rigueur du système colonial: *on* commence par occuper le pays, puis *on* prend les terres et l'*on* exploite les anciens propriétaires" (36); "Peut-*on* du moins trouver une compensation à cette misère (...). Si nous avions cette consolation, peut-être pourrait-*on* garder quelque espoir" (37) "Nothing demonstrates better the rigour of the colonial system: you begin by occupying the country, then you take the land and you exploit the former owners. Can we at least find some compensation for this dire poverty? (...) If we had that consolation, perhaps we could maintain some hope".

Three areas where there was an attempt to retain the style of the source text, but where it was not always possible were: phonetics; some instances of tense use; and word order. Some of our problems derived from homophonic aspects, such as alliteration. For example, the amusing and punchy alliterative effect of "puceaux de la peur" is probably intended (136), but one cannot rely on the target language obligingly to supply the required alliteration. It apparently cannot be achieved here; something like "virgins with regard to fear" seems to be the best solution. As such features are rare in the source text, undertranslation of this kind, when it occurs, is slight and relatively harmless.

Sartre's use of the historic present is standard French practice for historical narratives. As Chuquet and Paillard rightly state, "[l]a fréquence de cet emploi du présent en français pose souvent des problèmes de traduction".[27] We almost always rendered the French historic present by the simple past in English, a solution confirmed by Chuquet and Paillard: English-speakers, they affirm, "confrontés à ce type de narration ont tendance naturellement à passer au prétérit en anglais" (86). This was, we felt, a justifiable domestication in the interests of comprehensibility: when French uses the historic present to describe a past event, it can use the future tense to refer to another event situated after the first but before the present of the text. As this device is rare in English and therefore not easily understood, we rejected it as potentially confusing.

However, Sartre sometimes wavers between the historic present and the perfect or the past historic. This change of tense often signals a perspective change. A passage describing Lumumba's belief in the need for African co-operation is related in the historic present ("Il n'y *a* donc à ses yeux qu'une seule tâche" (216), etc.) ("In his view, therefore, there was only one task"). When the result of this belief is revealed, however, the perfect tense is introduced, presumably to underline the final nature of the event ("le panafricanisme déclaré de Lumumba lui *a valu* quelques-uns de ses plus redoutables adversaires" (217)) ("Lumumba's declared pan-Africanism earned him some of his most formidable opponents"). A similar process occurs in a description of Jacqueline and d'Abdelkader Guerroudj's resistance against the French in Algeria. Their work in the movement is described in the historic present: "Elle *entre* dans le Mouvement bien après lui" (69) ("She joined the Movement well after him"), but when Sartre recounts their fate at the hands of French justice, he makes the transition into the past historic: "le commissaire du Gouvernement *demanda* la tête des inculpés [...] Il l'*obtint*" (69) ("the Government Commissioner demanded the heads of the accused. [...] He got them"). The historic present suggests immediacy, promise, energy; the switch to a past tense proper suggests a definitive end, the dissipation of the future. In Chuquet and Paillard's words, the passé simple expresses a "procès envisagé globalement et rupture par rapport au moment de l'énonciation".[28] As the simple past seems more appropriate in English than the historic present, these nuances will in most cases be lost in translation.

"Alors qu'il est fréquent de trouver en français différents éléments insérés entre le $C_0$ et le verbe ou entre le verbe et le $C_1$ sous forme d'incise, l'anglais au contraire évite en général de 'faire éclater' ce bloc"; thus Chuquet and Paillard summarise the French tendency to make insertions which to the anglophone ear and eye break up the sense of the sentence.[29] The following are just a few of the numerous examples of this phenomenon: "Cette furie contenue, *faute d'éclater*, tourne en rond et ravage les opprimés eux-mêmes" (179); "en outre, Lumumba sait, *après ce foudroyant départ*, que le lièvre s'est soudain changé en tortue" (202); "De fait, l'année même où Iléo, *dans son manifeste*, exige l'indépendance à terme, Patrice en est encore à tracer l'esquisse d'une 'communauté belgo-congolaise'" (204) ("Instead of exploding, this contained fury goes round and round in circles and devastates the oppressed themselves"; "What is more, Lumumba knew that, after this spectacular departure, the hare had suddenly changed into a tortoise"; "In fact, the very year that Iléo was demanding eventual independence on his manifesto, Patrice had got no further than sketching out a 'Belgian-Congolese community'"). In some cases, the original French word order can be maintained. Often, however, we felt that the maintenance of the French order — a foreignising move — would appear too unnatural to English-speaking readers, and so we rearranged the information. For instance, in the last example, a re-ordering sounds more appropriate.

We anticipate that the translation will be published with a critical apparatus within the next year. The availability in English of Sartre's major contribution to the post-colonial debate should lead to significant new work by scholars active in that field who have not had this opportunity in the past.

Stephen Brewer & Terry McWilliams

### Notes

1 Jean-Paul Sartre, Paris: Gallimard, 1978.
2 *Gender in Translation. Cultural Identity and the Politics of Transmission*, London: Routledge, 1996, 7.
3 "Introduction. Of colonies, cannibals and vernaculars", in S. Bassnett and H. Trivedi (eds), *Post-colonial Translation. Theory and Practice*, London: Routledge, 1999, 6.
4 *The Translator's Invisibility. A History of Translation*, London: Routledge, 1995, 18.
5 "Post-colonial writing and literary translation" in *Post-colonial Translation. Theory and Practice*, 31.
6 See, for example, the discussions in *Post-colonial Translation. Theory and Practice*.
7 See André Lefevere, "Translation. Universe of Discourse", in *Translation, Rewriting and the Manipulation of Literary Fame*, London: Routledge, 1992, 87-98.

8   This issue is addressed by some of the contributors to *Post-colonial Translation. Theory and Practice.* For example, G.J.V. Prasad ("Writing translation: the strange case of the Indian English novel", 41-57) discusses techniques employed by post-colonial writers to transfer their (marginal) culture to the (dominant) culture of their readers at the "centre". They include: using loan words (with and without gloss); suggesting the syntax and morphology of language of the marginal culture accurately or synthetically; referring to cultural practices (with and without gloss). Prasad concludes that post-colonial writing displays some of the characteristics of translation.
9   *The Translator's Invisibility*, 23-4.
10  'Post-colonial writing and literary translation', in *Post-colonial Translation. Theory and Practice*, 30.
11  'Post-colonial writing and literary translation', 22.
12  *The Translator's Invisibility*, 18.
13  André Lefevere (ed.), *Translation/History/Culture. A Sourcebook*, London: Routledge, 1992, 2.
14  'Post-colonial writing and literary translation', 23.
15  Well expressed by Venuti in *The Translator's Invisibility*, 18: "a foreign text is the site of many different semantic possibilities that are fixed only provisionally in any one translation, on the basis of varying cultural assumption and interpretive choices, in specific social situations, in different historical periods. Meaning is a plural and contingent relation, not an unchanging unified essence". Or again by Sherry Simon: "Equivalence in translation, as contemporary translation theory emphasizes, cannot be a one-to-one proposition" (*Gender in Translation*, 12).
16  The pessimistic myth that translation always results in a diminution of meaning has recently been questioned in translation theory literature. For example, Bassnett and Trivedi write: "Students of translation almost all start out with the assumption that something will be lost in translation, that the text will be diminished and rendered inferior. They rarely consider that there might also be a process of gain". ("Introduction. Of colonies, cannibals and vernaculars", in *Post-colonial Translation. Theory and Practice*, London: Routledge, 1999 (4). It is possible, for instance, that our annotated translation of *Situations, V* may enhance the meaning even for native speakers of French by virtue of the extra information it contains.
17  In the section 'Emprunts et calques', H. Chuquet and M. Paillard note that loan words are used 'faute d'équivalent dans la langue d'arrivée ou pour faire couleur locale' (*Approche linguistique des problèmes de traduction anglais — français* (Paris, Ophrys, 1987), 221.) *Situations, V* provides examples of the first case — institutions and concepts specific to the French colonial

experience (e.g. évolué, indigénat). 'Pour faire couleur locale' is an unfashionable way of referring to the incorporation of cultural otherness into the rewriting. The 'either/or' assumption seems erroneous: a loan word can be used for both reasons.

18 'Post-colonial writing and literary translation' in *Post-colonial Translation. Theory and Practice*, 25.
19 *Approche linguistique des problèmes de traduction anglais — français*, 300 & 401. The authors simply abandon any attempt to translate the allusions to the British TV soap opera Coronation Street and the Biblical reference to the 'writing on the wall'.
20 All subsequent italics within quotations are our own.
21 *Approche linguistique des problèmes de traduction anglais — français*, 137.
22 *Gender in Translation*, 124-5.
23 'Cartier-Bresson's photos catch people in full flight'; 'Colonialism denies human rights to people whom it has subjugated by violence'; 'as all people have the same rights, the Algerian will be made a sub-human'; 'a petrified ideology takes pains to consider humans as animals that talk'.
24 'What remains is men/people/men and women who resemble each other as men/people/men and women'.
25 'And what are the sacrifices that the State makes for the colonist, this man cherished by the gods and the exporters?'; 'no one can treat a man like a dog unless they first consider him as a man'; 'Because it is indeed the man that they want to destroy, with all his qualities as a man'; 'What if I were to discover a criminal complacency in the man who has just shaken my hand?'.
26 *Approche linguistique des problèmes de traduction anglais-français*, 67.
27 *Ibid.*,84.
28 *Ibid.*, 93.
29 *Ibid.*,155-6.

## 10.
## SUBTITLING AND DUBBING, FOR BETTER OR WORSE? THE ENGLISH VIDEO VERSIONS OF *GAZON MAUDIT*

The choice available between subtitling and dubbing as modes of linguistic transfer in the case of film material invites a comparison of losses, particularly since attitudes towards the merits of both modes frequently owe more to subjective judgments largely determined by sociocultural canons than to objective criteria.

Our purpose here is to compare and contrast the nature of the losses observed in the English subtitled and dubbed video versions of the French film *Gazon maudit (French Twist)* focusing on some of the most important sources of losses, namely the way in which marked speech is rendered under each set of constraints.

Beyond the obvious advantage of its availability in both formats, *Gazon maudit* seemed an interesting choice for two reasons. Its resounding success in France was followed by successes abroad in a variety of countries, including the United-States, which suggests that, whatever effect translations may have had on the film, they have not lessened its appeal or hampered its commercial career abroad. More importantly, it offers an interesting range of characteristics in terms of our focus, as we shall see.

Before we say more about the film and attempt to identify the nature of the losses in order to assess their impact, we must remind ourselves very briefly of the specific factors which constrain the linguistic transfer and of the respective advantages and disadvantages of subtitling and dubbing, since losses can only be fully appreciated in the wider context of these parameters.[1]

In the case of subtitling, the linguistic transfer is constrained by the length and structure of utterances; frame changes (since they can divert the attention of the viewer away from the subtitles); the medium (video and television subtitling normally require larger fonts and therefore allow fewer characters); the viewers' reading speed, which will vary according to their degree of literacy as well as according to whether it is a cinema audience or a television/video one, which carries implications in terms of the age range.

A number of features associated with subtitling can be regarded as advantages. The presence of the source language helps to preserve a degree of cultural coherence, if the language of the source dialogue coincides with the culture. Although, of course, audiences will not be particularly aware of the cultural incongruity of a Samurai speaking German or a cowboy chatting in Arabic, if the target language happens to be their own. For viewers with some knowledge of the source language, subtitles can in theory act as a supplement to the original dialogue, though in practice viewers may well confine themselves to one method of processing the dialogue. Original voices and the natural link between speech and body language are preserved. Finally, although it has sometimes been claimed that the combination of a dialogue in a foreign language with subtitles in the mother tongue offers some instructive value in terms of second language acquisition, the evidence points to the contrary.[2]

Such advantages are set against a number of disadvantages. The most obvious amongst them is the sustained effort required on the part of the viewer to keep up with the subtitles, an effort which diverts his or her attention away from the picture. The simultaneous availability of the source and target dialogues may encourage viewers with a knowledge of the source language to start "picking holes in the translated text",[3] even though they are more often than not ignorant of the constraints which characterize this form of linguistic transfer and the strategies required to overcome them. This will constitute a further source of distraction. Aesthetically, subtitles are unsightly and ruin the composition of the picture. The combination of static text with certain dynamic camera shots can both ruin the intended filmic effect and seriously hinder deciphering. The move from speech to writing requires a substantial amount of compression due to the difference in processing speed. In order to enable the viewer to deal with the subtitles at an appropriate pace, two criteria must be satisfied: legibility and readability. Although they overlap to a degree, the former can be seen as concerning essentially the physical and visual dimensions of the text (colour and size of font, number and position of lines, position of line breaks, use of punctuation marks, timing, etc.), whereas the latter encompasses various linguistic characteristics of the dialogue likely to affect the viewer's reading speed. Given that, as a rule, the more marked the language, the more difficult it will be to process, subtitling leads to a linguistic levelling out of dialogues by neutralising or eliminating marked features concerning a whole range of dimensions: syntax (long or complex sentences), levels of speech, social or geographical origin, style (ungrammatical, muddled, technical, rude, slangy, poetic, archaic, etc.). Finally, the systematic use of subtitles could represent a form of linguistic and cultural imperialism and, as such, constitute a threat to the target culture.

Dubbing is constrained by a number of factors: the syllabic flow (e.g. the distribution of stressed syllables may affect lip movement and gestures); lip movement; the position of the speaker in the frame (close-up, medium shot, long shot, speaker off-screen) since it will impact on the visibility of lip movement; body language (gestures punctuating oral discourse).

Given that the dialogue is delivered orally, it remains in a similar form (intonation, volume, speed) and therefore demands much less from the viewer whose attention is not divided.

Although it makes it possible to avoid a number of quantitative and qualitative losses inherent in subtitling, dubbing is not without its drawbacks. Amongst them, the cost, which is considerably higher; the risk of poor synchronisation both in terms of lip movement and body language; the combination of speech and body language which do not belong to the same culture; unnatural syntax due to the pressure of synchronisation which could be erroneously interpreted as instances of emphasis; unnatural intonation (to the point where, dubbed material can apparently be identified as such in blind tests for this very reason); ill-matched voices; the inaccessibility of the original actors' voices (a situation which, of course, does not prevent foreign viewers who have never heard an actor's voice to pass judgments such as: "Richard Burton était brillant"); the possibility of different actors being dubbed by the same voice, and, conversely, one actor being dubbed by more than one voice.[4] Given the obliteration of the source, dubbing also increases the temptation to adapt or censor.[5]

Keeping in mind the pros and cons of subtitling and dubbing as modes of linguistic transfer, let us now focus on the chosen film. *Gazon maudit*, by director Josiane Balasko, was released in France in 1995. The English dubbed and subtitled video versions, which were produced by Guild Pathé Cinema, followed in 1996.[6]

The plot is based partly on a real-life story. Loli (Victoria Abril) is a sweet, tolerant, faithful housewife and mother of two who feels increasingly frustrated and unfulfilled in her relationship with her inattentive husband, Laurent, a successful high-class estate agent (Alain Chabat). Although she is initially unaware of it, he is in fact an inveterate philanderer. One day, Marijo (played by the director, Josiane Balasko), a butch, no-nonsense lesbian, knocks at the door, her van having broken down outside the house. She immediately falls for Loli's charm and spirited personality. After a while, Loli gives in to Marijo's advances. She also discovers the extent of Laurent's womanising. Marijo moves in with the couple and an uneasy *ménage à trois* develops. Eventually Loli sleeps three nights a week with each person (everybody resting on the remaining day). Not surprisingly, macho homophobe Laurent is devastated by the fact that his hitherto faithful wife is having an affair with a butch lesbian with whom he has to share her favours and attention. He is nevertheless prepared to put up with the situation because he loves her and is convinced that she will ultimately abandon Marijo. After a whole series of incidents and crises (including Marijo's departure), they all end up living under the same roof again. The plot ends on a final twist which may upset the freshly restored balance of their relationship.

Regarding the title, which was suggested by director Bertrand Blier, Balasko declares:

> It's a very old expression. 'Gazon' is like grass, it also can mean pubic hair. 'Maudit' means forbidden, suggesting that since this grass was touched by women and not men, it was evil. One of Baudelaire's poems uses it; it's called 'The Damned Woman' and it speaks about lesbians as condemned.[7]

Preserved, for instance, in the Spanish version (*Felpudo* [= doormat/ pubic hairs] *maldito*), the reference has disappeared in the English title (*French Twist*).

Director Josiane Balasko's purpose was to make a film about lesbian love which was not by lesbians for lesbians but instead appealed to the widest possible audience. With this in mind, she deliberately rooted her characters in French vaudeville stereotypes (the cheating husband, the faithful wife, the *ménage à trois*) in addition to more recent stereotypes (e.g. the butch lesbian). However, she subverts them in order to portray a triangular relationship involving lesbian love and to satirize gender roles, macho double standards and homophobia, while putting forward utopian solutions beyond social and moral norms. The result is somewhere between a comedy of manners and a sex farce.

A number of critics were clearly negative, some of them mildly, others more damningly so.[8] Esther Iverem (*Washington Post*) questions the overall message: "those sensitive to issues of gender and sexuality may wonder if the nuclear-family ideal and a perverse sort of patriarchy don't win out in the end."[9] The film was considered more theatrical ("boulevardier") or televisual than truly cinematic[10] and characterised by a hamfisted approach with coarse humour and over-the-top farcical scenes uncomfortably mixed with light drama. Its length and characterization also came under repeated attacks. Both major and minor characters were deemed to lack depth and credibility to the point of totally undermining any idea of love (as opposed to mere physical attraction) between them. However, the strongest and most frequent criticisms were aimed at the script. The plot was felt to unravel in mid-film, lurching from crisis to false ending.

Interestingly, the very same aspects which drew criticisms from some, generated praise amongst others. Many deemed the film to be engaging, funny, hilarious even, and refreshingly original in its treatment of the genre and of stereotypes. For Edward Guthmann (*San Francisco Chronicle*), it "pulverizes evil-lesbian icons and creates a new archetype: the twinkle-eyed, soft-hearted butch."[11] Characterization was lauded for developing well-constructed rounded characters, both convincing and true to life, out of the initial caricatures. Damian Cannon (*Movie reviews UK*) sees the film's appeal in the fact that "beneath the coarseness lie the dreams of the vulnerable." Even the script is commended: for Barbara Shulgasser (*San Francisco Examiner*), it "boils over with quick funny plot switches."[12] In fact, for *Gazon maudit*, Josiane Balasko and Telsche Boorman won the César Award for

Best Writing (1996) and the film was also nominated for a Golden Globe (1996).

For their part, audiences voted with their feet making it a box office success in France (fifth position at the French box office in 1995 with almost four million spectators) and abroad, where it was generally well received in a number of countries (e.g. United States, Spain, Brazil, Italy, Switzerland and Belgium).

When considering the language of the dialogue, one finds a number of features which characterise it as marked and will potentially represent a challenge in terms of linguistic transfer. We shall focus on four aspects: the geographical origin of the speakers; the use of colloquial, slangy and strong language; dramatic exploitations of the *Tu* and *Vous* forms of address, and, briefly, rapid speech.

Geographically marked varieties of language present the translator with a familiar problem, whether in the form of accents, dialects, regional syntactic and lexical usage or speech influenced by a foreign language because the speaker is not a native speaker.

Linguists will be quick to point out that literary representations of accents are phonetically inaccurate, often betraying an insufficient degree of familiarity on the part of the author with the variety concerned[13] as well as a highly stereotypical perception of features. As a rule, the ad hoc phonetic transcriptions used are inadequate and inconsistent and can be very difficult or virtually impossible to decipher for the reader. On the other hand, it could be argued that scientific accuracy is not the concern of literary representations. Their function is to trigger an appropriate response from the reader, who is meant to identify the variety in question with all the connotations which may be relevant to characterization. Under the circumstances, dubious stereotyping and flawed transcriptions could be deemed legitimate if they actually enable the writer to achieve the intended effect.

For the translator, the strategy which would consist in representing an equivalent target regional accent is blatantly fraught with difficulties: preserving connotations, maintaining cultural coherence, avoiding offensive stereotyping, achieving readability are all highly problematic. One solution could be, in certain instances, to reverse the process used by the author in the source text. As Altano points out: "Dialects are used primarily for the scope of characterization, and thus permeate the text when the characters converse. Thus, instead of descriptive characterization — writers telling us how the character speaks, looks, and thinks — we are presented with analysis through the spoken word, which is certainly much more expressive."[14] So the translator could resort to "descriptive characterization", adding metalinguistic comments in order to enlighten the reader (e.g. "... he replied in his broad southern accent").

The subtitler's position is even more constrained than the literary translator's. Ad hoc phonetic representation is out of the question, since it would completely ruin any chance of attaining the level of readability required by the viewer. As for additional metalinguistic comments, they represent an unlikely option given the normal pragmatic constraints (e.g. absence of narrator) and the degree of compression required for a subtitled dialogue.

In the case of dubbing, foreign and regional accents pose different problems. In principle, a foreign accent can be rendered as long as it does not coincide, of course, with the target language. And even then, neutralisation is not necessarily unavoidable. Thus, in the Spanish (Catalan) version of *Fawlty Towers*, the Spanish character Manuel is still portrayed as a native speaker of Spanish, but of Mexican origin. However, when it comes to regional accents, no solution is really satisfactory for the reasons mentioned previously.

In *Gazon maudit*, the dimension of accents manifests itself in two ways: Loli's Spanish accent and the meridional accents of some of the characters. Victoria Abril (Loli), although resident in France, is Spanish[15] and, in spite of a very good command of French, has retained a Spanish accent which, very occasionally, can be quite marked. This aspect is predictably lost in the subtitles, however it has been preserved in the dubbed version.

Given that most of the action in *Gazon maudit* takes place in Provence, various characters tend to speak with an *accent du Midi*. This includes minor ones (neighbours, café owners, etc.) as well as Antoine, Laurent's friend. For their part, Laurent and Marijo do not have a southern accent. As was the case with Loli's accent, there is no trace of the regional accents of the characters in the subtitles. The same applies to minor characters in the dubbed version. However, Antoine is treated differently: his name is changed to "Antonio" and he is dubbed with an Italian accent. This interesting strategy concerning a regional accent in order to maintain the contrast with other characters turns out to be quite successful, although it may strike one as strange at first sight. The difference in accents is very marked in the original version and the solution adopted manages to preserve it without any detrimental effect in terms of characterization (the grafted foreign origin being in complete harmony with the image of the irredeemable Latin philanderer) or cultural coherence. It is worth noting that, when Antoine first appears on screen, he greets the owner of a café in Occitan ("Que me dises?", i.e. "Qu'est-ce que tu racontes?" subtitled as "How is it going?" and dubbed as "How goes it?"), so regional markedness is not merely confined to his accent. This ability to speak a language other than French in the original version may well have played a part in the decision to attribute to him a foreign accent.

As far as accents are concerned, therefore, the dubbed version does greater justice to characterization by avoiding the neutralisation inherent in subtitling.

The use of a foreign language for parts of the dialogue represents an interesting problem for the translator. In the case of subtitles, Ivarsson suggests that italics should normally be used for "isolated words or phrases in a foreign language".[16] However, one issue which Ivarsson does not address is whether these occasional words or phrases ought to be translated in cases where no step was taken in the original version to make them less opaque to the source viewer. This is in fact what happens in *Gazon maudit*, where about a dozen instances of Spanish can be found without any subtitles in the original. Apart from three examples (Spanish musicians in a restaurant scene; Marijo in the same scene and Diego, the Spanish client whom Laurent meets at the very end of the film) all are uttered by Loli. Virtually all occurrences are emotionally charged: talking to her children affectionately; enjoying her first evening with Marijo (discussing funny slang terms for female pubic hairs — "la moqueta, el conejo"); begging Laurent to make love ("Un poquito, un poquito"); making love to him ("Si, si, te quiero"); swearing or hurling abuse in the course of various arguments ("Hijo de puta!", etc.); trying to calm down pregnant Marijo when she starts experiencing unexpected contractions late at night out in a street. The last scene between Laurent and Diego, which contains a mixture of Catalan and Spanish, is also emotionally charged. All these instances of Spanish, which punctuate the film and are often directly or indirectly linked with its main sexual theme, are therefore much more than sprinkled touches of exoticism: they actually represent significant contributions to characterization. In the case of Loli, and in conjunction with her foreign accent, they add to her charm as a sensuous, passionate Latin lover (even more Latin than French) with perhaps also a hint of the hot-headed, impetuous Spanish female stereotype. Besides, one cannot help feeling at times that some of them may well be unscripted lines or expressions added spontaneously by Victoria Abril, who does switch into Spanish in her interviews, which lends more spontaneity and credibility to the character which she successfully portrays.

In the subtitled version, all instances of Spanish have disappeared apart from two expressions which are rendered in italics ("Son of a bitch", "Yes, yes, I love you"), in accordance with the convention referred to earlier. Even then, one can wonder whether viewers without a sufficient command of French and Spanish would actually notice the subtle typographical change and interpret it appropriately. By contrast, Spanish utterances are all retained in the dubbed version, thus preserving the differences and their role in terms of characterization.

The next category of losses corresponds to colloquial, slangy or strong language which constitutes a challenge for the translator because the factors which come into play in order to arrive at suitable equivalences are numerous.

The grammar of authentic informal speech can differ widely from non-informal grammar. This is particularly obvious in a language like French.[17] Literal transcriptions of authentic oral corpora are notoriously difficult to process for this very reason and because of mistakes, broken constructions, the absence of meaningful intonation, idiomatic fillers, etc.[18] Certain taboo words are also characterised by an unusual degree of grammatical and pragmatic flexibility — one only has to think of the possible constructions and pragmatic uses associated with a word like *fuck* in English.[19] Language variation works in continuums which usually overlap: an extremely informal expression (situational variation) can also be socially and regionally marked, which leads to a proliferation of connotations. By nature, slang undergoes a permanent process of lexical renewal which means that slang terms are often strongly linked to a specific period, social group or fashion, and this, of course, affects their frequency of use and usability as translation equivalents. The nature of the medium (spoken v. written) may also have an impact. As Ivarsson remarks about swear words and obscenities: "such expressions seem to have a stronger effect in writing than in speech, especially if they are translated literally".[20] The strength of a word or expression varies greatly according to the context and is dependent on very subjective judgments conditioned by complex culture-specific social conventions related to taboos. Censorship, self-censorship, or general translation norms may influence the outcome. Subtitles are generally expected to provide a high degree of transparency, even when the original may well prove incomprehensible to source viewers (how many French native speakers can comfortably follow the dialogue of a film like *La Haine*?). Given all these dimensions, matching colloquial, slangy or strong language in terms of syntax, denotation, connotation and strength often proves extremely difficult, or even impossible if one is also submitted to the constraints of audiovisual translation. Consequently, as Fawcett points out, a degree of toning down can often be observed: "Slang seems to be quite regularly expunged or weakened in the translation of films."[21]

In *Gazon maudit*, the language used by all main characters is usually colloquial, frequently vulgar and quite strong and the tendency referred to by Fawcett is certainly observable. In principle, subtitled and dubbed dialogues can be (a) equivalent to the French source, (b) weaker or (c) stronger, which produces eight theoretically possible permutations for a given example (both weaker, both stronger, subtitles weaker/ dubbing equivalent, etc.). In practice only six can be found in *French Twist*.

# Subtitling and Dubbing, For Better or Worse?
## The English Video Versions of *Gazon maudit*

Both are weaker (25 examples):

— Putain, ça fait du bien de s'arrêter cinq minutes.
(S) — It feels good to take a break.
(D) — God, it's good to break for five minutes.

— "Mort aux mecs!"
(S) — "Death to men!"
(D) — "Men are morons!"

— Il me fait chier Antoine.
(S) — Antoine is a pain.
(D) — Antonio is a pain.

— Y en a d'autres qui auraient fait la gueule.
(S) — Some men would mind.
(D) — And you really don't object.

— Ne te fous pas de ma gueule par dessus le marché!
(S) — Don't try to be funny!
(D) — Don't try to be clever with me on top of everything!

— Tu lui pelotais la moule, c'est ça?
(S) — So you felt her up?
(D) — So you felt her up, is that it?

— Tu crois que ça va m'empêcher de te foutre mon poing dans la gueule!
(S) — I'll still knock your teeth out!
(D) — Do you think that will stop me putting my fist through your face.

— Ah, ben, c'est pas trop tôt! Mais magne-toi, il est huit heures. Ça cogne déjà.
(S) — Finally! Hurry! The sun's already up!
(D) — Get a move on. It's eight o'clock. It's already boiling hot.

— Alors, collez-moi votre poing sur la gueule, si ça peut vous détendre.
(S) — So take a swing at me.
(D) — So you can beat me up, if you really have to.

— Arrêtez de vous engueuler tous les deux!
(S) — Stop arguing you two!
(D) — Won't the two of you stop quarrelling!

— Une femme qui trompe son mari, ça c'est dégueulasse.
(S) — But a wife cheating, that's sick!
(D) — A woman who cheats on her husband, that's disgusting!

— Et puis, une engueulade par-ci, par-là, ça a du bon, hé.
(S) — And a tiff, is good sometimes.
(D) — Hey, a bit of a battle is good for you.

— Oh, la honte, con.
(S) — How humiliating.
(D) — How awful.

— Avec qui? Avec qui? Du con! T'es mon ami ou merde!
(S) — With who? With who? You idiot! Are you my friend or what?
(D) — Who with? Who with? You fool! And you're a mate of mine!

— Je passe ma vie à faire gaffe.
(S) — I'm extra careful.
(D) — I spend my life trying to be careful.

— Je suis con, je suis con.
(S) — I'm an idiot. An idiot.
(D) — I'm a fool, I'm a fool.

— Elle m'a plaqué pour une gonzesse. Ça vous fait pas rigoler ça?
(S) — She dumped me for a woman. Isn't that funny?
(D) — Threw me over for a woman. Don't you find that funny?

— Je te file mon numéro, tu m'appelles sans faute.
(S) — Here's my number, call me.
(D) — You've got my number, use it.

— Je vais vous le foutre sur la gueule le beurre!
(S) — I'll rub your nose in the butter!
(D) — Get it yourself, the butter!

— Et oui, mais je suis chez moi et chez moi, je me balade à poil si je veux.
(S) — And in my house, I walk around naked...If I feel like it.
(D) — Oh yes, but this is my home and in my house I can dance around without my clothes if I want.

— Tiens, je t'avais bien dit, j'ai pris du cul.
(S) — I told you I put on weight.
(D) — She's quite right, I spread a bit.

Subtitling and Dubbing, For Better or Worse?  
The English Video Versions of *Gazon maudit*

— De toute façon, tu penses qu'à ton cul!  
(S) — You are so selfish!  
(D) — You only think of yourself!

— On dort vachement bien chez vous.  
(S) — I slept like a charm.  
(D) — I had a wonderful sleep last night, thanks.

— Je sais que tu viendras pas m'emmerder.  
(S) — You won't nag me.  
(D) — I know you won't bother me.

— No mecs! (sic)[22]  
(S) — No men!  
(D) — No men!

Subtitles weaker, dubbing roughly equivalent (13 examples):

— Encore un emmerdeur.  
(S) — What a pain.  
(D) — What a bloody nuisance.

— Qu'est-ce qu'elle a à être encore là l'autre engin. Elle est plus collante qu'un morbac.  
(S) — What's the diesel doing here?  
(D) — What the hell is she still doing here. She's harder to shake off than a case of crabs.

— C'est ça, tire-toi, hé!  
(S) — That's it, leave me!  
(D) — Get lost.

— Tu fais chier hé maintenant, à la fin!  
(S) — You're being a real pain!  
(D) — You're really starting to piss me off!

— Tu commences à me pomper l'air!  
(S) — You were getting boring!  
(D) — You're getting on my tits!

— Et merde alors, les amis c'est fait pour ça, sinon à quoi ça sert?  
(S) — What are friends for, damn it?  
(D) — Oh, for Christ's sake, what are friends for?

— Une fois elle m'a trouvé avec une gonzesse, ça suffit.
(S) — She caught me once, that was enough.
(D) — Once she found me with a tart. Once was enough.

— Chiale pas, merde!
(S) — Stop bawling!
(D) — Oh, shut up, shit!

— Où t'as foutu tes putains de balles?
(S) — Where are the bullets?
(D) — Where've you hidden the bloody bullets?

— Le mieux, pour nous, pour tout le monde c'est que vous vous cassiez comme vous êtes venue dans votre minibus.
(S) — Why don't you just drive off in that pretty little van of yours?
(D) — So the best for us and everybody is if you hit the road just as you came in that pretty minibus.

— Ça vous fait bien chier que je reste.
(S) — It makes you sick that I'm staying?
(D) — I guess you're well pissed off I'm staying.

— Qu'est-ce que c'est que ce bordel?
(S) — What's this mess?
(D) — What the hell is this now?

In one particular instance, the requirements of lip synchronisation produced a mixture of English and Spanish (*putois* > *puta*):

— C'est toi qui va réveiller les enfants à gueuler comme un putois!
(S) — Now you are going to wake up the kids.
(D) — It's you who'll wake the children shouting like a puta.

Subtitling weaker, dubbing stronger (8 examples):

— Qu'est-ce que j'en ai à foutre de l'autre grosse gouine!
(S) — Leave the fat dyke!
(D) — I don't give a shit about the fucking dyke.

— Attends Antoine, la philosophie de comptoir à huit heures du mat, merci!
(S) — Keep your two-bit wisdom!
(D) — Oh, shut up Antonio! Who needs your crap philosophy!

# Subtitling and Dubbing, For Better or Worse? The English Video Versions of *Gazon maudit*

— Fous le camp!
(S) — Get out!
(D) — Fuck off!

— Ça me fait chier de me taper 40 bornes à transpirer comme un porc!
(S) — I'm not doing 30 miles sweating like a pig!
(D) — I'm fucked if I'll pedal for miles till I sweat like a pig!

— Pourquoi, pourquoi avec cet espèce d'ersatz?
(S) — But why, why with that poor substitute?
(D) — Why, but why with that substitute dick?

— A la rigueur, je comprendrais avec un mec, je comprendrais.
(S) — At least with a man I'd understand.
(D) — At any rate, it'd make sense if it was a guy she was fucking.

— Je vais me faire une chèvre.
(S) — I'm going for the goat!
(D) — I'm going to fuck the goat!

— Toi, fous-moi la paix!
(S) — Leave me alone!
(D) — Piss off bitch!

## Subtitling stronger, dubbing weaker (2 examples):

— Avec votre fromage à la con!
(S) — With your fucking cheese!
(D) — With your stupid cheese!

— Les conneries, on finit toujours par les payer.
(S) — You always pay for your fuck-ups!
(D) — It's true, friend: crime doesn't pay.

## Subtitling stronger, dubbing roughly equivalent (2 examples):

— Dès qu'il avait le dos tourné, hop, hop, elles broutaient un peu le gazon!
(S) — As soon as he was away, they'd start fucking!
(D) — The second he goes out of the room, hop, they're at it: a little bit of grazing!

— Habille-toi au lieu de dire des bêtises.
(S) — Get dressed and cut the bullshit.
(D) — Hurry. Stop your nonsense and get dressed.

Subtitling roughly equivalent, dubbing stronger (2 examples):

— Ah, tu peux pas la fermer!
(S) — Can't you shut up!
(D) — Why don't you shut the fuck up!

— Je me suis jamais tapé de vieille.
(S) — It'd be my first old bag.
(D) — I've never fucked an old one before.

The above examples clearly illustrate how arduous the translators have found the task of pitching the target language at an appropriate level and how the solutions adopted can diverge substantially, even allowing for the possibility of deliberate compensations for some of the equivalences which do not match the source (stronger language being used to make up for weak translations elsewhere or vice versa). Besides, the tendency to tone down and neutralise referred to by Fawcett is plainly observable, particularly in the subtitled version, as shown by the table below:

*Colloquial, slangy and strong language compared to the source dialogue*

|            | weaker | stronger |
|------------|--------|----------|
| Subtitling | 46     | 4        |
| Dubbing    | 27     | 11       |

One cannot help wondering whether this tendency is always explicable in terms of the kind of linguistic or sociolinguistic factors mentioned previously or whether, in some instances where equivalents would seem available, we are not in the presence of some translation norm influencing, consciously or not, the choices made by the translator. Be that as it may, the dubbed version does again greater justice to characterization than the subtitled version, since, in the latter, characters will be perceived as less informal and more refined than they actually are.

Pronouns of address present a familiar challenge for the translator either because one of the languages concerned does not offer a morphological contrast of the *Tu-Vous/Du-Sie/Tu-Usted*, etc. type, or

## Subtitling and Dubbing, For Better or Worse?
## The English Video Versions of *Gazon maudit*

because usage patterns diverge substantially from one language to the other.[23] The factors governing the use of such pronouns are numerous and their interaction is both subtle and complex. Thus, referring to a study by Friedrich on Russian, Anderman quotes the following possible dimensions: "age, generation, sex, kinship status, group membership, jural and political authority as well as emotional solidarity".[24] Sociolinguistic norms vary from group to group as well as over time, and sometimes quite rapidly.

Given the wide spectrum of emotions which can be conveyed through pronouns of address and pronominal switching (intimacy, remoteness, contempt, respect, affection, anger, etc.), they are frequently exploited in literature as a dramatic device. Needless to say, the point made by Anderman about the theatre applies to film material:

> In order to maintain the continued interest of the audience, drama, to a larger extent than prose, is crucially dependent on conflict. By simply switching from a pronoun expressing a certain degree of intimacy to another, indicating greater formality or vice versa, the emotional temperature of an exchange on stage may swiftly be raised or lowered, in accordance with the playwright's intentions.[25]

Understandably, rendering connotations built into the morphology of one language through lexical means in another presents the translator with a thorny problem. Vinay and Darbelnet suggest a number of possibilities to render French *tutoiement* in English: using first names, nicknames, initials or, in the case of pronominal switching, equivalences such as "My name is Violet, but my friends call me Vi". Vocatives can also represent an option (*man, chum, mate, brother, sister, etc.*) as does informal syntax. One can, of course, easily conceive formal alternatives to these procedures for *vouvoiement*. Anderman also underlines the option of visual solutions to the problem in the case of drama when the director is aware of the feature in the source text.[26] Although she does not elaborate, one can envisage gestures, physical contact, closeness or remoteness conveying analogous meanings.

*Gazon maudit* offers several instances of *Tu-Vous* contrasts involving various relationships between characters: Loli-Marijo, Laurent-Marijo, Laurent and an old prostitute, Diego-Laurent.

Loli and Marijo use the *Vous* form initially. Then, in the course of the first meal they have together in Laurent's absence, Marijo suddenly moves to *Tu* as they discuss various names for female pubic hairs ("Et tu sais comment ils appellent ça au Québec?"); Loli follows suit. Yet, Marijo reverts to *Vous* when saying good night to Loli, in front of Laurent, who has just returned ("Votre lapin: génial! Un délice."), to change back to the more intimate *Tu* again later on in the same evening, when she calls, feigning to have forgotten her wallet, to say goodbye to Loli ("Je voulais juste te dire au revoir") and kiss her. Predictably, these nuances are not rendered in English, though what they signify is arguably conveyed by the manner in which the conversations develop, the characters' actions and the acting which all indicate more familiarity and closeness or the opposite.

Having realised that there is something going on between his wife and Marijo, Laurent erupts, shouts abuse at Marijo and, in the process, drops the formal *Vous*, which he had been using to distance himself from her (e.g., referring to a cricket bat she is holding in response to his physical threats, "Tu crois que ça va m'empêcher de te foutre mon poing dans la gueule!"). Although, having calmed down a little, as a result of the neighbours' coming out because of the disturbance, he reverts to *Vous* for further abuse ("Si je vous revois dans le coin, je vous démolis la tête. Et en prime, la batte de cricket, je vous l'enfonce dans le cul!"). When Marijo moves in with them, the formal pronoun is the norm between them, even when tension rises and the language turns stronger: [27]

> Laurent: Vous avez amené le beurre?
> Marijo: Je vais vous le foutre sur la gueule le beurre!
> (S) — I'll rub your nose in the butter!
> (D) — Get it yourself, the butter!

The humorous mixture of the polite *Vous* with vulgar language is lost in the translations, and although one could in theory argue that, when more neutral renderings are provided, they constitute a sort of stylistic average of the polite and the vulgar, the impact is obviously different.

In addition, Laurent's strategy in terms of form of address contrasts with Antoine's, since the latter is quick to resort to the friendly *Tu* when talking to Marijo. As the possibility of driving Marijo away from his wife (by stirring up Loli's feelings of jealousy towards Marijo's former girlfriend) dawns on Laurent, he decides to be excessively affable towards Marijo and suggests they abandon the mutual *vouvoiement:*

> Marijo: — Dites-moi, il y a un truc qui me chiffonne.
> Laurent: — Quoi?
> — Pourquoi vous êtes si sympa d'un seul coup avec moi?
> — Je me détends. Ça arrive. Et puis, on arrête de se vouvoyer, ça fait vieux cons.
>
> (S) — Why are you so nice, suddenly?
> — I'm lightening up. It happens. Let's stop acting like assholes.
>
> (D) — Hang on, there's something I don't get.
> — Yeah?
> — Why are you so nice to me all of a sudden?
> — I'm loosening up. That can happen. And, by the way, consider me a friend from now on.

Of course, neither solution is fully satisfactory, at the same time it is hard to envisage what alternative could successfully convey the move to a less formal form of address in the context.

Laurent's encounter with an old prostitute, at a point where he is deeply depressed and feels sorry for himself, offers another instance of subtle play on pronouns. His opening remarks are most abrupt:

> — Pourquoi t'es triste comme ça?
> — A cause des femmes, des putes comme toi.
> — T'as plutôt une tête à faire souffrir.
> — Te fatigue pas, je suis pas client.
> — T'es pas venu là par hasard, et moi je suis la dernière.
> — Je me suis jamais tapé de vieille.

He finally follows her, yet changes his mind once in the bedroom, clearly regretting his initial offensive remarks, and switches to *Vous*, which sounds all the more respectful since it is in the context of a prostitution transaction and she retains the *Tu:*

> — Je vais partir. Je vous paie, ne vous inquiétez pas, je vous paie.
> — Trop vieille?
> — Excusez-moi, j'ai été dégueulasse.
> — Je suis habituée à pire. J'ai vraiment plus les moyens de faire la difficile.

> — Madame, s'il vous plaît. C'est pas que vous soyez vieille, c'est pas ça. Vous êtes belle. Regardez-moi.

The subtitles provide:

> — Why are you so sad.
> — Why? because of whores like you.
> — You're more the heartbreaker. With your looks.
> — Stop it, I'm not interested.
> — You're not here by chance. Why not?
> — You'd be my first old bag.
> — I'm leaving. I'll pay, don't worry.
> — Too old?
> — Sorry, I was cruel.
> — I'm used to worse.
> — I can't be picky anymore.
> — Madame, please... It's not your age. Look at me. You're beautiful.

The dubbed version offers:

> — Why the long face, pretty fellow?
> — Why not? Because of women, whores like you.
> — I bet you've made a few girls shatter, a good looking young man like you.
> — Forget it, I'm not paying for that.
> — You mean you're here by accident? Well I'm the last in line.
> — I've never fucked an old one before.
> — I've got to go. I'll pay you, don't worry, I'll pay.
> — Too old?
> — I'm sorry that was unkind of me.
> — I'm accustomed to worse, and I'm hardly in a position to make a fuss.
> — Madame, please. It's not because of your age, it's not that. Look at me. You're beautiful.

The nuance imparted by the play on pronouns is lost in the target dialogues. The use of *Madame* would tend more to connote foreignness than act as a linguistic marker of respect equivalent to the *Vous* form. Nevertheless, the change of mood is apparent in the manner in which the situation develops.

# Subtitling and Dubbing, For Better or Worse?
## The English Video Versions of *Gazon maudit*

The last occurrence of pronominal switching is to be found at the very end of the film. Laurent, who is an estate agent, calls at a vendor's with the intention of purchasing his beautiful property. The man, Diego, is young and handsome and the scene soon takes on homosexual undertones, although Laurent has constantly been portrayed as a womanizer up to this point. The more intimate *Tu* comes in the answer to a question from Laurent:

— Sans être indiscret, vous êtes espagnol?
— Si. Tu connais l'Espagne?

The use of the Spanish *si* where one would normally use *oui* in French, could well be linked here, since Diego is clearly reacting in Spanish, a language in which the use of the informal form *Tu*, as opposed to *Usted,* is more widely spread and can appear more easily than French *Tu* in conversations with complete strangers. They clink glasses together and Diego uses a common Catalan formula which makes reference to male sexual vigour ("Salut i força al canut!") and is explained to Laurent with an appropriate gesture. The conversation ends with the promise of a further encounter the following Saturday. Not surprisingly, the subtlety of the pronoun change has no linguistic equivalent in the target versions:

(S) — Yes! You know Spain?
(D) — Si. Do you know Spain?

Yet, once again, the evolution of their relationship in the course of this very brief conversation remains clear because of all the other clues available to the viewer of either English version. Like drama, films offer the possibility of interpreting the dialogue in conjunction with the visual information available to the spectator.

Since oral language can be processed much faster than its equivalent in written form, rapid speech is always a casualty in subtitling. Good subtitles will normally succeed in preserving the essence of the dialogue, as in the following example:

— C'est pas du tout le genre à se faire draguer à la sortie de l'école en attendant les mômes, si tu vois ce que je veux dire.

(S) — She's the faithful type, get it?
(D) — She's not the type to get chatted up in the playground waiting for the kids to get out from school, you get my drift?

Many similar examples can be found in the subtitled version of *Gazon maudit*, which successfully condenses the frequent occurrences of fast speech without any inadequate equivalences. However, the cumulative effect of such systematic compression results in a less colourful and rather bland dialogue, whilst the dubbed version can remain, stylistically and in terms of content, much closer to the original.

A number of points emerge from this brief analysis. The *Tu/Vous* contrasts are equally neutralised in both modes of transfer. Yet the resulting losses of this particular neutralisation are to some extent lessened by the fact that the dialogue is only one of the interacting dimensions of film discourse. Although, on one hand, the sound track and the visuals constantly hinder the translator-adapter in his/her task, on the other, they provide him or her with a permanent source of solutions and compensations, a reminder, if need be, of the holistic nature of filmic discourse.

Geographically marked language (Loli's Spanish accent; meridional accents, particularly Antoine's; the various instances of Spanish), colloquial/slangy/strong language and rapid speech (well condensed, but bland) all come out worse in the subtitled version.

Apart from rapid speech, the dimensions levelled out in the transfer are mostly sociolinguistically marked. The cumulative impact of such neutralisations does not affect the plot or the overall message of the film. The humour and satire are occasionally weakened by the comparative blandness of the language, but the comic, which essentially arises from situations, is for the best part preserved. The main casualties are undoubtedly characterisation and general colourfulness, and, as we have seen, this is particularly true of the subtitled version. The dubbed version avoids some of the pitfalls of this mode of transfer like ill-matched voices. The lip synchronization, although occasionally problematic and quite noticeably so in places when the film is analysed closely, is perfectly acceptable and unobtrusive under normal viewing conditions. Therefore, *Gazon maudit* definitely fares better in its dubbed version than in its subtitled one.

In terms of sociocultural norms, subtitling is commonly perceived as more likely to be favoured by the cultural elite, whilst dubbing is considered as more appropriate to less discerning audiences. The difference in the markets targeted is certainly plain in the manner in which the two English video versions are packaged. The dubbed one carries a quote from the *Sunday Mirror* depicting the film as "a deliciously vulgar sex comedy" and is preceded by a series of trailers, which, leaving aside the noticeable exception of *Richard III*, all advertise mass audience films offering action, erotic tales or light comedy (*Down Periscope, The Tomorrow Man, Broken Arrow, The Temptress, Girl 6*). In marked contrast, the subtitled version entices its viewers with a quote from *The Times* characterising the film as "endlessly entertaining" and invites them to watch two further subtitled films: *Nelly & Monsieur Arnaud*, by Claude Sautet, and *Une femme française*, by Régis Wargnier, both dramas featuring Emmanuelle Béart. The truth is that the greater authenticity often attributed to subtitling by the culturally sophisticated is largely dependent on the nature of the film. The case of *Gazon maudit* shows that subtitling would be best suited to material with, amongst other features, little or no sociolinguistically marked language and fast speech. The authenticity argument, though correct in terms of original voices and cultural coherence, is flawed by the fact that, unless viewers enjoy a high command of the source language — in which case the prop of subtitles would be largely redundant — they will not be in a position to appreciate the linguistic subtleties of the dialogue and will therefore be at the mercy of all the losses and neutralisations inherent in subtitling as a mode of linguistic transfer.

Finally, underlying the authenticity argument is the notion, linked to the "sourcier/cibliste" debate,[28] that subtitling is more film-oriented whereas dubbing is more viewer-oriented, since the original film remains present with subtitling and dubbing is kinder on the viewer. However, in cases where the source remains largely opaque to the viewer of the subtitled version and is only accessed through a highly filtered dialogue due to the constraints inherent in this mode of audiovisual translation, the film can actually suffer a great deal more in a subtitled version than it would in a sympathetically dubbed version.

Jean-Pierre Mailhac

**Notes**

1. For the constraints, advantages and disadvantages of both modes, see, for instance, Jan Ivarsson, *Subtitling for the Media. A Handbook of an Art*, Stockholm: Transedit, 1992; Jean Yvane, "Le doublage filmique: fondements et effets", in Yves Gambier (éd.), *Les transferts linguistiques dans les médias audiovisuels*, Villeneuve d'Ascq: Presses Universitaires du Septentrion, 1996, 133-143.
2. Gary D'Ydewalle & Ubowanna Pavakanun, "Le sous-titrage facilite-t-il l'apprentissage des langues?", in Yves Gambier (éd.), *Les transferts linguistiques dans les médias audiovisuels*, 218.
3. Morten Krogstad, "Subtitling for cinema films and video/television", in Yves Gambier (ed.), *Translating for the Media*, Turku: Centre for Translation and Interpreting, 1998, 60.
4. For an interesting example of public reactions following the death of the Columbo German dubbing actor, see Karin Wehn, "Re-dubbing of US-American television series for the German television: the case of *Magnum, P. I.*" in Yves Gambier (ed.), *Translating for the Media*, 186.
5. For instances of both adaptation and censorship, see *ibid.*
6. I am extremely grateful to Steve Opray (Pathé Distribution Ltd) for kindly providing a copy of the subtitles by Eric Collins. Information about the author of the dubbing script was not available.
7. Peter Keough, "About *Gazon maudit...*", Movie reviews, *The Phoenix*, http://www.phx.com/alt1/archive/movies/reviews/01-11-96/GAZON_MAUDIT.html, 1995.
8. In addition to reviews quoted elsewhere in this article, see the following for critical comments: James Berardinelli, *Gazon Maudit* (1995), *Internet Movie Database*, 1996, http://us.imdb.com/Reviews/47/4767; Roger Ebert, *French Twist*, *Chicago Sun-Times*, 23 February 1996, http://www.suntimes.com/ebert/ebert_reviews/1996/02/1021845.html; John Hartl, "Tired French Farce", *Film.com Movie Reviews*, http://www.film.com/reviews/index.jhtml?review _url =/film-review/1995/10352/109/default-review.html; Christopher Null, *Gazon Maudit* (1995), *Internet Movie Database*, 1996, http://us.imdb.com/Reviews/48/4818; Steve Rhodes, *Gazon Maudit* (1995), *Internet Movie Database*, 1996, http://us.imdb.com/Reviews/50/5003; Bob Thompson, "Flaky crust, no filling", *Toronto Sun*, http://www.canoe.ca/JamMoviesReviewsF/french_twist.html.
Essentially positive reviews include: Alex Albanese, *French Twist*, *Boxoffice Magazine*, http://www.boxoff.com/cgi/getreview.pl?where=Name&filename= All&terms=FRENCH+TWIS; Damian Cannon, *French Twist*, *Movie Reviews*

*UK*, 1997, http://www.1worldfilms.com/frenchtwist.htm; Richard Corliss, "Bedtime Story", Time Magazine, 147, 3, 15 January 1996, http://pathfinder.com/time/magazine/archive/1996/dom/960115/cinema.frenchtwist.html; Karine Weinberger & Julien Vermorel, "'J'aime pas faire le même chien avec un autre collier', ou Victoria, la Latin-Loveuse", interview de Victoria Abril, *France.com*, http://www.france.com/mag/cinema/gazonmaudit/victoria.html.

9  Esther Iverem, 'French Twist', *Washington Post*, 16 February, 1996, http://www.washingtonpost.com/wp-srv/style/longterm/movies/videos/frenchtwistriverem_c0478a.htm.

10 *Gazon maudit*, Jean-François Houben, *Guide Critique des Films*, 1997, http://www.cinemaniacs.be/pages/critique/AGAZON.htm.

11 Edward Guthman, "A 'Twist' on Sexual Stereotypes", *San Francisco Chronicle*, 19.1.1996, http://www.sfgate.com/cgi-bin/article.cgi?f=//chronicle/archive/1996/01/19/DD3022.DTL&type=printable.

12 Barbara Shulgasser, "A threesome with a real Twist", *San Francisco Examiner*, 19.1.1996, http://www.sfgate.com/cgi-bin/article.cgi?f=/examiner/archive/1996/01/19/WEEKEND2814. dtl&type=printable.

13 W. Brian Altano, "Translating Dialect Literature: the Paradigm of Carlo Emilio Gadda", *Babel*, 34, 3, 1988, 153.

14 *Ibid.*, 152.

15 Her international film career includes films with Spanish director Pedro Almodóvar.

16 Jan Ivarsson, *Subtitling for the Media. A Handbook of an Art*, Stockholm: Transedit, 1992, 116.

17 See Gadet, F., *Le français ordinaire*, Paris: Armand Colin, 1989 and Gadet, F., *Le français populaire*, Que sais-je?, n° 1172, Paris: Presses Universitaires de France, 1992. For a discussion of translation problems concerning this aspect, see Jean-Pierre Mailhac, "Levels of speech and grammar when translating between English and French" in Beverly Adab and Christina Schäffner (eds.), *Developing Translation Competence*, Benjamins Translation Library, Amsterdam: Benjamins (forthcoming).

18 In this respect, two of the recommendations put forward by Jan Ivarsson and Mary Carroll in their *Code of Good Subtitling Practice (Language Today*, April 1998) amount to a contradiction: "The language register must be appropriate and correspond with the spoken word", "The language should be (grammatically) correct since subtitles serve as a model for literacy" (20). Such guidelines can only apply if "spoken word" does not refer to authentic informal speech.

19 Geoffrey Hughes, *Swearing. A Social History of Foul Language, Oaths and Profanity in English*, London: Penguin, 1998, 30-33.
20 *Subtitling for the Media. A Handbook of an Art*, 126.
21 Peter Fawcett, *Translation and Language. Linguistic Theories Explained*, Manchester: St Jerome Publishing, 1997, 119. For a discussion of the issues touched upon here, see the chapter devoted to sociolinguistics (116-122).
22 The remark is made by a female bouncer refusing Laurent access to a lesbian night club.
23 See: J.-P. Vinay & J. Darbelnet, *Stylistique comparée du français et de l'anglais. Méthode de traduction*, Paris: Didier, 1960, 189-190; P. Friedrich, "Structural Implications of Russian Pronominal Usage", in W. Bright (ed.), *Sociolinguistics*, The Hague: Mouton, 1966, 214-259; Jan Ivarsson, *Subtitling for the Media. A Handbook of an Art*, 125; Mona Baker, *In Other Words. A Coursebook in Translation*, London: Routledge, 1992, 94-98; Gunilla Anderman, "Untranslatability: The Case of Pronouns of Address in Literature", *Perspectives: Studies in Translatology*, 1993, 1, 57-67.
24 *Ibid.*, 65.
25 *Ibid.*, 59-60.
26 *Ibid.*, 61.
27 Interestingly, Anderman ("Untranslatability: the Case of Pronouns of Address in literature", 61-62) refers to a scene in Shakespeare's *Richard III* in which pronominal switching between *You* and *Thou* follows exactly the same pattern from formality to a loss of self-control due to anger back to a more respectful form of address when the characters regain their composure.
28 See, Jean Yvane, "Le doublage filmique: fondements et effets", in Yves Gambier (éd.), *Les transferts linguistiques dans les médias audiovisuels*, 134.

## 11.
## ADVENTURES ACROSS TIME: TRANSLATIONAL TRANSFORMATIONS

One morning, I found the children watching a cartoon on television. A handsome fox with a posh English accent and a top hat was making plans for a journey, with a cockney hamster and a beautiful lady cat in a sari. Something about the dialogue rang a distant bell, and I was told that the programme was *Willy Fogg goes to the Centre of the Earth*.

Aficionados of Jules Verne will recognize the reference instantly: the fox, Willy Fogg, was the hero of an animated cartoon series that ran for dozens of episodes in the 1980s based on Verne's *Around the World in 80 Days*. Now the characters from that series were back, this time undertaking a journey to the centre of the earth. Somehow, the protagonist of *Around the World in 80 Days*, Phileas Fogg, had become Willy, the wily fox, and his companions had metamorphosed into other animals. Moreover, not content with occupying the pages of one novel, they had invaded another, for as we know, the characters who travel round the world in a balloon never appear in the *Journey to the Centre of The Earth* at all. The two novels have been conflated, and the basic narrative of the journey in both cases provides a frame for a successful children's cartoon series.

This essay explores some of the transformations of Verne's novel, *Voyage au centre de la terre* that appeared in 1864 and underwent its most recent cinematic translation in 1993. It is the second novel in his *Voyages extraordinaires* and he was to go on and write over 50 more before his death in 1905. He was a prolific writer, who enjoyed immense popular acclaim at home and abroad, and some of his novels, most notably *Around the World in 80 Days* (1872), *Michael Strogoff* (1876), *Twenty Thousand Leagues under the Sea* (1869), and *From the Earth to the Moon* (1865) have become classic adventure stories and are regularly reprinted in many languages.

Commenting on Hillis Miller's argument in his 1986 Presidential Address to the MLA, that our "common culture" is less and less a book culture and more a visual and audio culture, André Lefevere pointed out that literature reaches those readers who are not "professional students" by way of the images constructed of it in translations. In other words, although there may be an "original" somewhere, the versions that reach the widest number of readers may bear little relation to that original, no matter how venerable it may be. He goes on to add:

> What impacts most on members of a culture...is the 'image' of a work of literature, not its 'reality', not the text that is still sacrosanct only in literature departments. It is therefore extremely important that the 'image' of a literature and the works that constitute it be studied alongside its reality. This...is where the future of translation studies lies.[1]

We need only think of the huge success of Andrew Davies's 1996 television adaptation of Jane Austen's *Pride and Prejudice*, which shifted the focus away from Elizabeth Bennet, the female protagonist, towards Mr Darcy. This shift was accomplished in subtle ways that had everything to do with image: the series opens with Mr Darcy and Mr Bingley riding across fields and discussing whether to buy a house. In this way, the emphasis on property that was to feature strongly in Davies' version was established from the outset, and only after the introduction to the two men does the camera cut to Elizabeth Bennet, observing them on her daily walk. Later, in the crucial scene that was such a hit that the BBC used it to remind viewers to pay their television licence fees, Mr Darcy takes a dip in his lake at Pemberley and is caught desirable and dripping wet by both the camera and Miss Bennet. This, of course, is not in the Austen "original", but it is an image so powerful that we can be sure that it will henceforth be read into the novel and into subsequent film versions. The covert sexuality of Jane Austen's world has been overlaid with the more overt sexuality of the late twentieth century. There has been a shift of image, a translation process that we can clearly see.

The transfer of written texts into the visual medium enables us to see in more ways than one. On the one hand, we can see a visual representation unfold before us; on the other, through a reading of this new semiotic system we can see evidence of the process of translation that the text has undergone. The transfer of a book into a film is the clearest evidence of what every translator knows and yet so many people refuse to admit: that the translation is no more and no less than one individual's reading of the original. Once this basic fact is recognized, we can set aside the debates about faithfulness and the notion of the definitive translation. There can never be a definitive translation, because individual translators, the product of different times and different cultures, will inevitably produce divergent readings.

This does not, of course, mean that the alternative is a postmodern deluge in which anything goes and there are no ground rules of any kind. The text is always a product of its time, and the translation is likewise a product of its time. Both texts are firmly embedded in a context, just as all eventual readers also read within a context. The dialectical relationship between the production of the original, the production of the translation and the reading is therefore what concerns the translation studies student, for in mapping out the links between those three moments we can learn about how cultures renew themselves and how ideas are transmitted interlingually and interculturally.

One of the lines that connect translation studies to that other interdisciplinary field that also emerged in the 1970s, Cultural Studies, is a repudiation of textual hierarchies into "high" and "low" literature. The history of translation offers clear evidence of how such categorization disintegrates with processes of textual transfer. A text deemed canonical and high status in literature A may become a popular best-seller in literature B or may sink without trace. In contrast, a text that is regarded as marginal or to use the German phrase *trivialliteratur* in one literary system, may rise to a position of high status in another. Evidence of these transformations abounds, and is particularly obvious once we start to look at the fortunes of non-European literatures in European language translation. Moreover, as so many scholars have shown, the material processes of textual production impact upon the strategies of the translator, and probably of equal importance is the horizon of expectation of readers in the receiving culture. We need to bear these points in mind when we move on to our present case-study.

In a useful essay that explores the problem of how to determine what norms in translation might be, Theo Hermans struggles with the question of whether we can determine what constitutes "translation" at all.[2] Drawing parallels with anthropologists, such as Clifford Geertz,

Hermans finally falls back on Gideon Toury's semiotic definition of translation, which he claims "clearly underdetermines concepts of translation current in the Western tradition."³ Let us remind ourselves of Toury's definition at this point. Translation, says Toury, is an act or process that is performed over and across systemic borders:

> it is a series of operations, or procedures, whereby one semiotic entity, which is a constituent (element) of a certain cultural (sub) system, is transformed into another semiotic entity, which forms at least a potential element of another cultural (sub) system, providing that some informational core is retained 'invariant' under transformation and on its basis a relationship known as 'equivalence' is established between the resultant and initial entities.⁴

Toury here is referring to the ever-vexatious problem of what Anton Popovič called the 'invariant core', that aspect of a text which remains constant in both translation and original.⁵ Efforts to define the invariant core have often foundered on the reef of form versus content divisions, but although we may not agree on a definition of the invariant core, we probably all agree that this is the aspect that connects a translation and its source, otherwise why would we bother with the terminology of translation at all? Where I part company from Toury, though, is when he suggests that the relationship between translation and original (resultant and initial entities) is known as 'equivalence', for when we discuss the translation of written text into film, or film translation, the terminology of equivalence is surely redundant? We need not ask how a film may be equivalent to a book, but rather why we should ever want to think in terms of equivalence here at all. Once we start to apply theories of reading to translation, then the debates about equivalence become very difficult to sustain. Let us assume, therefore, that equivalence is redundant in film translation, for we are dealing with different semiotic systems. However, the problem of the invariant core is highlighted in film translation.

Let us return now to Jules Verne. The first translation of *Voyage au centre de la terre* was published in 1871 and went through numerous editions.⁶ Others followed: a version by Frederick Amadeus Malleson in 1876, the same year that saw the publication of translations of *A Voyage round the World* and *Five Weeks in a Balloon*, which was then reissued with illustrations in 1891, a version by T.C Dugdale in 1911, and several editions specifically for French language learners. Edward Arnold brought out one such edition in 1899, with notes and introduction, whilst in 1913 the text adapted and edited by Eugene Pellissier also contained a word and phrasebook as well as a key to the appendices. Yet another edition edited by E.R. Shearer came out in 1915.

What can be seen from the evidence of the translations and the language-learning editions is that the work was widely used in schools in the late nineteenth and early twentieth centuries. There then appears to have been a dip in the fortunes of the novel, with only one new translation, in 1938 (adapted and rewritten by H.E. Palmer) until a run of translations started to appear in the post-Second World War period: an edition published by Ward and Locke in 1961, Isabel Fortey's translation reprinted in 1949, 1959 and 1964, Willis Bradley's version in 1960, Joyce Gard's version in 1961, John Howson's version in 1964, Hayden Perry's version in 1961 and the version used here by Robert Baldick.[7] Apart from its availability, this version has been selected because it is not abridged and is included significantly in the "Penguin Science Fiction Series". What can be inferred from the run of translations in this period is that Verne was re-emerging in the general revival of interest in science fiction of the 1950s and early 1960s. However, as H.G.Wells, with whom Verne was frequently compared by British journalists, had pointed out, there were clear distinctions between his particularly British science fiction writing and that of the French master:

> His work dealt almost always with actual possibilities of invention and discovery, and he made some remarkable forecasts. The interest he invoked was a practical one; he wrote and believed and told that this thing or that thing could be done, which was not at that time done. He helped his reader to imagine it done and to realize what fun, excitement or mischief would ensure. Many of his inventions have "come true". But these stories of mine collected here do not pretend to deal with possible things; they are exercises of the imagination in a quite different field.[8]

The sudden run of translations in the late Fifties was also accompanied by several films of Verne's novels, but the interest was short-lived, there has been no similar flurry of translations in the past 30 years. Oxford University Press brought out a new translation by

William Butcher in 1992, as part of their World's Classics series, but most of the editions available today are reprints of earlier translations, and the categorization of these texts is worthy of note. The OUP edition is classified under "French fiction", but a 1991 reprint by Macmillan, and a 1995 reprint by the Readers' Digest Association list the novel under "French fiction/children's stories". Versions published in 1979 and 1980 are specifically targeted at children and are described as "retellings" and even "retelling in simple language". A 1977 edition published by Nelson and "retold by Donald McFarlane" is specifically for English language learners, and is consequently classified under "text books for foreign speakers". From this evidence, we can draw a rough picture of the fortunes of Verne's novel in the twentieth century: he starts out as a widely-read author, whose books are used as language-learning aids, becomes a classic adventure-story writer in the inter-war years, then undergoes a resurgence in the post-World War Two Sci-fi boom, only to be once again relegated to the shelves of books for children, heavily abridged, adapted and illustrated by the end of the century.

In his recent book on Jules Verne, *The Mask of the Prophet* (1990) Andrew Martin's opening sentence declares that "Jules Verne is in danger of joining the ranks of the great unread."[9] He goes on to qualify this statement, explaining that the epic journeys of protagonists like Captain Nemo and Phileas Fogg have "secured for them a permanent home among the residents of popular mythology." Such characters and their travels are buried in the collective unconscious, and Jules Verne appears to belong to another age:

> Thus the task of writing about Verne has acquired the dusty flavour of an exercise in trying to raise the dead. Verne has become the object of bibliophile fervour, material for extravagant de-luxe editions, an antiquarian collector's item. He is a literary brontosaurus, a harmless monster doomed to extinction by some uncongenial shift in the ecology, superseded by hardier species, and destined to survive only as a museum piece.[10]

This is not a judgement with which most people would quarrel. Jules Verne's works have indeed become household names in some cases, but remain largely unread. However, that they remain household names is because of the role played by translations in prolonging their afterlife, for, as Walter Benjamin reminds us, the translation can ensure the survival of a text, can prolong its life-span or even resurrect it from the dead.[11] For although we may note a dearth of new translations, English versions of Verne's works are continually being reprinted. Someone, somewhere, must still be reading him.

In his time, Verne's writing touched a number of highly sensitive strands of contemporary thought. Voyage literature, travel or exploration literature was hugely popular in both France and England. The number of travel accounts published from the 1850s to the 1900s is staggering and reflects the existence of a mass readership. Many of these texts were first-hand accounts of journeys undertaken, but what concerns us here is the fictional version of the genre. Peter Hulme, in his *Colonial Encounters*, notes the emergence of the "adventure novel", and draws attention to the period when this genre was especially successful:

> It might be said that the 'pure' adventure story, which has to take place outside metropolitan Europe and preferably in as remote an area as possible, reached its apogee as the tentacles of European colonialism were at their greatest reach in the late nineteenth century.[12]

Hulme makes this comment in the light of a discussion of *Robinson Crusoe*, but it can serve our purposes here, even though we need to distinguish between the French version of the adventure story and the English one. The latter can be seen in novels of J.M. Ballantine such as *The Coral Island, The Young Fur Traders, The Gorilla Hunters* or in the novels of Rider Haggard and G.H. Henty, writers whose books extolled the virtues of both the imperial ideal and the proper attributes of manliness. Not for nothing have scholars such as Joseph Bristow drawn parallels between educational developments in England, popular adventure fiction and the spread of empire.[13]

The French version of the genre is less obviously concerned with supplying readers with idealized images of masculinity. The impact of Edgar Allen Poe cannot be underestimated, and the emergence of the *roman jaune* likewise owes much to Poe. What marks Verne's fictions out as distinctive, however, is the way in which he transforms Science into effectively a protagonist. Haggard's heroes, Allan Quatermaine, Captain Good, Umslopogaas and Sir Henry are good with their guns, physically resilient, cool as ice regardless of whatever horrors they are confronting and happier bivouacking in the jungle than seated in a drawing room. The contrast between the beauty and majesty of the natural environment compared to the stultifying nature of urban society is a constant theme in the English adventure story. But above all, English heroes are not intellectuals, and have no time for excessive book-learning. Whatever knowledge they acquire is knowledge that comes from experience or, in the case of some of the stories of ancient Egypt, from an idiosyncratic passion.

In contrast, Verne's characters seem highly intellectual, concerned as so many of them are with pushing back the frontiers of scientific knowledge. The reader is drawn into this process and the novels are full of scientific details, reflecting his auto-didactic forays into fields of medicine, anthropology, palaeontology, geology, physics, chemistry, astronomy, mineralogy or engineering. *Journey to the Centre of the Earth* is full of passages giving the reader information on such diverse points as the nesting practices of the eider duck, life in rural Iceland, vulcanology, the history of prehistoric reptiles, problems created by atmospheric pressure, code-breaking and runic inscriptions. His stories, as Kennett Allott points out, "reflect the neurosis of a generation."[14] Science, that obsessed the nineteenth century mind, finds a popular outlet in the writings of Verne, whose novels also deal with the fundamental problematics of the relationship between scientific knowledge and belief in the divine.

The insecurity about the relationship between man and God raised by Darwin's theories could be counter-balanced by a belief in human progress. The nineteenth century expanded the great positivist tradition begun with the Enlightenment: things were getting better, people were getting better, the task of education was to reinforce the notion of human progress, and the revelations offered by science confirmed the validity of that viewpoint. It is a remarkably optimistic view, and if it seems naive today at the end of the twentieth century, we can only marvel that it lasted so long.

Let us turn now briefly to *Journey to the Centre of the Earth*. As the title indicates, it is just that. The narrator is Axel, an unheroic, slightly comic figure who is forced to accompany his eccentric uncle, Professor Lidenbrock, on his attempt to follow in the footsteps of a

Renaissance alchemist, one Arne Saknussem who has left a message written in runes giving instructions on how to descend into the centre of the earth via an Icelandic volcano. Lidenbrock finds this message accidentally, but once he has decoded it, with Axel's help, there is no holding him back, and the two men set off for Iceland, where they acquire the services of the intrepid guide, Hans.

The book is divided into forty-five short chapters, and presented as a breathless narrative in the first person. Occasionally, the narrative is varied by a series of devices that are intended to create an impression of the veracity of the enterprise, a standard feature of the adventure story in the nineteenth century. Such devices here include samples of texts, including the runic message, lists of items, details of geographical and weather data, as well as dates purporting to be diary entries. The first sixteen chapters deal with the preparations for the voyage, and the arrival in Iceland. After chapter seventeen, the travellers descend into an extinct crater and then undergo a series of adventures: they run out of water, discover an underground river, Axel gets lost and is found again, they discover an underground sea, over which they sail, watch a battle between a plesiosaurus and an ichthyosaurus, are swept away by a gigantic storm, find evidence of an early form of human life, and are finally shot up still on their raft back to the earth's surface by a jet of boiling water, emerging on the slopes of Mount Stromboli just off the coast of Sicily. During the course of the journey Lidenbrock is proved right about everything, Hans is incredibly brave and resourceful and the rather dim Axel comes through it all and marries his sweetheart, Grauben, Lidenbrock's ward. It is perhaps worth noting that one of the funniest episodes in the novel occurs in chapter seven, when Grauben, contrary to everything Axel is hoping she will say, tells him that accompanying his uncle on the mad journey will make a real man of him. The masculine heroic idealism of English adventure novels is treated parodically in Verne's fiction.

Verne's novels were successful in their day, in France and England, and in the United States, because of their heady combination of boyish adventure, comedy, pell-mell narrating and pseudo-scientificity. The characters are stereotypes or caricatures. In this novel, we have the dour Nordic guide, the mad professor and the awkward student nephew in love with the perfect virginal young maiden. Nobody is injured, nobody dies and all ends happily ever after. During the course of the narrative, we learn all kinds of facts about volcanoes, minerals and early life forms. We are also told quite a lot about Iceland, showing that once again Verne was really keyed in to contemporary fashion. Interest in Iceland developed steadily from the 1840s onwards, fuelled by a series of factors: interest in the language, as a direct result of the growth of Germanic philology, interest in the sagas, becoming known through translations and widely seen as prototypical epic texts, interest in the natural landscape of this most unusual of European islands and interest in the racial purity of the Icelandic people. English writers as different as William Morris, the pre-Raphaelite and later utopian socialist thinker, and Sir Richard Burton, orientalist, explorer translator and pornographer, made their own journeys to Iceland, producing books that were widely read. Morris's interest was that of an antiquarian primarily, and a medievalist, whereas Burton was interested in the geography and geology of the island, and in the racial characteristics of the people. Reading Burton's two volume Ultima Thule that appeared in 1875 is a good way of accessing some of the material that Verne must undoubtably have used in compiling his own novel, including the interesting fact of the thesis established by Baron Sartorius von Waltershausen in 1838 that argued that the basis of Iceland was the Palagonite, which forms the foundation of volcanic tufas on Etna, the Azores, Tenerife and the Cape Verde islands. A voyage below the surface of the earth from Iceland to Sicily can be therefore held to be based on scientific fact. By cunningly throwing in authentic scientific material and debating the ideas of such men as Humphrey Davy who are named in the novel, Verne establishes an idea of authenticity for his narrative. Readers are constantly invited to juggle scientific knowledge with romantic imaginings, and this combination proved a great hit in its day.

In the twentieth century, the acceleration of technological innovation altered public attitudes to Verne's work. No longer seen as at the cutting edge of pioneering new thinking, Verne came instead to be increasingly regarded as a rather quaint precursor. The excitement of battles with giant squid or journeying by raft over a subterranean ocean remained to some extent, though now increasingly the novels were shifting from the domain of the general reader, and coming to be seen more as children's literature. There is no space here other than to touch on this fascinating question, but the way in which texts shift from being categorized as mainstream fiction to a categorization that places them in children's literature deserves a lot more critical attention than it has hitherto received. In one distinctive way, however, Verne's novels were translated anew: some of his works were adapted into film.

If the second half of the nineteenth century can be characterized as the age of adventure fiction, it is interesting to note the importance of adventure cinema of the post-war period. There was a run of films, both British and Hollywood-produced, over roughly two decades from the 1940s onwards that are versions of the adventure novel: fast-moving films with linear plot structures and stereotypical characterization. The adventure genre is, of course, closely linked at this point with science fiction. Moreover, the post-war filmic manifestation of the sci-fi adventure novel has some distinctive characteristics that have a great deal to do with realignments of gender relationships in society at large. Indeed, the film versions of *Journey to the Centre of the Earth* provide one of the clearest ways of seeing shifts in gender balance both in film as such and in the world inhabited by prospective audiences.

The 1959 film version was directed by Harry Levin and starred the unlikely team of James Mason, who was big at the box office at the time, Pat Boone, the singer and Arlene Dahl. In its transposition into film, the novel underwent all kinds of transformations and significant additions include a love interest, an armed villain and an attack by a killer chameleon.

What remains of Verne's novel, the "invariant core", if it can be so termed, is the rough framework of the journey of a scientist driven by a desire for greater knowledge aided by his nephew. The characterization is totally different however: Mason's persona is gentle, kindly and sympathetic, not at all like the Lidenbrock of the novel and Pat Boone is (unbelievably) a star student, unlike the bumbling Axel. The action begins in Edinburgh, which Anglo-Saxonizes Verne's original German setting (Hamburg) thereby enabling the director to include some footage of Scots soldiers marching in kilts and Pat Boone singing Robert Burns' "My love is like a red, red rose."

There are several significant additions to Verne's narrative: the character of the Swedish explorer's widow, with whom James Mason falls in love, despite her addressing him at one point as a "dried-up walnut of a man!", and the character of Arne Saknussem's descendant, a homicidal madman who is finally dispatched by a fortuitous landslide after he has committed the most barbaric act of the film: he murders Gertrude, the tame duck belonging to Hans, in the novel a trusty Icelandic guide but in the film a Swedish-speaking beefcake hunk.

The implications of these additions are obvious: as the genre of the romantic Hollywood adventure film dictates, there has to be conflict and there has to be a love interest. Whereas Verne wrote primarily for men and boys and women readers then joined their ranks, the film is aimed at a mixed family audience. The publicity for the film makes this point:

> Remaining faithful to Verne's story, it is a sweeping adventure that offers enough thrills and entertainment to satisfy every explorer in the family.[15]

The question that translation studies scholars might ask is what "remaining faithful" means here. True, the title is the same, the basic elements of the narrative are recognizably similar, but the characters have been altered, and new characters have been introduced, the emphasis is not only now on the events as such and the chronology of the journey, but on the complexity of human emotions and the relations that are established during the journey. The love interest is brought to the foreground, and the relationship between the sexes is a major line throughout the film. *Journey to the Centre of the Earth* is no longer a narrative about three men driven to undertake bizarre hardships in order to advance the cause of science, it is a narrative about individuals testing themselves against nature and, with the exception of Count Saknussem, triumphing over all the odds and discovering their own inner selves. This notion of self-discovery is particularly clear as the film moves to its climax, when the travellers discover the lost city of *Atlantis* that has somehow slid under the earth's surface. Unable to escape up the shaft that the dying Arne Saknussem has indicated (his mummified corpse is pointing his successors in the right direction) because it is blocked, the explorers decide to use the gunpowder they have found beside his skeleton. As the fuse is lit, and the team climb into a conveniently-shaped giant dish, even more conveniently made of asbestos and therefore heat-resistant, Pat Boone (a born-again Christian in real life) prays, and the huge fire lizard that is creeping up on them is swept away in the explosion that unleashes the lava that will eventually drive the dish and its passengers up to the surface. Here the camera suddenly shows Arlene Dahl, clothes and hair dishevelled, leaning back in what in other circumstances might appear to be orgasmic ecstasy, and gazing up at the pin-point of light at the top of the shaft towards which the dish is heading.

In the final scenes, back at the University of Edinburgh, James Mason tells the cheering students that "The spirit of man cannot be stopped", and the film ends with the student body led by Pat Boone singing "Here's to the Prof of Geology" in chorus. The emphasis in this film version is on individualism and the human spirit. Science is not the protagonist, rather it is Nature, a nature red in tooth and claw that can, however, be dominated by men of noble spirit (and a noble woman and a heroic duck). The message accords well with the optimistic messages that Hollywood adventure movies were projecting at that time.

The 1993 version was made as a pilot for an adventure series and so ends inconclusively. In this film, a party descends into the centre of the earth in a machine, and by the end, they are setting off on the next lap, in no way ready to return to the earth's surface, thereby opening the way for a future episode. The crew consists of seven people, four men: the blond Captain Greg Turner, the Italian video-game champion with the world's fastest eye-hand coordination, the elderly Englishman who is the world expert on ancient myths and legends, the black ex-Seal who is almost always seen carrying some form of lethal weapon and communicates by shouting insults, and three women: the ice-cold scientist who is imposed on Captain Turner by his millionaire sponsor as commander, the sweet-natured Chinese who is the world expert on food science and is the ship's medical officer, and the attractive blonde in shorts who is a psychologist and the world's leading rock climber. On their journey, they encounter a gentle creature with whom they are able to communicate and who helps them escape from an evil-minded tribe of troglodytes who are about to burn some of the party and eat them. Even worse than the troglodytes is the ghastly Evil Thing that is trying to regain possession of a piece of text carried in the baggage of the elderly Englishman, because if he can accomplish this, his evil powers will be wholly restored.

What, we may ask, remains of Verne's novel in this 1993 film version that owes a debt to the Star Trek genre? Quite a lot, surprisingly: the descent into the volcano, the idea of a man following in the footsteps of someone else (at the start of the film we see the beloved uncle of the protagonist attempting the first descent and failing, hence the compulsion to honour his memory) and, bizarrely, several scenes of underground discovery, most notably the moment when the crew discover an underground sea.

Moreover, if Science is a protagonist in Verne's novel and Nature is a protagonist in the 1959 film, then in this instance the protagonist is a singularly Nietzchean one: the film glorifies human achievement and strength. All the twenty-something perfectly formed members of the crew are world experts in their own fields, the ship is equipped with an unbelievably big weapon, a sonic blaster than can cut through mountains. This team of explorers are not driven by any desire to know, but have a clear mission: they are each earning a million dollars in cash and their task is to see if there are ways of improving the ecological balance of the earth's surface by learning about its depths.

It could, of course, be argued that Verne's novel was a potboiler in the first instance, and that both these films are entirely in keeping with the genre. Hence, in genre terms of popular adventure, the three versions are equivalent. This alters the concept of equivalence somewhat, but recognizes the function of the three texts, which is to entertain. There are also arguably equivalences of tone, in that adventure, spectacle, wonder and amazement are combined in all three texts with comic elements. Beyond this, what is most striking are the differences in narrative structure and characterization. These differences can be explored in all kinds of ways, and related to such questions as changes in taste, horizon of expectation, casting and budget constraints. However, what is of importance here are those elements of Verne's novel that recur in the different versions, for this is where the debate about what constitutes the invariant core can be most clearly seen.

The frame of the journey determines all three versions, and the theme of the precursor who is brave enough to attempt the impossible is also a key feature. In addition, there are certain other elements in the narrative, including the underground sea and the ability of the underground world to provide its own sources of light. Can we consider such narrative units as paralleling the stable, basic and constant semantic elements in the text which Popovič argued comprise the invariant core? His point was that transformations or variants do not modify the core of meaning but simply influence the expressive form. The invariant is therefore that which exists in common between all existing translations of a single work, a dialectical relationship that confirms that a translation is indeed a translation of another text.

With film translation, this theory is further problematized. There is no doubt that the 1993 *Journey to the Centre of the Earth* is less obviously a translation of Verne's novel than it is a translation of the 1959 film of Verne's novel. This is most clearly indicated by the shift in gender roles. The women in the 1993 version are all tough world experts, whilst the women in the 1959 version are homemakers and sex kittens. Moreover, whilst Verne's Axel is an anti-hero and the 1959 Axel is a romanticized anti-hero, the testosterone-charged heroes of 1993 testify to a radically different view of masculine characteristics. The villainous count who was added in the 1959 version is transmogrified into an ancient creature of evil in the 1993 version. Yet the 1993 version also returns with startling directness to the language of Verne's novel as the underground sea scene shows.

What we have therefore is a plurality of translations, with subsequent translators/directors/screenwriters drawing upon more than one original source. The English translation of Verne's novel is used as the starting point for the 1959 film version, whilst the 1993 version draws not only upon translations in book form but also upon the preceding film. This plurality renders a theory of the invariant core applicable to film translation very difficult to formulate and calls into question assumptions about equivalence in translation. What exactly remains invariant other than the title, some of the names, the idea of a journey into the centre of the earth are certain isolated formal features which appear almost as quotations in the film versions. A case-study such as the one offered by *Journey to the Centre of the Earth* raises some very fundamental questions about relationships between texts and about the very definition of translation. Investigation into the field of intersemiotic translation is far less-developed than other areas in translation studies, but it offers enormously exciting potential for further research.

Susan Bassnett

### Notes

1 Susan Bassnett and Andre Lefevere (eds), *Translation, History and Culture*, London: Cassell, 1995, 11. First edition, London: Pinter, 1990
2 Theo Hermans, "Norms and the Determination of Translation", in Roman Alvarez and Carmen-Africa Vidal (eds), *Translation, Power, Subversion*, Clevedon: Multilingual Matters 1996, 25-52.
3 "Norms and the Determination of Translation", 47.
4 Gideon Toury, "Translation: A Cultural-Semiotic Perspective", in Thomas Sebeok (ed.), *Encyclopaedic Dictionary of Semiotics*, Berlin: De gruyter 1986, vol 2.
5 Anton Popovič, *A Dictionary for the Analysis of Literary Translation*, Edmonton, Alberta: University of Alberta, 1976.
6 *A Journey to the Centre of the Earth, from the French of Jules Verne*, With illustrations by Riou London: Griffith and Farrar, 1871.
7 *Jules Verne, Journey to the Centre of the Earth*, trans. Robert Baldick, Harmondsworth: Penguin, 1965.
8 H.G.Wells, *Preface to the Scientific Romances of H.G.Wells*, London: Gollancz, 1933, cited in Kennett Allott, *Jules Verne,* London: The Cresset Press. No date.
9 Andrew Martin, *The Mask of the Prophet. The Extraordinary Fictions of Jules Verne*, Oxford: Clarendon Press, 1990.
10 *op. cit.*, ix.
11 Walter Benjamin, "The Task of the Translator", in *Illuminations*, trans. H. Zohn, New York: Schocken Books, 1969.
12 Peter Hulme, *Colonial Encounters: Europe and the Native Caribbean 1492-1797* London: Routledge, 1987, 182-3.
13 Joseph Bristow, *Empire Boys. Adventures in a Man's World*, London: Harper Collins, 1991.
14 Kennett Allott, *Jules Verne*, London: The Cresset Press, 98.
15 Unattributed statement on video cassette of *Journey to the Centre of the Earth*.

## 12.
## TRANSLATING STEREOTYPES IN THE CINEMATIC REMAKE

The remake can take many forms and cannot be abstracted from other types of cinematic adaptation. However the term will be used here to describe Hollywood remakes of French cinematic works, a group of films which merits a category apart by virtue of its sheer numbers. Since 1930 and the early days of sound cinema over fifty such remakes have been produced in Hollywood. Some are well known, usually due to their commercial success (for example *Three Men and a Baby*, Leonard Nimoy's 1987 remake of Coline Serreau's *Trois Hommes et un couffin*). Others are less familiar: as Julien Duvivier's *Pépé le Moko* (1937) enjoys a well deserved re-release in British cinemas, many will be surprised to learn that the film was remade three times, twice in Hollywood (in 1938 and 1948) and once, as a parody entitled *Toto le Moko* in Italy in 1949.

These films overwhelmingly give rise to critical condemnation, notably amongst French critics: they are described as a form of "vampirisation" as Hollywood sucks the life-blood of French production: they are yet another example of American cultural imperialism as big-budget Hollywood production swallows up and spits out its much smaller, but of course far more valuable, French counterpart. These anxieties can be seen to emerge from, and indeed reinforce, a number of discourses. Firstly they must of course be connected to the very long and very complex history of Franco-American political and cultural relations. I will not attempt to provide an overview of these relations here. Suffice it to say that the United States has figured large in French discourse about political and cultural identity. It has served both as a model (for example in the 1950s when a France in dire need of modernisation saw in the United States an image of all that progress and technology could achieve) and perhaps most importantly as a rival (strikingly of course in the domain of cinema, witness French reactions to the Blum-Byrnes agreements of 1946 and, more recently, the GATT).

However, this negativity, this rejection of Hollywood's appropriation of French culture, should also be linked to wider discourses about production and reproduction and it is perhaps here that the pertinence of the remake to discussion about translation and rewriting in a more general sense becomes apparent. It is worth stressing the very noticeable tendency amongst the critics of the remake to describe it as a threat, a process that inevitably undermines both the identity and the status of the original. Now clearly this position can be partly attributed to the material conditions that influence the remake process. The practice emerges from a cinematic landscape dominated by Hollywood in which French products have very little chance of penetrating American markets. The purchase of remake rights frequently allows United States' distributors to delay the release of the source film until after that of the remake and in many cases the French work will not be distributed in the USA at all. Thus the French film becomes secondary to its reproduction, its status as original, with all the connotations of value that implies, is undermined.

However, this anxiety is also bound up with a whole set of binary oppositions, the highly manichean dualities that structure our readings of texts into confined and confining value judgements. It emerges from the distinction between art and mass culture that underwrites so many accounts of French cinema and its relations with Hollywood: it also emerges from the positing of clearly defined national cultures and national cinemas which enables straightforward distinction between the French cinematic "creation" and the American product. However, such oppositions become quite untenable when we look more closely at the remake process. To describe the French source text in terms of the discourses of art and high culture is highly problematic when we consider that the majority of films chosen for remaking are extremely popular works, frequently the domestic comedies so successful at the French box-office. Moreover, to attribute clear-cut national identities to these films is no easy task. Many of the films are co-productions, indeed some of those remakes condemned as an American threat to French culture are in fact the product of both French and American production companies. Moving beyond conditions of production to consider reception, it is vital to acknowledge the unstable nature of the filmic text, notably in terms of its identity as "national" product. Evidently films do interrogate and invoke their particular contexts of production, yet different audiences will understand this in different ways. Thus a film such as *La Haine*[1] which deals with a very specific socio-cultural phenomenon and a clearly defined geographical space, is likely to be received by a non-French audience as a film which deals more generally with police violence, racial tension and so on. This argument is borne out by the subtitled version of the film released on video in Britain: the subtitles borrow from the language of the hood, contemporary Afro-American slang, and the text inside the video box draws parallels with Spike Lee's *Do the Right Thing*.[2] Thus the film's specificities are transformed and the film becomes something other to its new audiences.

The very attempt to posit an "original" film is extremely problematic. Whatever we may think of the ethics of the distribution methods mentioned above, the fact remains that for many cinema audiences the remake *is* the "original" film either because they see it before the French source or because they are unaware of its identity as a remake. Films are highly intertextual artefacts, both in terms of production, as they borrow from and quote other texts, and in terms of reception as audiences' interpretations of films are shot through with their own knowledge, their own position and their own identity.

To claim an original text is to deny this hybridity and to maintain a hierarchical relationship that underwrites distinctions between "art" and "entertainment" and opposing national cultures. If however we discard the original/copy relationship we are able to move towards a far more complex vision of the adaptation process. I would certainly not want to deny the negative possibilities of the remake process, or indeed of any form of rewriting. The material factors that influence the practice can also be seen to encourage the type of appropriation which Lawrence Venuti describes as a "fluent translation strategy": the French source film is remade and assimilated into the ideologies and aesthetics of the target culture.[3] Nevertheless, to position French cinema and Hollywood in a particular relation of dominance is highly problematic. Hollywood may be materially more powerful than its French counterpart, but it is French cinema which tends to hold the cultural capital that prohibits any attempt to see it as entirely subordinate. Moreover, the remake does not necessarily mean the disappearance of the source text within the target culture. Those films that lead to successful remakes are often re-released on video or in movie theatres, as "the film upon which such and such a remake was based". Thus the remake becomes the French film's "afterlife". Rather than destroying the identity and status of its source, it satisfies its demand for translation and becomes the means of its continuing dissemination.

If we turn our attention to the two films I would like to discuss here, it will become even more apparent how vital it is to rethink the critiques of the remake process outlined so far. The films in question are *La Cage aux folles*, a Franco-Italian co-production directed by Edouard Molinaro and released in 1978, and *The Birdcage*, directed by Mike Nichols and released in 1996.[4] The material trajectories of each film do not correspond to the "vampirisation" so often invoked to categorise the remake process. *La Cage aux folles* (a co-production and thus not a straightforwardly "national" product) was nominated for an Academy Award and is still one of the top grossing foreign language films in the United States. Evidently this success may appear limited when compared to the career of the domestic product, nevertheless it does suggest that this particular source text has not been, and cannot be entirely assimilated by the target culture through the production of the remake. Furthermore, the film gave rise to two sequels, released in 1980 and 1985 respectively, revealing a dissemination or afterlife which extends beyond the remake and problematises the binary relationship between the two films.

The career of *The Birdcage* is particularly fascinating as it illustrates the process of exchange and interaction which I believe typifies the remake. Nichol's film was produced by MGM-UA, a Hollywood studio whose enduring significance does not need to be underlined. However, the studio was, at that point in time, owned by the French bank, *Crédit Lyonnais*, a fact which immediately complicates attempts to define the remake as straightforwardly "American". Moreover, Nichol's film earned eighty million dollars in under four weeks when released in the United States thus proving to be Hollywood's biggest earner of that year so far. This immense box-office success reversed the failing fortunes of MGM-UA subsequently enabling *Crédit Lyonnais* to put their acquisition on the market. The losses incurred by the studio had pushed the state-owned bank into technical bankruptcy, forcing the French government to support it through public subsidies worth more than four billion dollars. Thus the success of this particular Hollywood remake can be seen to have important financial repercussions both within the United States and France. The French government was able to divest itself of a possession whose retention was neither politically nor financially advisable whilst the future of a "great" Hollywood studio was, at least for the time being, secured. What this demonstrates is the need to perceive the remake as a far from solitary manifestation of the interaction and cross-fertilisation of the emergent global economy. *The Birdcage* is neither an isolated example of Hollywood's reproduction of French film nor an American threat to French culture. Rather it is a hybrid text that cannot easily be attributed a "national" identity and whose very success has positive implications in France *and* the United States.

Nevertheless, at first glance the two films may seem to fall easily into the original versus copy relationship. Their narrative structures are almost identical and they share various lines of dialogue and even a certain number of gags. Each film takes place in a drag club (the "Birdcage" or "Cage aux folles" of the title). Armand, the proprietor of the club (played by Ugo Tonazzi in the source film and Robin Williams in the remake) is preparing a surprise for his temperamental star chanteuse and life companion (played by Michel Serrault in the source and Nathan Lane in the remake). The surprise is the return of Armand's son, the result of an unfortunate heterosexual encounter twenty years previously. However, the son also has a surprise and announces that he is getting married, not only to a woman but to the daughter of an arch-conservative politician, played by Michel Galabru in the source and Gene Hackman in the remake. The father's initial resistance to the marriage is put aside when his party for moral order is caught up in a sex scandal. He and his wife decide to distract the media by staging a traditional white wedding. Of course they have yet to meet their prospective in-laws and the central focus of the film is the dinner party in which Armand attempts to pass for straight and his partner disguises himself as the boy's mother. The film concludes with the media's discovery of the politician's presence in the apartment (situated of course above the club) and his escape through the club disguised in heavy drag. The closing sequence shows the wedding of the young couple, highly traditional but for the array of drag queens seated amongst the guests of the bridegroom.

As I think this plot summary makes clear, the film's narrative and indeed its comedy, are constructed via the representation of stereotypes.

Thus each film involves a limp-wristed and hysterical drag queen, a neo-conservative and ultimately hypocritical politician, and his supportive wife. Clearly the stereotype serves a useful narrative and comic function as it connotes certain information in an apparently straightforward manner, eschewing complexities and difference. As Richard Dyer explains in an essay on stereotypes:

> The effectiveness of stereotypes resides in the way they invoke a consensus. Stereotypes proclaim, 'This is what everyone — you, me and us — thinks members of such-and-such a social groups are like', as if these concepts of these social groups were spontaneously arrived at by all members of society independently and in isolation.[5]

This invocation of consensus seems to be borne out by the mobilisation of stereotypes in this pair of films. Despite their differing temporal and spatial contexts of production, the two films employ seemingly identical stereotypes. As such they suggest that these are stereotypes which transcend national boundaries and the rigid definitions of gender and identity that they construct.

These films do then appear to underwrite the critiques of the remake outlined above: the Franco-Italian source is reproduced in the United States, cultural specificities are ignored and a copy is produced based upon a set of consensual and normative stereotypes. However, such an account of the films does seem to be overly reductive. Without a doubt their narrative structures and comedy are based upon some rather problematic clichés yet these same clichés also enable a far more complex understanding of gender, sexuality, the family and their relations to the nation than this rather simplistic, and I think essentialist, assessment suggests.

Through its reconstruction of the stereotype of the drag queen, *The Birdcage* seems to claim that this is an identity able to transcend national boundaries. Indeed drag's ability to position itself outside rigid constructions of identity is revealed by its explicit subversion of gender. Its very excess and emphasis on performance underlines the non-essential nature of gender, what Judith Butler has described as its "performativity". Indeed Butler invokes the cultural practices of drag as instances of the subversive power of gender parody, claiming that in imitating gender "drag implicitly reveals the imitative structure of gender itself — as well as its contingency".[6] Certainly this notion of performance is at the heart of both of these films, not only through the drag acts of the club but also through Armand and Albert's attempts to "play straight", to "perform" a "normal" family life. This is made particularly clear in the sequences which show the couple trying to perform what they perceive to be an unproblematic heterosexual masculinity. It is striking that in both films the model for such a notion of masculinity is John Wayne. John Wayne provides an iconic version of masculinity, a straight, white masculinity reinforced by his connotations of conservatism and a red-blooded antipathy to liberal agendas. This version of masculinity has a particular resonance in the United States, where Wayne's performances in the Western establish connections to a "national" masculine embodied in the myths of the Far West and the Final Frontier. However, as a Hollywood produced masculinity it is able to transcend national boundaries, a fact revealed by its presence in both films. Nevertheless, this version of masculinity, however far-reaching its resonance may be, is *no more* than a performance. It emerges from the cinematic, thus from performance and artifice, and this is underlined in the sequences in which the characters mimic Wayne's construction of masculinity, ultimately revealing it to be no more "natural" than their own constructions of gender.

This revelation of artifice can be seen as a key theme in each of these films. Just as gender is revealed to be about performance through the contrast between the characters' "natural" gay and/or drag identities, and their performed heterosexuality, so the family is shown to be a locus of semblance and hypocrisy. In both *La Cage aux folles* and *The Birdcage*, the father of the would-be bride is an important member of a party devoted to moral order and the reinstatement of "traditional" values. The hypocrisy of this movement is soon made visible by the death of the party's leader whilst in bed with an under-age, black prostitute. The wedding is agreed to in an attempt to minimise the ensuing scandal, thus the senator's use of his daughter for his own political ends provides a striking contrast to the gay couple's selfless attempts to help their son. Both films stress the closeness and affection shared by this couple and the coldness and apparent frigidity of the straight marriage. As the dinner party ends in confusion and the revelation of each participant's true identity, so the gay home is shown to be the "true" family as the son declares his love for his "parents" (both of them male) and their affection is set against the continuing political posturing of the senator and his wife.

Both films seem to want to claim for themselves a liberal agenda established through their deconstruction of normative notions of gender, sexuality and family. This is particularly true of the remake which makes constant references to contemporary politics thus explicitly criticising the rise in a highly reactionary conservatism in American society in the 1990s. In a notable exchange during the dinner party sequence, Senator Keeley condemns Armand as a typical European, claiming that he mistreats his "good, old-fashioned" American wife, and going on to state that all Europeans, apart from Margaret Thatcher, are involved in extra-marital affairs. This opposition between European decadence and traditional American values derides and undermines a specifically national construction of morality (the "true" woman is constructed as a "true" American and yet *we* know she is a man), and yet simultaneously reveals the film's "national" construction of politics and identity. It is striking that such contemporary references are more or less absent from the Franco-Italian source. In place of the politically constructed moral code, the film suggests a bourgeois Catholic morality which is not confined to a specific national culture. Nevertheless, although these constructions and representations are not as explicitly confined to contemporary discourse as those of the remake, it would be erroneous to deny the film's evocation and interrogation of its context of production entirely. Indeed, the film's very status as a co-production and its roots, which can be seen in theatrical traditions of vaudeville and farce traceable in both France and Italy, can be understood to give rise to its specific representation of gender and family.

This obviously presents us with another vision of the remake process. Despite their mobilisation of seemingly identical stereotypes, it is evident that the films' construction, and more importantly mockery of notions of gender, family, morality and so on, emerge from and interrogate very specific cultural and political contexts. This is particularly true of the remake, a fact which must surely undermine accounts of the film as a mere copy. Both films do represent a drag culture which through its performativity transgresses rigid notions of gender and suggests the utopian possibility of a non-essentialist identity politics. However, somewhat paradoxically, this representation is firmly anchored in a very specific geographical and temporal space. Indeed, *The Birdcage*'s specificities are quite striking as Hollywood production usually tends to avoid such detail in its quest for global audiences. Such overt references to contemporary American politics and society reveal the film to be a new text, something other which does not simply reproduce its French source and which also demands new forms of reception shot through with a knowledge of its particular context of production.

So these films can then be seen as clear examples of the complexity and hybridity of the remake process. Rather than merely copying a French text within Hollywood, the process has produced another text which reworks the narrative and its concerns in new ways. The films' mobilisation of stereotypes may suggest a rigidity and denial of difference in keeping with the critiques of the remake discussed earlier. However, as I hope the preceding comments have demonstrated, both *La Cage aux folles* and *The Birdcage* can be understood as quite open texts based upon notions of alterity and performance.

Nevertheless, I think it would be wrong to embrace wholeheartedly the films' apparent espousal of a liberal agenda. Ultimately they do reinstate the conservative ideologies that they set out to deride. Although the films mobilise stereotypical identities in order to reveal the hypocrisy that lies at the heart of normative constructions of gender, sexuality and family, the very use of these stereotypes prevents anything more than a very limited problematisation. Stereotypes are always already defined against a norm, and as their function is to provide consensus and information which can be readily understood, so nuance and difference must be discarded. Thus the gay characters of both films remain little more than the two-dimensional caricatures, constructed by and for dominant (and here read heterosexual) ideology. In a review of *The Birdcage* in *The Washington Post*, one critic remarked:

> the depiction of homosexual life here is romanticized: there is no sex and no AIDS, and the characters are gay in that cuddly, non-threatening, all-American way that Liberace was gay. [...] With a flash of sequins and ostrich plumes, *The Birdcage* offers an alternative definition of the nuclear unit. In shaping a homosexuality acceptable for mass consumption, though, the

filmmakers have come close to turning gays into colorful cartoon creatures. That's a costly stereotype, and, ultimately, too high a price to pay for a place at the table.[7]

The films' apparent destabilising of identity is in fact confined to various forms of stereotypical excess which must of course be defined against some notion of normality. So the films' gay characters, despite their generally sympathetic roles, are unable to escape the confines of a very limited perception of what gay identity may be. The problematising of fixed identities suggested by the drag performance is curtailed by the films' narrow and negatively stereotypical representation of gay sexuality. This is problematic in the source film but is perhaps exacerbated in the remake where the very contemporary political references are matched by a vision of gay culture which ignores the present reality of gay politics and fixes its representations in a highly outmoded notion of effeminacy and hysteria.

This curtailment of the films' purportedly liberal agenda is reinforced by the ultimate reinstatement of the family as the ideal social group. Certainly the gay family is held up in both films as the better unit, more loving and lacking the hypocrisy of its conservative counterpart. Nevertheless, this critique of the nuclear family is confined to mockery of the politician's family and the desirability of the family unit is never called into question. This is reinforced at the end of each film as the young couple are married so reinforcing traditional moral and social values. Again, this can perhaps be seen to be most problematic in the remake. Whereas *La Cage aux folles* remains ultimately a comedy rooted in the traditions of vaudeville and farce, *The Birdcage*, through its contemporary references, sets out explicitly as a critique of certain ideological discourses. However, by confirming the need for family and by showing the wedding, with its happy mix of Jewish and Catholic doctrine, gay and straight guests, as an idealised vision of the melting pot, the film ends by reaffirming long-standing notions of American society and national identity, the very same notions which have enabled the rise of the arch-conservatism it apparently sets out to deride.

Ultimately the films should perhaps be seen as highly ambivalent texts, each incorporating various discourses which are open to further "translation" as they are viewed by different audiences. Indeed it is this very ambivalence which makes this particular pair of films so very interesting in terms of a discussion of the remake, and of translation and adaptation more generally. For the films can in many ways be seen as a metaphor for the remake process. Just like the remake, the narrative concerns of each film can be seen to both transcend national boundaries and fixed notions of identity whilst simultaneously rooting themselves within, and reaffirming, particular constructions of the nation. Just as *The Birdcage* can be seen to both undermine and yet ultimately reaffirm gender and sexual stereotypes, so the remake process calls into question constructions of national cinemas, of production and reproduction, and yet finally demands the retention of both. The remake, and indeed all forms of translation, reveal the performative nature of the text, an instability which manifests itself through its very translatability. Films can be remade, texts can be translated and thus they are not fixed in immutable identities. However, through the very process of rewriting these texts are reinscribed within new contexts which assign to them new forms of identity. It is only through subsequent rewriting, or through an acknowledgement of the circles of intertextuality and hybridity which link source and target, that the non-essential nature of these identities become apparent once more. Which brings me back to the stereotype. In his essay "The Other Question: The Stereotype and Colonial Discourse"[8], Homi Bhabha argues that the racial stereotype of colonial discourse can be read as a fetish in that it serves to mask difference and affirm the wholeness of the coloniser (in other words, sameness of skin and colour) and thus offer the fantasy of a pure origin. In just the same way, those discourses which maintain the binaries of original and copy, those rewritings which deny the plurality of both source and target texts, posit an unbroken, vertical trajectory of translation which reaffirms the authenticity and the uniqueness of individual works. Thus they are akin to the limited performance of gay identity and drag in the films discussed here. Whilst their very status as remake or translation must reveal the plurality and non-essential nature of the text, their reinscription of texts within certain sets of discourse may curtail this plurality and offer the fantasy of a whole text, entire unto itself.

I would like to leave Armand, star of *The Birdcage*, to conclude this argument. In response to his partner's anxious queries as to the authenticity of his attempts to walk like John Wayne, Armand says "No, no, it's perfect. I just never knew that John Wayne walked like that."

Performance and reproduction make us see things in new and different ways. So let us look at the remake and its source as texts that are at once both different and the same, as texts which enable us to see that we never really knew what each one looked like anyway.

Lucy Mazdon

### Notes

1 *La Haine* (France, 1995, Mathieu Kassovitz, Grammercy Pictures/Les Productions Lazzenac/Le Studio Canal Plus/La Sept Cinéma/Kasso Inc. Productions).
2 *Do the Right Thing* (USA, 1989, Spike Lee, 40 Acres and a Mule Filmworks).
3 Lawrence Venuti, *The Translator's Invisibility*, London: Routledge, 1995.
4 *La Cage aux folles* (France/Italy, 1978, Edouard Molinaro, United Artists/ PAA/Da Ma). *The Birdcage* (USA, 1996, Mike Nichols, United Artists).
5 Richard Dyer, "The Role of Stereotypes", in *The Matter of Images: Essays on Representations*, London: Routledge, 1993, 14. First published in Jim Cook & Mike Lewington (eds), *Images of Alcoholism*, London: BFI, 1979.
6 Judith Butler, *Gender Trouble: Feminism and the Subversion of Identity*, London: Routledge, 1989, 137.
7 Hal Hinson, *The Washington Post*, 8 March 1996.
8 Homi Bhabha, "The Other Question: The Stereotype and Colonial Discourse", *Screen*, Vol. 24, No. 6, Winter 1983, 18-36.

## 13.
## CAN INTERTEXTUALITY BE TRANSLATED? BAUDELAIRE'S "LE GUIGNON" AND "LE FLAMBEAU VIVANT" IN ENGLISH

The translation of Baudelaire's poetic works into English raises complex issues such as the relationship between form and content, the nature of poetry, the questions of rhyme and rhythm and of equivalence or non-equivalence of French and English poetic forms, the untranslatable (particularly invoked when it comes to the question of poetry) and, finally, the relationship between creativity and translation.

But, in addition to these issues, which are common to most translations of poetry in general,[1] we have the more specific question of the translation (and retranslation) of a canonical writer, whose reception in the English-speaking world, since Swinburne's 1861 article in *The Spectator*, illustrates a special relationship with French poetry. Patricia Clements' *Baudelaire and the English Tradition*, for instance, shows indeed how, "from the beginning, Baudelaire appears in England as *influence*".[2] Thus different periods have constructed a different Baudelaire to suit their literary purpose and concerns — from Swinburne to Wilde to Symons and of course T.S. Eliot. And when looking at the corpus of English-language translations of Baudelaire's works, one is struck by the extent of the experiments with translation approaches and the number of versions of his works in English, from the first translations which appeared in late 1860 to Shapiro's 1998 *Flowers of Evil*. The 1968 *Sunday Times* translation competition organised by George Steiner is a case in point: the basis for this competition was one of the *Spleen* poems ("Je suis comme le roi d'un pays pluvieux"), and the poem gave rise to countless experiments, most remarkably perhaps Nicholas Moore's thirty-one versions entered under different names, and explained by the translator himself as a consequence of the "impossibility of translation", a point to which I shall return.[3]

This special place of Baudelaire in the English tradition is mirrored by the poet's own obsession with English and American literature, particularly manifest in his own lifelong experiments with translation. Indeed, the Baudelairean corpus includes the whole gamut of possible translational approaches, from the relatively close approach of the Poe translations to the manipulations and appropriations at work in his presentation of De Quincey's *Confessions of an English Opium Eater* and *Suspiria de Profundis* in *Les Paradis artificiels*, or in some poems of *Les Fleurs du Mal*, such as "Le Guignon" and "Le Flambeau vivant" which are heavily based on English hypotexts and can be seen as forms of translation. It is in fact arguable that Baudelaire experimented with the limits of translation.[4]

In the same way as Baudelaire's poetic experiment is at the source of modern poetry and its evolution, Baudelaire's own translation experiments have a lot to tell, theoretically, on what constitutes translation, and may offer a key into the possible translation approaches to poetry. In addition, English (re)translations of these texts and the varying choices made by translators to bring back to the fore or not the English hypotexts shed light on the question of the subversion of authorship achieved by translation in general and Baudelaire's treatments of his source texts in particular.

My aim is two-fold, therefore. First of all, I would like to see to what extent Baudelaire's translating activity may answer the question of the untranslatable in poetry. And second, I shall look at a specific case within the wide field of Baudelaire in English: that of the retranslation into English of Baudelaire's own hypertextual poems based on English texts. Through this study I am hoping to explore issues such as the status of translated works in relation to their original, the question of the "double signature du texte traduit",[5] and, more generally, the so-called "impossibility" of poetry translation.

In his writings, Baudelaire seems to subscribe to the topos that poetry is untranslatable. In his essay on *Edgar Allan Poe, sa vie et ses ouvrages* (itself mostly a compilation of extracts of American articles on Poe translated and/or paraphrased into French), he notes "traduisible, cela ne l'est pas" about the The Bells.[6] A similar idea is expressed about Poe's poetry in general when Baudelaire writes in *Notes Nouvelles sur Edgar Poe*: "une traduction de poésies aussi voulues, aussi concentrées, peut être un rêve caressant, mais ne peut être qu'un rêve".[7] A dream that Baudelaire intended to realise in the 1850s (see 1854 letter to Paul de Saint-Victor,[8] and 1856 letters to Maxime Du Camp to whom he promises "quelques poésies de Poe, de quoi faire une ou deux feuilles";[9] and to Sainte Beuve, to whom he announces "quelques échantillons de Poésie[10]").

He notoriously did NOT translate Poe's poetry except as part of his presentation of Poe's *Philosophy of Composition* (*Genèse d'un poème*), in which "The Raven" is presented in prose. In fact his only other attempts at translating poetry were quite minor, compared to the bulk and nature of his translations of Poe's prose and De Quincey's autobiographical works: Baudelaire translated some English songs by T. E. Walmisley and Dr Cooke, as requested by Alfred Busquet who inserted them in an account of London entitled *Londres fantastique*, published on 29 January 1853. There was also the aborted project of Longfellow's *Song of Hiawatha*, also done to order, this time for Alfred Stoepel, and published on 28 February 1861. And, finally, we have the translation of Thomas Hood's "Bridge of Sighs", dictated to Arthur Stevens in 1865. None of these translations seems to have reached the status of the Poe translations and the treatment of De Quincey's text in *Un Mangeur d'opium*.

Reference to the untranslatable is not limited to the examples quoted above. Even more striking are indeed the passages in the art criticism where Baudelaire's admiration is expressed in relation to a "volupté", a "suggestion" which cannot be translated. In the *Salon de 1859*, he writes, for instance:

> Certes je n'essayerai pas de traduire avec ma plume la volupté si triste qui s'exhale de ce verdoyant exil.[11]

Similarly, in *Le Peintre de la vie moderne*:

> [ces images] sont grosses de suggestions, mais de suggestions cruelles, âpres, que ma plume, bien qu'accoutumée à lutter contre les représentations plastiques, n'a peut-être traduites qu'insuffisamment.[12]

It is these very "voluptés absentes du rythme et de la rime" which make the translation of poetry impossible according to Baudelaire.[13]

This view of poetry as untranslatable is not an admission of failure, however, but rather a challenge and the first step towards an exploration of the limits of translation. The concept of the untranslatable in fact refers to close, direct translation ("translation proper" in

Jakobson's classification,[14] or "translation in the usual sense" as Marilyn Gaddis Rose calls it,[15]) an approach generally adopted by Baudelaire in the Poe translations. Baudelaire's answer to the untranslatable is to develop a much freer approach to the foreign text. In the same way as the aesthetic effect of paintings cannot be conveyed literally and in fact needs to be transposed into poetry, poetry poses the same difficulties, which can only be solved by an open definition of translation. So Baudelaire's repeated mentions of the untranslatable, and of the "lutte" involved in translation, have to be seen in conjunction with a definition of translation which turns out to be broad, quasi-metaphorical: his recurrent use of the word "traduction" and its cognates to refer to the act of criticism, in particular as applied to verbal recreations of visual texts, suggests a very strong creative, transpositional dimension of translation.[16] Perhaps the most striking example of this may be found in the "transpositions d'art" (mainly in *Les Fleurs du mal*).[17] In such cases, a visual text is recreated in poetry, a transfer based on Baudelaire's belief in the specificity, and yet transposability of each art.[18] That such transpositions may be considered as translations has since then been confirmed in now classic theories of translation, such as Roman Jakobson's "Linguistic Aspects of Translation" which lists "intersemiotic translation" as part of the three types of translation.

So Baudelaire's answer to the untranslatable seems to be the choice of a translation approach which is often very close to transmutation and alchemy — he talks about an amalgam in the case of his translation of De Quincey's works — and the transformative/appropriative dimension of the act is consciously exploited in many of his translations. In the case of De Quincey, the transformations are justified by clearly domesticating concerns (De Quincey is indeed considered "conversationniste" and "digressionniste", and Baudelaire largely reshapes the autobiography to make it, in his own words, more "dramatique").[19] Thus *Un Mangeur d'opium* mixes summaries, translations, commentaries and paraphrases. Translation becomes a blend, an explicitly double-authored text:

> jusqu'à quelle dose ai-je introduit ma personnalité dans l'auteur original, c'est ce que je serais actuellement bien empêché de dire. J'ai fait un tel amalgame que je ne saurais y reconnaître la part qui vient de moi, laquelle, d'ailleurs, ne peut être que fort petite.[20]

The links between poetry and translation are both apparent in Baudelaire's use of the same alchemical metaphors to refer to the translation activity and to the work of the poet,[21] and, even more strikingly, in his description of the work of the poet as that of a translator. He writes, for instance: "qu'est-ce qu'un poète (je prends le mot dans son acception la plus large), si ce n'est un traducteur, un déchiffreur?".[22] And, in another instance, he talks about the viewer of paintings as "traducteur d'une traduction toujours claire et enivrante".[23]

The significance of the concept of translation as applied to poetry is particularly clear in poems such as "Correspondances" which emphasize, among other things, the role of the poet as an interpreter of the secret language of nature. But besides this metaphoric dimension of the translating role of the poet, we do find in *Les Fleurs du mal* poems which are literally based on translation, the most striking of which are perhaps "Le Guignon" and "Le Flambeau vivant". These poems are not direct translations, and instead, like *Un Mangeur d'opium*, blend Baudelairean elements with passages translated from English. The blend means that the result is a Baudelairean poem in its own right, a fact which is made even more potent by the full integration of the poem into *Les Fleurs du mal*. As a consequence, and in addition to a dialogue with its English sources, the French text is engaged intertextual links with the poems that surround it, and more generally, the collection as a whole. If we follow André Lefevere, then, these poems cannot strictly speaking be called translations:

> The translator, as opposed to the version-writer and the imitator, should possess the ability to reinterpret the source text along the lines of the interpretation laid down by the original author. He should not superimpose his own interpretation on it. He should, in a word, try to achieve an 'equivalent effect' (...). The translator should neither wilfully heighten (version) nor involuntarily weaken (translation concentrating exclusively on one aspect of the source text) that effect.[24]

For Baudelaire, however, translation, version and imitation are all part of the same creative process, based on the appropriation and transformation of a source text. Baudelaire's choice of translation as alchemical transmutation creates, to use Gérard Genette's terms, a hypertext, that is to say a text based on another, but existing in its own right, independently from its hypotext (or source).[25] Baudelaire's approach to his hypotext clearly challenges the concept of authorship and authority since it brings to it a new author who takes over the text. As Lawrence Venuti puts it, such translation projects erase "the distinction that an individualistic notion of authorship draws between author and translator, creator and imitator".[26] Or, as Terry Eagleton writes: "what is being displaced (...) is the mythological notion of the founding text".[27] From this point of view, "Le Flambeau vivant" and "Le Guignon" can be seen as emblematic of what happens in translation and of the subversion of authorship at play in the act, since the two poems use translation as a means of appropriation and transformation of English sources.[28]

"Le Guignon"
Pour soulever un poids si lourd
Sisyphe, il faudrait ton courage!
Bien qu'on ait du cœur à l'ouvrage
L'Art est long et le temps est court.
Loin des sépultres célèbres,
Vers un cimetière isolé,
Mon cœur, comme un tambour voilé,
Va battant des marches funèbres.

— Maint joyau dort enseveli
Dans les ténèbres et l'oubli,
Bien loin des pioches et des sondes;

Mainte fleur épanche à regret
Son parfum doux comme un secret
Dans les solitudes profondes.

"A Psalm of Life" (lines 13-16)
Art is long, and Time is fleeting,
And our heart, though stout and brave,
Still, like muffled drums are beating
Funeral marches to the grave.[29]

"Elegy Written in a Country Church Yard" (lines 53-56)

Full many a gem of purest ray serene,
The dark unfathom'd caves of ocean bear:
Full many a flower is born to blush unseen.
And waste its sweetness on the desert air.[30]

The two quatrains of this sonnet develop what is expressed in the corresponding quatrain from Longfellow's "Psalm of Life", while the two tercets are based on a quatrain drawn from Gray's "Elegy Written in a Country Churchyard". The title and the first two lines of the sonnet, which are the only elements *not* borrowed from Longfellow or Gray, set the tone of the poem and influence our reading of the rest of it. Removed from their original context, Longfellow's and Gray's verses take on the meaning intended by Baudelaire: Longfellow's poem does not have in general a negative tone, but is rather an encouragement to action, while Baudelaire focuses on the difficulties of artistic creation and recognition. By "cutting and pasting" the two poems, Baudelaire links them together and to his title, and blends them with his own poetry. This is confirmed by the fact that Baudelaire, rather than merely translating the two extracts word for word expands on them in order to produce a poem close to his own thematics of *guignon*.[31]

"Le Guignon" of course fully belongs to Baudelaire's thematic concerns, and as such appears frequently in English anthologies, not to mention full English editions of *Les Fleurs du mal*. Compared to other texts — *Un Mangeur d'opium*, for instance — "Le Guignon" fully amalgamates the source text to the new poetic purpose, and as such presents specific translation challenges. English translations of this poem have varied in their strategies. There are two distinct trends regarding the French poem's hypotext — the translator either chooses to restore the hypotext, or does not. In other words, translators in their strategies have to take a stance on the status of Baudelaire's sources in the poem. The examples I have selected illustrate a small portion of the range of strategies adopted towards Baudelaire's text. We have Carol Clark's "plain prose translation" as she calls it in the introduction to her bilingual edition:[32]

> "Bad Luck"
> To lift such a heavy weight, Sisyphus, a man would need your courage. Though we work with a good heart, Art is long and Time is fleeting.
> Far from the tombs of the famous, towards a lonely graveyard, my heart, like a muffled drum, goes beating funeral marches.
> Many a gem sleeps buried in dark forgetfulness, far, far from picks and plumb-lines;
> Many a flower unwillingly loses its perfume, sweet as a secret, in deep solitudes.

Obviously Clark is relying on the confrontation between the French and English texts to "put the reader in touch with the magical original".[33] The other examples all match Baudelaire's sonnet structure but vary in rhythm and rhyme pattern:

"The Hoodoo"
Sisyphus, man must be as strong
Of will as you, to lift such weight!
For even though his heart be great,
His Time is brief, and Art is long.

Away from famous burial grounds
And towards a lonely grave apart,
The muffled drum that is my heart
Moves, and beats out funereal sounds.

Full many a buried precious stone
Is sleeping, shadowed and unknown,
Far from the pickaxe and the spade;

Full many a Flower spreads in vain
Its perfume, for it must remain
In outer solitudes to fade.[34]

"Artist Unknown"
Flesh is willing, but the Soul requires
Sisyphean patience for its song.
Time, Hippocrates remarked, is short
And Art is long.

No illustrious tombstones ornament
the lonely churchyard where I often go
to hear my heart, a muffled drum, parade
incognito.

'Many a gem,' the poet mourns, abides
forgotten in the dust
unnoticed there;

'Many a rose' regretfully confides
the secret of its scent
to empty air.[35]

"Ill Fortune"
One must have courage as strong
As Sisyphus, lifting this weight!
Through the heart for the
work may be great,
Time is fleeting, and Art is so long!

Far from the tombs of the brave
Toward a churchyard obscure
and apart,
Like a muffled drum, my heart
Beats a funeral march to the grave.

But sleeping lies many a gem
In dark, unfathomed caves,
Far from the probes of men;

And many a flower waves
And wastes its sweet perfumes
In desert solitudes.[36]

"Bad Luck"
As Time is not as long as Art
And won't conform to my desires,
To shoulder such a weight requires
A stubborn, Sisyphean heart.

Far from the great Triumphal Arch,
Towards a lonely grave I come,
Still beating on a muffled drum
The Unknown Artist's long dead-march.

In such a dark sleeps many a gem,
Oblivion is full of them,
Beyond the reach of pick or drill.

And flowers that waste in desert air
A secret they would rather share,
In solitude are blushing still.[37]

"The Jinx"
Sisyphus, one must be as strong
And brave as you to lift this weight!
Though one be tireless, obdurate,
Yet Life is short and Art is long.

Far from the tombs of glorydom,
In some lone graveyard, set apart,
Beating the deadman's-march, my heart
Pounds out its pace, like muffled drum.

— Many a gem lies buried deep
In darkness, overlooked, asleep,
Far from the pick and probe, alone.

Many a flower, alas, was meant
To spread the fragrance of its scent
In secret solitude, unknown.[38]

There is, however, a tendency to attempt some rhyme dimension, from the totally mimetic (Duke, Martin, Shapiro), to the more vaguely form derivative (McGowan). In the case of Richard Howard, we have some vague rhymes although very little regularity, a choice mirrored with variations in rhythmical patterns. In fact Howard notes in his foreword that he has "not sought to make the verse rhyme". Instead, he says "I have employed all the artifices in my power to make up for, even to suggest, the consentaneous regularly that the persistent use of rhyme affords". He describes his approach as the sacrifice of terminal consonance for the sake of cumulative effects. These examples are fairly typical — other translations, such as H.C.'s (1894 translation) Arthur Symons's, George Dillon's, attempt a mimetic rhyme pattern, and there are only very few examples, such as Wallace Fowlie's, which make no attempt at rhyme at all.

As far as the rhythmical pattern is concerned, there also seems to be an attempt to copy an octosyllabic structure — and, a choice, therefore, to import into English a French metrical system. On top of this French-inspired metre, we also have, of course, the rhythm created by English prosody, and, therefore, a hybrid form.

Turning to my main interest in choosing this poem, that is to say the presence of English hypotexts within Baudelaire's text, there is, in most texts, an awareness of the hypotexts (for instance often noted in footnotes — endnotes, a fact which emphasizes of course the metatextual nature of translation). In some instances, however, the hypotext is almost ignored — it is the case, for example, in Francis Duke's "Hoodoo", which avoids any mention of the hypotext (apart from the "muffled drum" and the repetition of the phrase "full many"). Shapiro's version, which also uses the phrase "muffled drum" but also "many a gem", is similar. In these translations, Baudelaire's voice is perceived as having almost completely erased his source texts. In other poems, we find a stronger surfacing of the hypotexts. Carol Clark's prose version blends translation and unmarked quotations from the source texts: "Art is long and Time is fleeting", "muffled drum", "beating funeral marches", "many a gem", "many a flower". James McGowan's version is more complex, as it operates small modifications of Baudelaire's English sources which match the appropriation at work in the French poem. We have, as in "The Hoodoo" and "Bad Luck", the same reference to "muffled drum", "many a gem", "many a flower"; but this must be seen with other passages — "Time is fleeting, and Art is *so* long!", where the added word "so" enables a trochaic rhythm which is idiosyncratic to the English poem. The use of the singular in "Beats a funeral march" achieved a transformation of both Longfellow's text and Baudelaire's who had kept the plural of his source, and enacts here again the appropriation at work. In the third stanza, the second line, "In dark, unfathomed caves" is entirely based on Longfellow, but here again we have a slight rhythmical modification. And in the final stanza, the "sweet perfumes" and "desert solitude" are respectively derived from "sweetness" and "desert air".

The other two versions I have selected have adopted different strategies. Both Richard Howard and Walter Martin refer to the context of the poem — and the history of its composition — by using its first title "L'Artiste inconnu", which they have translated as "Artist Unknown" in the title (Howard) or included in the text itself (Walter Martin: "The Unknown Artist's long dead-march". In Walter Martin's case, this is the strongest extratextual reference — the only other ones being the use, as in most of the other examples I have presented, of "a muffled drum", "many a gem", and maybe more interestingly, "blushing", which seems based on Gray's "to blush unseen". Richard Howard's version is perhaps the most adventurous one, since it attempts to point out the intertextual dimension of the poem, not by actually quoting Baudelaire's sources but by emphasizing the dialogic dimension of the text. Rather than Longfellow, it is Longfellow's own source, Hippocrates, which resurfaces. Finally, the two quotations "Many a gem", and "Many a rose" as well as the reference to the poet — the main subject of the poem or the author of its source? — complete this "quoting" text. Of all these versions, this is perhaps not the most satisfying, but it does push towards its limits the intertextual dimension of Baudelaire's poem.

Another interesting — and problematic — treatment by Baudelaire of the *untranslatable other* may be found in "Le Flambeau vivant",[39] which also exemplifies Baudelaire's transformation of an English text to create a poem which is his own. This poem is loosely based on the last 19 lines of Poe's "To Helen":[40]

"Le Flambeau Vivant"
Ils marchent devant moi, ces Yeux pleins de
lumières,
Qu'un Ange très savant a sans doute aimantés;
Ils marchent, ces divins frères qui sont mes
frères,
Secouant dans mes yeux leurs feux diamantés.

Me sauvant de tout piège et de tout péché grave,
Ils conduisent mes pas dans la route du Beau;
Ils sont mes serviteurs et je suis leur esclave;
Tout mon être obéit à ce vivant flambeau.

Charmants Yeux, vous brillez de la clarté
mystique,
Qu'ont les cierges brûlant en plein jour; le soleil
Rougit, mais n'éteint pas leur flamme
fantastique;

Ils célèbrent la Mort, vous chantez le Réveil;
Vous marchez en chantant le réveil de mon
âme,
Astres dont nul soleil ne peut flétrir la flamme!

"To Helen" (lines 48-66)
But now, at length, dear Dian sank from sight,
Into a western couch of thunder-cloud;
And thou, a ghost, amid the entombing trees

Didst glide away. *Only thine eyes remained.*
They *would not* go — they never yet have gone.
Lighting my lonely pathway home that night,
They have not left me (as my hopes have) since.
They follow me — they lead me through the years.
They are my ministers — yet I their slave.
Their office is to illumine and enkindle —
My duty, to be saved by their bright light,
And purified in their electric fire,
And sanctified in their elysian fire.
They fill my soul with Beauty (which is Hope),
And are far up in Heaven — the stars I kneel to
In the sad, silent watches of my night;
While even in the meridian glare of day
I see them still — two sweetly scintillant
Venuses, unextinguished by the sun!

Baudelaire's poem combines direct translation, compression and transformation of Edgar Allan Poe's "To Helen". Passages such as "Ils sont mes serviteurs et je suis leur esclave", and "Astres dont nul soleil ne peut flétrir la flamme!" are directly translated from Poe's "They are my ministers — yet I their slave" and "Venuses, unextinguished by the sun!". In other passages, however, several of Poe's lines become one in Baudelaire: "Ils marchent devant moi" is based on "Lighting my lonely pathway home that night" and "they lead me through the years"; "Ces yeux pleins de lumière" summarises all the references to eyes in Poe's text; "Me sauvant de tout piège et de tout péché grave" compresses four lines "Their office is ... elysian fire"). Elsewhere, Baudelaire adapts the source text to his own thematics ("They fill my heart with Beauty (which is Hope)/they lead me through the years" becomes "Ils conduisent mes pas dans la route du Beau", which refers in Baudelaire to poetic creation far more explicitly than in Poe. Similarly, Poe's Christian imagery ("To be saved", "purified", "sanctified", "Heaven") is developed by Baudelaire ("Ange", "divins", "sauvant", "péché", "cierges"). The third stanza of "Flambeau vivant" develops Poe's two lines: "While even in the meridian glare of day/I see them still".

In addition, Baudelaire omits the atmosphere and background created by Poe in the fifty lines that are suppressed — and instead concentrates on the theme of his Muse's eyes. Similarly, while Poe's text is in the past tense (his favoured tense, used to create a sense of melancholy, the most appropriate to poetry according to him), Baudelaire's text is in the present tense — operating again a distinctive shift. Finally, the sonnet chosen by Baudelaire completes the transformation.

What of the English translations, then? Carol Clark produces a prose version, to be read as a guide to the French text:

"The Living Torch"
They walk before me, those light-filled eyes, which a very wise Angel magnetized, no doubt; they walk, those divine brothers who are my brothers, shaking into my eyes their glittering fires.
Saving me from all snares and all grave sins, they lead my steps in the path of the Beautiful; they are my servants and I am their slave; all my being obeys this living torch.
Enchanting Eyes, you shine with the mystical brightness of candles burning in daylight; the sun reddens, but cannot extinguish their eerie flame;
They celebrate Death, you sing of Awakening; you go forth humming the awakening of my soul, stars whose flame no sun can wither.

Other translations generally keep the sonnet form. There is the same mimesis of a rhyme pattern, albeit often quite approximate as in the case of Walter Martin:

"The Living Torch"
Identical, electrifying Eyes —
Scattering cosmic fire across the night!
A subtle Seraph must have magnetized
My brethren, for they lead me to the light.

They follow, yet they lead me through the snares,
And guide me past the pitfall of the grave,
Directing me to Beauty, faithful stars,
They are my ministers and I their slave.

Beguiling Eyes, you blaze with strange desires,
Like tapers burning through the day; the day
Is powerless to quench your subtle fires.

You celebrate Rebirth, not Death's decay,
Encouraging my soul to rise, and shine —
Twin planets, unextinguished by the sun![41]

Richard Howard, in this poem as in "Le Guignon" is one of the rare translators to have moved away from rhyme:

"The Living Torch *after Poe's* To Helen"
They pass before me, those electric eyes
some abstruse Angel must have magnetized —
celestial twins, yet mine as well, they pass
and share with me their supernatural power;

protecting me from trespasses and snares
they lead to Beauty, as the poet says:
'They are my ministers — yet I their slave,'
and all my being serves that living torch.

Enchanting eyes! you glisten with the light
of candles burning in broad day — the sun
challenges but does not change their flame;

they burn for Death, you for the New Life:
you sing my soul's awakening — bright stars,
'Venuses unextinguished by the sun.'[42]

Some translators avoid any reference to Baudelaire's sources and stay as close as possible to Baudelaire's text:

"The Living Torch"
They move in front of me, hypnotic Eyes that shine
With such assurance only Angels could inspire;
They move, those godlike brothers, brothers which are mine,
Who glitter in my eyes like diamonds set afire.

From every snare and every sin I have been saved;
And, following their steps, to Beauty's path I came;
Indeed they are my ministers — yet I'm their slave;
My entire being must obey this living flame.

Enchanted Eyes that shine mysteriously bright,
Like candles at midday, pink in the reflection
Of the sun, yet burning with fantastic light;

Some celebrate the Death, you sing the Resurrection;
You walk around me singing of my risen soul,
Two morning stars whose flame no sun can ever dull![43]

# Can Intertextuality Be Translated? Baudelaire's "Le Guignon" and "Le Flambeau vivant" in English

"The Living Torch"
They march before me, those eyes filled with light
Made magnets, likely, by some angel wise;
They march, those heavenly twins, my brethren bright,
Stewing their diamond-fires into my eyes.

Keeping me safe from snares iniquitous,
They lead me in the path of Beauty; they
Are both my servants and my masters; thus
Does my whole being this living torch obey.

Bewitching eyes, you glow with mystic blaze,
Like tapers burning in the sun, whose rays
Never can dim their flame fantastic, pure;

But they chant Death, you sing Awakening:
Yes, as you march, my waking soul you sing
O stars whose flame no sunlight can obscure![44]

In other examples, however, the sources are brought back to the surface. When this is the case, translators seem to have focused on specific key phrases to reveal the link with a hypotext, as they have in "Le Guignon": Martin engages with Baudelaire's sources ("electrifying eyes"), and amends slightly the source to reflect Baudelaire's modifications ("They are my ministers and I their slave"). Howard also refers to the "electric" which is absent from Baudelaire's poem but is present in his hypotext. As in his translation of "Le Guignon", he has a strategy of clearly indicating quotations and thereby underlining the hypertextual dimension of the text: (in "they are my ministers — yet I their slave" and "Venuses unextinguished by the sun", quotation marks within the text point out the dialogic nature of the text); similarly, Baudelaire's hypotext is emphasized in the title ("*after Poe's* To Helen").

This brief survey of translational approaches to the dual authorship of "Le Guignon" and "Le Flambeau vivant" reveals a certain ambivalence on the part of translators. The choice to restore Baudelaire's sources makes the intertextuality of the poem more blatant than in the French texts, where the English hypotexts are not acknowledged, and are instead amalgamated to Baudelaire's voice. So in effect the most adventurous translations, those which treat Baudelaire's text with the most freedom, are in fact those which also give the most importance to

Baudelaire's own sources and challenge Baudelaire's ownership of his text by pointing out the original authorship of his hypotext. For them, a translation is ancillary to its sources which it is their duty to restore. On the other hand the translations which stay the closest to Baudelaire's hypertext and ignore his English sources, both adopt a source-oriented approach and acknowledge the appropriative, transformative dimension of Baudelaire's target-centred approach.

"Le Flambeau vivant" and "Le Guignon" reveal a type of untranslatability similar to that analysed by Jacques Derrida in "Des Tours de Babel".[45] Indeed Derrida stresses the difficulties of translating multilingual texts — Baudelaire's poems are in effect multilingual and it is their return to English, that is to say a monolingual context, which makes translation difficult. The solution to the problematic rendering of intertextual poems may be the production of several translations of the same poems, such as Nicholas Moore's experiment, or the recent Penguin edition of *Baudelaire in English*, which provides several versions of each poem.[46] Untranslatability becomes a positive dimension, therefore, since it generates renewed and fascinating versions which emphasize the richness of their source and the inventiveness of their authors.

Emily Salines

## Notes

1 See for instance Edwin Honig, *The Poet's Other Voice*, Amherst: University of Massachusetts Press, 1985; Burton Raffel, *The Art of Translating Poetry*, University Park and London: Pennsylvania State University Press, 1988; Daniel Weissbort, *Translating Poetry*, London: Macmillan, 1989.
2 Patricia Clements, *Baudelaire and the English*, Princeton: Princeton, 1985, 14.
3 Nicholas Moore, *Spleen*, London: The Menard Press, 1990 (first edition 1973). See Moore's preface "The Impossibility of Translation", 11-16.
4 See my doctoral thesis, *Alchemy and Amalgam: Translation in the Works of Charles Baudelaire*, University of London, 1998; see also my article, "Baudelaire and the Alchemy of Translation" in Jean Boase-Beier and Michael Holman (eds), *Translation Creativity and Constraints*, Manchester: St Jerome, 1999.

5   Sherry Simon, "Conflits de juridiction, la double signature du texte traduit", *Meta*, 34, 2 (1989), 195-208.
6   Charles Baudelaire, *Oeuvres Complètes II*, Paris: Gallimard, 1976, (hereafter abbreviated as *ŒCII*), 274.
7   *ŒCII*, 336.
8   Charles Baudelaire, *Correspondance I*, Paris: Gallimard, 1973, hereafter abbreviated as *CI*, 294.
9   *CI*, 342.
10  *CI*, 345.
11  *Salon de 1859*, *ŒCII*, 702: "I will not try to translate with my pen the exquisite pleasure that emanates from this green exile." (My translation).
12  *Le Peintre de la vie moderne*, *OCII*, 722. "[these images] are laden with suggestions, cruel, harsh ones which my pen, although used to fight against plastic representations, may have translated incompletely." (My translation).
13  *Avis du traducteur*, *ŒCII*, 347.
14  Roman Jakobson, "Linguistic Apects of Translation", in Reuben A. Brower (ed.), *On Translation*, Cambridge, Mass.: Harvard University Press, 1959, 232-43.
15  Marilyn Gaddis Rose, *Translation and Literary Criticism*, Manchester: St Jerome, 1997, p. 31.
16  See Michele Hannoosh, "Painting as Translation in Baudelaire's Art Criticism", *Forum for Modern Language Studies*, 22 (1986), 22-33.
17  These "transpositions d'art" are poetic re-creations and explorations of visual sources — examples include "Le Masque", based on a statue by Ernest Christophe, "Une Gravure fantastique" which transposes into words an engraving by Josephe Haynes, "L'Amour et le crâne" based on an engraving by Goltzius, "Sur *Le Tasse en prison*" based on Delacroix's "Le Tasse dans la maison des fous".
18  This belief is repeatedly expressed in the art criticism, in particular in *L'Art Philosophique*, *ŒCII*, 590-605.
19  *Exorde et notes pour les conférences données à Bruxelles, en 1864*, *OECI*, 519.
20  Letter to Auguste Poulet-Malassis, 16 February 1860, *CI*, 669. "To what extent I have introduced my personality into the original author, I would be presently incapable of saying. I have made such an amalgam that I could not distinguish the part which comes from me, and which, anyway, cannot but be minimal."). (My translation).
21  See for instance *Alchimie de la douleur* in *Les Fleurs du Mal*.
22  *Salon de 1859*, *ŒCII*, 133. "What is a poet? (I take the term in its broadest sense) If it is not a translator, a decipherer?" (My translation).
23  *Le Peintre de la vie moderne*, *ŒCII*, 698. "translator of a translation which is for ever clear and intoxicating". (My translation).

24 André Lefevere, *Translating Poetry, Seven Strategies and a Blueprint*, Amsterdam: Van Gorcum, 1975, 103.
25 Gérard Genette, *Palimpsestes*, Paris: Seuil, 1982.
26 Lawrence Venuti, *The Translator's Invisibility*, London: Routledge, 1995, 166.
27 Terry Eagleton, "Translation and Transformation", *Stand*, 19, 3, 1997-98, 73.
28 See Alan Astro, "Allegory of Translation in Baudelaire's *Un Mangeur d'opium*", *Nineteenth-Century French Studies*, 18, 1-2, Fall-Winter 1989-90, 165-71.
29 Henry Wadsworth Longfellow, "A Psalm of Life", in *Selected Poems*, London: Everyman 1993, 9.
30 Thomas Gray, "Elegy Written in a Country Church Yard", in *The Poems of Thomas Gray, William Collins, Oliver Goldsmith*, ed. by Roger Lonsdale, London & New York: Longman, 1969, 127.
31 See Paul Bénichou, "À propos du «Guignon», Note sur le travail poétique chez Baudelaire", *Etudes Baudelairiennes III*, 1973, 232-40.
32 Charles Baudelaire, *Selected Poems*, London: Penguin Books, 1995.
33 *Ibid*, xxxii.
34 *The Flowers of Evil and Other Poems*, trans. Francis Duke, Virginia: University of Virginia Press, 1961, 29.
35 *Les Fleurs du mal*, trans. Richard Howard, Brighton: The Harvester Press, 1982, 20-21.
36 *The Flowers of Evil*, trans. James McGowan, Oxford: OUP, 1993, 29.
37 *Complete Poems*, trans. Walter Martin, Manchester: Carcanet, 1997, 37.
38 *Selected Poems from* Les Fleurs du mal, *English Renderings by Norman R Shapiro*, Chicago: University of Chicago Press, 1998.
39 *Les Fleurs du Mal*, OECI, 43.
40 Edgar Allan Poe, "To Helen", in *The Complete Tales and Poems*, New York: Dorset Press, 1989, 80-83.
41 Walter Martin, 113.
42 Richard Howard, 47-48.
43 *The Flowers of Evil and Paris Spleen*, trans. William H. Crosby, Rochester, NY: BOA editions, 1991, 41.
44 *Selected Poems from Les Fleurs du Mal*, 83.
45 Jacques Derrida, "Des Tours de Babel", in Joseph F. Graham (ed.), *Difference in Translation*, Ithaca and London: Cornell University Press, 1985, 209-48.
46 Carol Clark and Robert Sykes, *Baudelaire in English*, London: Penguin, 1997.

## 14.
## BACK TO THE ORIGINAL: TRANSLATING MAGHREBI FRENCH LITERATURE INTO ARABIC

*Literature is not innocent. Neither is translation.*[1]

### Introduction

That translation may involve acts which could be regarded as manipulatory or discriminatory is not an entirely new concept. In the nineteenth century Jungmann wrote:

> The subject matter, the topic, the stuff of the mind, so to speak, is a product of the age; it does not lie in our power, and it would be absurd to care whether it is original or taken over from elsewhere. But the way in which we adopt it, the form we give it is of primary importance.[2]

Since the early 1980s Translation Studies has given prominence to the view of culture-Modelling through translation, with scholars such as Bassnett, Lefevere, Venuti and others, ushering in questions and issues that transcend the convential notions of equivalence and accuracy. According to some, the process of translation has come to denote acts of discrimination, interpretation, inclusion and exclusion, making it synonymous with domination, appropriation and the (mis)representation of cultures. Lawrence Venuti succinctly sums up this view of translation within the Anglo-American tradition:

> The violence of translation resides in its very purpose and activity: the reconstitution of the foreign text in accordance with values, beliefs and representations that pre-exist it in the target language, always configured in hierarchies of dominance and marginality.[3]

Elsewhere, Venuti attempts to exorcise the ideological in the process of translation. Using the terms *domestication* and *foreignization*, he argues that over the last three centuries the Anglo-American (by extension Western) translation theory and practice have had normalizing and neutralizing effects, subduing the dynamics of source texts in order to represent foreign and alien cultures in terms of what is familiar and unchallenging to the dominant Western culture[4]. In his seminal work, *Orientalism*, Edward Said[5] sees that the Orient, particularly the Arab World and Islam, has become an imaginary space construed by the ideology, the cultural sets of values, and norms of the West.

The conflation of Said's and Venuti's views indicates that the Arab-Islamic world, as well as the so-called Third World, become signs that have been invisibly and violently construed, defined, and stereotyped; each as an imaginary homogeneity. Given this ideology, translation becomes a significant technology of domination, and the site of conflictual relationships of power and struggle between the cultures being translated and those doing the translating.

The assumed and imaginary basis for invisibility and violence in translation, in orientalism, lies in the Western obsession with fixed texts and its preoccupation with the mechanisms of this fixedness. Translating texts from cultures which have only oral traditions into fixed texts has meant taking liberties, i.e. being invisible, violent, appropriationist and subverter, in order to shift the texts into mainstream world culture and literature. World culture and literature means, of course, adoption of the Western canons of production that also stand as signs of universalism and humanism.

The Arab World and Islam are expressed and represented within an established framework of institutions with its own vocabulary. Within this relationship of power and knowledge, the West, satisfied and content with its own representations of the Arabs and Muslims, has not bothered itself with appreciating and knowing the literatures of these peoples. There are of course some exceptions but they do not affect mainstream trends. Edward Said aptly remarks:

> For all the major world literatures, Arabic remains relatively unknown and unread in the West, for reasons that are unique, even remarkable, at a time when tastes here for the non-European are more developed than ever before and, even more compelling, contemporary Arabic literature is at a particular interesting juncture.[6]

When Arab writers, for instance, Munif, a superb critic of the Middle Eastern oil based societies, are translated into English, critics either ignore or denigrate their writings. Dallal quotes a remark by John Updike about Munif's outstanding *Cities of Salt*:

> It is unfortunate [...] that Mr Munif [...] appears to be [...] insufficiently Westernized to produce a narrative that feels much like what we call a novel.[7]

This attitude stems from an ideology based on universalism, unitarism, and the homogeneity of human nature, which marginalizes and excludes the distinctive and unique characteristics of post-colonial societies and their discursive traditions. What Updike is saying is that the West needs to satisfy itself that it knows its natives: its others who should adapt to its norms in order to be welcomed as members of universalism and world culture and literature.

Western centric assumptions about others — races, nationalities, literatures — provide the site for critiques of representations, of language and of ideological control on writers from the ex-colonies. These assumptions return time and again to haunt the production, reception and circulation of post-colonial literatures, and in turn complicate the issue of translation.[8] Post-colonial literatures, however, are the products of the interaction between the ex-colonizer's culture, the complex of the ex-colonized's cultures, and the invisibility and violence of the translation enterprise. As the newcomer, the colonized is invited by the colonizer to join world culture and literature, with the proviso that the colonizer be the judge of any success.

Though the West has, in the 1980s and 1990s, opened up to Third World peoples, cultures and texts — to Latinos, for example — literatures of the Arab-Islamic world generally remain marginalized, despite the enormous and persistent attention which is accorded to the Arabs and to Islam, and the fact that a Nobel Prize for literature was awarded to the Egyptian writer Naguib Mahfouz in 1988. What further complicates translation from Arabic is the existence of what has come to be known collectively as Maghrebi French literature (MFL henceforth), which is produced by writers who originate from the Maghreb, or those who were born and grew up in the area.

The Maghreb forms part of the francophone world; a world into which French explorers and later colonialists brought their language and culture to "civilize" the natives. Post-colonial MFL represents a unique instance: it is written in French yet about cultures and values that are not French but Arab, Berber and Islamic in spirit. Among its aims is the emphasis on the identification and exploration of the struggle to achieve national identity, and the valorization of ethnic, social, political, cultural and literary values.

MFL's main text is French, but it also draws on the languages of sub-texts, whether these be in standard Arabic or Arabic as spoken in Morocco, Algeria and Tunisia; or Berber and its varieties; as well as either mainstream Islamic culture or the variations of this that exist in the Maghreb. The position of this literature is important particularly that in the Maghreb books which are written in French, whether imported or locally produced, still represent close to 50 per cent of total book sales.[9]

The translation of MFL into Arabic, in itself quantitatively insignificant, does not simply involve the conventional situation of distant languages and cultures, but involves translating source texts which are themselves target texts — translations or rather pseudotranslations — back into target texts which are themselves source texts, the input for the technically French source texts. The issue, then, is not only turning texts written in the French language into Arabic, but the re-writing of texts which are originally Maghrebi. Though most MFL can be seen as committed to challenging a dominant ideology, both external and internal, as well as the humanist and universal discursive values, some writers, notably Tahar Ben Jelloun, could be labelled as reinforcers of orientalist stereotypes and clichés about everything Arab and Islamic.

## MFL: Resistance and/or Compliance

Maghrebi societies are still subject to overt and covert forms of neo-colonial domination, and the existence of élites, educated primarily in the French language and its humanist, universalist culture, has not helped the shift from colonization. The members of these élites are the main producers of post-colonial MFL.

The growth of MFL, and the existence of a considerable Maghrebi minority community in France, has resulted in new challenges to, and redefinitions of, many notions of production and translation. Post-colonial MFL consists of texts with layerings of languages and cultures, which has resulted in a form of French with its own discursive strategies that defy the conventional definitions of source and target texts. Whilst the texts are generally written in standard French, they can rupture standard grammar and vocabulary by means of the infusion of indigenous vernaculars, customs and religious practices. French discourses and discursive strategies are investigated from a somewhat privileged position: within and in-between two languages and two cultures. Samia Mehrez writes:

> ...the ultimate goal [of MFL] was to subvert hierarchies by bringing together the "dominant" and the "underdeveloped", by exploding and confounding different symbolic worlds and separate systems of signification in order to create a mutual interdependence and intersignification.[10]

The aim of such literature should be to bring to the fore the problematics of interculturation, bilingualism and identity. As a postcolonial enterprise, MFL should engage in readings, interpretations, and rewritings of spaces already occupied as well as the "betweeness" of France, French and the Maghreb with its languages, religion, ethnic diversity, pasts, presents and futures.

> si le bilinguisme maghrébin contribue à inscrire la littérature comme sujet de l'histoire, à son tour, l'écriture refait l'histoire, celle d'un sujet qui, paradoxalement s'efface en elle. En ce sens, on peut dire qu'il existe "des français", comme il existe des écrivains et des langues. La littérature maghrébine que l'on dit d'expression française est en fait, selon Khatibi, "récit de traduction", traduction d'une langue familière autre, mais aussi traduction du français en français.[11]

Writers like Djebar, Khatibi, Kilito, Chraibi, and others have produced texts that aim to be both resisters and liberators. Their work shows alternations of two discourses which reflect on one another in the interrogation, modification and/or negation of certain histories as well as the (re)construction of awarenesses of these histories. Their texts are generally closer to standard French, but include considerable references, including names, to Arabic, Berber and Islamic signs, together with alternative narrative techniques.

The problem for MFL texts, which are mainly published in France, is whether the dominant culture will accept and interact equitably with the differences they present, or whether it will try and force them to assimilate into French value systems. Whilst certain texts have received attention from French academic and journalistic critics, as well as the general readership, only a few writers maintain noticeable presence in the French literary arena. This is because, as Jacquemond[12] argues, they need to conform to: a) dominant representations of Arabic culture and society, and b) dominant French ideological, moral, and aesthetic values.

Ben Jelloun, it would appear, opted to conform to both of these conditions. In *La Nuit sacrée*[13] for which he was awarded the Prix Goncourt in 1987 and which sold almost two million copies, as well as in his other writings since *Harrouda*, published in 1973, Ben Jelloun has inhabited the space of the *délire, fantasmes,* and *fabulation*. This article will focus on the apparent auto-orientalism of his text and on the way its translation into Arabic was carried out.

Written as a sequel to *L'Enfant de sable*,[14] *La Nuit sacrée* tells the story of a female given the Arabic name of Zahra after almost twenty years living as a boy with the name of Ahmed. Zahra-Ahmed, the child of a wealthy father in Morocco, is brought up as a boy to safeguard the honour and fortune of the father and to conform to the dominant patriarchal system. Ben Jelloun gives a number of accounts of fantasy, sex, irrationality and mental illness, the same accounts used in orientalist texts to describe the Arabs and Islam. Ben Jelloun produces an essentially Western text by building on certain concepts of Islamic mysticism, whilst ignoring their historical contexts.

In *La Nuit sacrée*, Ben Jelloun makes numerous references to Islam and to its Book. These include the questions of children to the blind teacher (the Consul): "Puisque l'islam est la meilleure des religions, pourquoi Dieu a attendu si longtemps pour la faire répandre?" (79) (Since Islam is the best religion, why did God wait so long before revealing it?). There are also implications that Islam condones rape and torture, sorcery and charlatanism. The text is littered with images of the dead and ghosts, precisely what some orientalist discourses maintain in their depiction of the Arabs and Islam.

> Ghosts are the remains of the dead. They are echoes of former times and former lives: those who have died but still remain, hovering between erasure of the past and the indelibility of the present — creatures out of time. Muslims too, it seems, are often thought to be out of time: throwbacks to medieval civilizations who

are caught in the grind and glow of 'our' modern culture. It is
sometimes said that Muslims belong to cultures and societies that
are moribund and have no vitality — no life of their own. Like
ghosts they remain with us, haunting the present.[15]

Ben Jelloun's text carries with it the implication that Moroccan life is irrational, depraved, childlike, raging, dark, angry and different, in opposition to what is rational, virtuous, mature and normal, and Islamic society is depicted in a contrast to Christendom, the West and modernity. Islam is almost always referred to in negative and antithetical terms. Hiding behind mysticism and straddling two cultures, one of which is attached to specific and diverse locales and histories in the Third World, Ben Jelloun, the alien yet half familiar writer from Morocco, addresses his text primarily to readers in the West.

Representation, stereotyping, strategies of signification and power: the network in which a culture is fashioned does appear as a texture of signs linked by endless connotations and denotations, a meaning system of inextricable complexity that is reflected, developed and recorded in the multifarious act of writing.[16]

In *La Nuit Sacrée*, Ben Jelloun is aware of the fact that he is invisible and subversive in his representations of Arabs and Islam. He is quoted by Samia Mehrez as having said in a French television talk-show that it would have been impossible for him to write in Arabic in the same way that he wrote in French due to the sensitivities and the taboo nature of the topics. This, I suggest, is rather an extraordinary statement. Is Arabic unable to handle his topics? Is the average Moroccan reader, or the wider Arab audience, unable to cope with what he, Ben Jelloun, has to say? His rationale is similar to that of a publisher who told Edward Said that Arabic was a controversial language.[17]

## Back to the Original — *La Nuit sacrée* in Arabic

*Laylatu l-Qadr*, the Arabic translation of *La Nuit sacrée*, appeared in 1987, the same year in which the text was published in French.[18] The Arabic text was published within a series named ᶜ*awdatu n-naS* (the return of the text), that aims to translate bestselling MFL works into Arabic, and which is sponsored by the Éditions du Seuil, the French publisher of *La Nuit sacrée*. Unfortunately the translation of texts like

Ben Jelloun's back into Arabic does not seem to serve any return of any kind because it does not stimulate any cultural innovation or positively assess indigenous traditions and identities. La Nuit sacrée, like most of Ben Jelloun's writing, presents thorny problems for translation, including a significant number of passages which the author "translated" from Arabic. Translating these embedded passages into Arabic eliminates the element of the play with the French language which is a vital aspect of the source. Such translations are mainly addressed to an élite of bilingual readers. Manipulative strategies are used in order to camouflage Ben Jelloun's initial invisibility and violence, and the language is highly formal, often archaic, including Islamic references in an apparent attempt to pacify Arab readers. Ben Jelloun's overt faithfulness to his target audience, that is the residents of metropolitan France, and his enthusiasm for the extremes of exotica, together with his representation of Moroccan locales as godforsaken places, pre-empt proper appreciation of his work in Arabic. The problem, thus, of translating texts such as La Nuit sacrée is not restricted to linguistic codes, but includes also the translation which is inherent in the French text and the invisibility that went into its creation.

Ben Jelloun opted for *La Nuit sacrée* (The Sacred/Holy Night) as the title of his text in French (FT henceforth), a phrase which, to his French readers, intertextualizes with *Les Mille et une nuits* (A Thousand and One Nights). This strategy keeps his choices and the narrative in line with "exotization" and "naturalization". Chapter two of the French text is entitled *La Nuit du destin* (The Night of Destiny), a choice approximately equivalent in signification to the Arabic translation. The Arabic translator chooses *Laylatu l-Qadr* (The Night of Destiny/fate/preordination) to render both this and the main title of the book. Regarding this translational choice, Mehrez notes:

> This Arabic title is not a literal translation of the French words which remain alien to the cultural referent provided by the Arabic sign. The bilingual reader, however, is bound to make these necessary translations as soon as he or she begins to read the French text. If anything, therefore, the French title (of the original) fails to translate the Arabic subtext in which the entire work is grounded. ... Consequently, the French title is decentered and deterritorialized by the Arabic sign which the bilingual reader is expected to read/translate into the French text.[19]

Though I would tend to agree with the thrust of Mehrez's argument, I do have two misgivings: borrowing from the *Koran*, a sensitive text, to translate the main title of the FT and that of its chapter two seems to be a calculated ploy to put some distance between the Arabic text (AT henceforth) and its receiving constituencies; and furthermore any translation is first and foremost intended for monolinguals, not Mehrez's bilingual readers.

The translator uses "*ar-rawD al-ᶜaaTir*" (fragrant or perfumed meadow or garden) to translate both the title of chapter four, "*Le jardin parfumé*" (The Perfumed Garden) as well as the structure "le jardin exotique" (the exotic garden) in chapter nine. This choice is another example of the foreignizing appropriation of the language to manipulate readers. The phrase "ar-rawD al-caaTir" not only usually refers to paradise in Islamic culture, but also appears as a constituent element in the titles of some medieval Arabic texts on sexuality and related topics: aphrodisiacs, genitalia, etc. The Arabic translator seems to play on these intertextual referents, bewildering the AT audience.

In rendering the title of chapter fourteen, *La comédie du bordel* (The comedy of the brothel), the translator opts for an archaism that is not easily intelligible to the average Arab reader, hence "kumiidyaa l-maakhuur" (the Comedy of the House of Prostitution, or the Comedy of the Whorehouse) is used. At once the Arabic translator transliterates the word "comédie", yet archaicises his translation of "bordel". A more fluent, domesticating option would have been to use a phrase such as "mahzalat l-bordeiil" (the farce/comedy of the brothel) where the French word "bordel" is transliterated, since this is already in common usage among the target audience.

The AT overflows with uncommon and strange linguistic forms that reveal the translator's hand: a systematic use of archaisms is apparent at the lexical level, with the frequent use of specialised language regarding body parts and diseases, which possibly indicates the desire to elevate the tenor with lofty and highbrow language. The translator also increases the conceptual density of the language and, thus, moves it away from the everyday usage of Arabic in Moroccan society and in the wider Arab World. In cases such as with our AT, argues Venuti[20], the translator's lexical choices rely on limited usage, and are not easily processable by the average reader. By their difficulty, such choices attract attention from and disturb the effects of the language that surrounds them.

The Arabic translator's lexical choices are in complete contrast with the unidiomatic lexis and style of the FT. The AT's transparent foreignizing strategy applies at several levels: lexical, syntactical and cultural, and can be easily illustrated. Phrases that are in common usage in French: "sans rien dire", "sans rien répondre", and "je ne dis rien" (without saying anything), all become "lam yanbus bibinti shafa" (literally "not utter the daughter of a lip"), an archaic collocation that is not easy to decipher. The translator could have opted for common usage in Modern Arabic: "sakata" (kept silent) or "lam yaqul shay'an" (did not say anything).

"J'ai pleuré" (34) becomes "inkharTtu fi l-bukaa'" (26) (I entered into/associated myself with crying) in lieu of "bakaytu" (I cried);

"ramène" (43) becomes "ya'uub" (34) (to come back with) instead of "jalaba" (brought back);

"filiformes" (65) becomes "khayTiyyataa sh-shakl" (50) (filamentous) instead of something like "naHifataan" or "naHiilataan" (skinny/thin);

"eau pure" (93) becomes "maa' namiir" (70) (good/pure/clear water) instead of "maa' Saafii" (pure water);

"il émane de votre peau" (99) becomes "yataDawwac min jildik" (75) (it exudes/emanates/diffuses from your skin) instead of a common translation like "yasiilu min jildik" (flows from your skin);

"les fesses" (90) becomes "ilyatayhaa" (68) (her two buttocks), an anatomical term, instead of the colloquial "mu'akhiratuhaa" (her backside);

"noircie par les vomissures" (115) becomes "mudlahimma bitaqayyu'aat" (90) (pitch-black/deep-black/tenebrous of vomit) instead of "swaddat bitaqayyu'aat" (blackened with vomit);

"coupé le nez" (118) becomes "satajda$^c$ anfii" (will amputate my nose) instead of the more intelligible "satqTa$^c$ anfii" (will cut off my nose);

"générosité" (136) becomes "a-laryaHiyya" (104) instead of either "karam" or "juud" (generosity), a more fluent and intelligible choice; and

"Il me fallait pas" (184) becomes "kaana laa manduHata" (145) (there was no alternative/choice/option for me) instead of the common usage "kaana ᶜalayya" (I had to).

Furthermore the AT frequently goes to the unusual lengths of providing vowels, in order to assist pronunciation, even though vocalisation does not normally feature in Arabic texts.

The AT also contains a number of transliterated adaptations of French words: "smoking" (11/9), "naphtaline" (124/97), "babouches" (187/148), and includes very technical terms for diseases and body parts, that occur in the passages referring to rape and sex. Consider: "al-ᶜuDwu l-jinsii l-'unthawii" (the female sexual organ) instead of the common term: "farj" (vagina). Such lexis would not be out of place in a Friday sermon at a mosque, or in technical dictionaries and medical textbooks.

The most telling example, perhaps, is the translation of "bougainvillées" (35) into Arabic as "jahnamiyyaatt" (26). Aware of the strangeness of the Arabic term, the translator provides a footnote. But the irony is that the footnote itself turns out to be too technical, itself needing a footnote; putting added burdens on the reader.

The language of the AT is highbrow and extremely poetic, through excessive reliance on archaisms that often prove strange or even incomprehensible, in an attempt, perhaps, to whitewash the exoticization which Ben Jelloun adopted in the FT. At times, the translator adopts the strategies of *concretization* or *particularization* so as to narrow the meaning. On occasions he renders the French word "erreur" (error) as either "Dalaal" (aberration), on others as "maᶜSiyya" (sin), both of them Arabic terms which have specific religious connotations in Islam. In fact the more mundane term "khaTa'" (error/mistake) would equate with the French "erreur".

One might argue that perhaps the translator's aim was to address a wider pan-Arab audience, and not just Moroccans or Maghrebis. But the fact that he used a typically Moroccan lexis to describe what is quintessentially Moroccan would tend to deny this. The use of the local

Moroccan Arabic terms for tea and its ingredients, "biit l-maa" (Lit. the room of water (ie., toilet)), words for food and clothing, those words used for streets and alleyways ("derb", "zanqa"), certain narcotics ("kif") would all impair intelligibility for Arabs from the Middle East. I should note here that in the translation words related to specifically Moroccan references are merely transliterated from the French, Ben Jelloun having transliterated them in his FT from Arabic.

At the level of syntax and punctuation, the AT adheres literally to the FT. In the following example, the transliteration of the passage in Arabic is a near copy in terms of the short sentences and punctuation. I have added extra spaces in order to highlight the punctuation marks in both excerpts.

> Alors il vaut mieux rire ... nous ne faisons que passer ... Ne permettons pas au temps de s'ennuyer en notre présence ; faisons en sorte qu'on lui donne quelques satisfactions , avec un peu de fantaisies , avec de la couleur par exemple ; le Consul adore les subtilités des couleurs ; il n'est pas étonnant que cette passion soit celle d'un aveugle ...
> (*La Nuit Sacrée*:105).[21]

> izan mina l-afDali an naDHak ... liannanaa ᶜaabiruun laa ghayr ... falaa yanbaghii an nasmaHa liz-zaman bi'an yas'ama fii HuDuurinaa ; linataSarraf biHaythu nurDiihi baᶜDa sh-shay'i ; biqaliilin mina l-khayaali , billawni mathalan ; 'inna l-qunSula yaᶜshaqu 'ashkaala r-riqqa l-latii lil'alwaan ; wa laysa mudhishan 'an takuuna hazihi lᶜaaTifa naabiᶜa min 'aHadi l-ᶜumyaan ...
> (*Laylatu l-Qadr*:80).

Besides the awkwardness of sentences, the punctuation is unusual to say the least. In a study elsewhere[22] I contrasted the punctuation in Arabic texts taken from prestigious Arabic international daily newspapers to which distinguished Arab writers contribute, with that in texts from British broadsheets. The twenty English texts used 414 commas, 23 semi-colons, and 432 full-stops; while the same number of Arabic texts used 193 commas, no semi-colons at all, and 388 full-stops. One passage in *Laylatu-l-Qadr* contains 4 semi-colons in 4 lines.

Aware of the sensitivity of handling passages from the *Koran* and of the pride the Arabs have in their poetry, Mohammed Sharghi, the translator, intervenes in the presentation of Koranic and poetry quotations, which are given in large, bold fonts, and appropriately introduced. So "Dieu a dit" (God said) becomes "fii qawlihi ta‑caalaa" (in His [exalted/raised far above] words) where the tense, past in the FT, is not marked at all. The French "quatre phrases" (four sentences), which introduces an excerpt from Arabic poetry, becomes "baytayn" (two verses or two lines), echoing the structure of the Arabic classical *Qasiida*, the canonized genre of Arabic classical poetry. What is more peculiar is that the Arabic translation of the poetry is not equivalent to the FT. An excerpt from page 41 of the FT runs as follows:

> Nous sommes les enfants, les hôtes de la terre.
> Nous sommes faits de terre et nous lui reviendrons.
> Pour nous, terrestres, le bonheur ne dure guère,
> mais des nuits de bonheur effacent l'affliction.

> We are the children, the guests of earth.
> We are made of earth, and return to it we shall.
> For us, terrestrials, happiness barely lasts,
> but nights of happiness remove the infliction.
> (My translation)

For which the Arabic translation, *Laylatu-l-Qadr*, gives the following:

> wa lammaa 'an tajahhamanii muraadii    jaraytu ma‑ca zzamaani
>                                         kamaa 'araadaa
> wa hawwantu l-khaTuuba ‑calyya Hattaa    ka'annii Sirtu
>                                          'amnaHuhaa l-widaadaa

> And, when my aim got sick of me,
> I ran the way time ran
> And, I lessened the effects of my misfortunes until
> I felt as if offering them affection.
> (My translation)

It would appear that the translator took the liberty of quoting from other parts of the poem, which he felt would be more effective. The wider aim could have been to modify the cognitive environment of the receivers of the AT, and achieve particular illocutionary effects.

Through a combination of archaisms, unusual syntax and punctuation, concretization and adaptations, the AT manages to portray the blurred relationship between reality and fantasy, strange events and characters that Ben Jelloun employs, perhaps, to camouflage his exoticization.

One final point worthy of note is that the translator also retains all intertextual references, as well as references to French literary figures, without offering any assistance which would allow the reader to locate them. For instance *Ulysses* and *Hamlet* are simply transliterated as ᶜ*uliis* and *hamlit* respectively.

Though *La Nuit sacrée* has been described by some as the model of North African literature that is both resister and liberator, it was the Prix Goncourt that located it within world literature and hastened its translation into Arabic. The novel's celebrated bilingualism or translingualism does not make it oppositional to the French cultural representations of the Arabs and Islam.

> Modern world culture has no difficulty in accommodating unstable signs and domesticated exotica, so long as neither conflicts radically with systems of profit.[23]

*La Nuit sacrée* would appear to fit this requirement, but its translation into Arabic reads like an alien text, despite and because of the fact that its source text originated from, but then went far beyond, its indigenous context. Maghrebi writers such as Fatima Mernissi, Abdelkebir Khatibi, Ahmed Bouzfour, Ahmed Madini have been described as resisters and liberators. They can be said to use literary virtuosity to form oblique critiques of life in Arab states, where political oppression and activism are features of daily life, but Ben Jelloun and Mohammed Shargi are not of this ilk. The complexity of male-female dynamics, for example, cannot be furthered by narratives such as Ben Jelloun's, but can only be appropriately and effectively considered within the contexts of the correlations as well as the contradictions between Islam, as religion, history, laws, social realities, traditional-modern family fabrics, modernist versus conservative Arab discourses, aspirations and economic dilemmas.

Ben Jelloun avoids all these issues, focusing instead on ghosts and saints, sex, rape and mutilation in the name of Allah, satisfying along the way desires of a West that is more interested in new translations of the *One Thousand and one Nights* than in the intricacies of contemporary Arab literature. Not surprisingly, he proceeds in a predictable, even predetermined direction: alien cultures, indigenous practices — some fabricated — are recuperated through pseudo-translations via a process of familiarization and assimilation to existing norms. And, true, Ben Jelloun presents in his text "nights" that intertextualize with the ever popular "nights". Not only does he fulfill Khatibi's request "*Apprends-moi à parler dans tes langues*"[24], but he has mastered dangerously the invisible translation of Morocco, Arabs and Islam, to his French readers. Instead of being an exploration of the relationships between opposites, racial, religious, social, linguistic, or a critique of 1980s society in Morocco, Ben Jelloun's *La Nuit sacrée* merely affirms its status as a Western text, but one which was written by a non-Westerner.

The following quote from Jacquemond bears relevance to *La Nuit sacrée*, a work which leans heavily on translation in itself, and throws light on *Laylatu l-Qadr*, its arabically alien translation: "Et ces «documents» sont d'autant mieux reçus qu'ils viennent confirmer à la fois l'altérité de l'autre culture (arriérée, autoritaire ...) et la représentation que la culture française se donne d'elle même (moderne, démocratique ...) — confirmation qui, venant de l'autre, n'est que plus gratifiante."[25] Ben Jelloun is the exotic entertainer of Paris, who manages to do a superb job for orientalism, as expounded by Edward Said in terms of its poetics and ideology.[26]

Said Faiq

### Notes

1 Carol F. Coates, "The Political Subtext of Translation: Examples from Francophone Literature", in Marilyn Gaddis Rose (ed.), *Translation Perspectives IX*, Binghamton: State University of New York, 1996, 215.
2 Josef Jungmann quoted in Vladimir Macura, "Culture as Translation", in Susan Bassnett & André Lefevere (eds), *Translation, History & Culture*, London: Cassell, 1990, 68.
3 Lawrence Venuti, "Translation as Social Practice: or, The Violence of Translation", in *Translation Perspectives IX*, 196.

4   Lawrence Venuti, *The Translator's Invisibility: A History of Translation*, London & New York: Routledge, 1995.
5   Edward Said, *Orientalism*, London: Penguin Books, 1995. The 1978 edition by Routledge & Kegan Paul.
6   Edward Said, "Embargoed Literature", in Anuradha Dingwaney & Carol Maier (eds), *Between Languages and Cultures*, Pittsburgh & London: University of Pittsburgh Press, 1995, 97.
7   Jenine Abboushi Dallal, "The perils of occidentalism", *The Times Literary Supplement*, 24 April 1998, 8-9.
8   Richard Jacquemond, "Translation and Cultural Hegemony: The Case of French-Arabic Translation", in Lawrence Venuti (ed.), *Rethinking Translation*, London & New York: Routledge, 1992, 139-58.
9   Richard Jacquemond, "Pour une économie et une poétique de la traduction de et vers l'arabe", in Miguel Hernando de Larramendi & Gonzalo Fernández Parrilla (eds), *Pensamiento y circulatión de las ideas en el Mediterráneo: el papel de la traducción*, Cuenca: Editiones de la Universidad de Castilla-La Mancha, 1997, 149-62.
10  Samia Mehrez, "Translation and the Postcolonial Experience: The Francophone North African Text", in *Rethinking Translation*, 122.
11  Isabelle Larrivée, "Khatibi Interlangues", in Mdaghri Alaoui & A Zeggaf (eds), *L'interculturel au Maroc*, Casablanca: Afrique Orient, 1994, 57.
    "...if Maghrebi bilingualism contributes to the inscription of literature as a subject of history, writing, then, rewrites history, a history of a subject that, paradoxically, melts within it. In this sense, we can say that there are "French" as there are writers and languages. Maghrebi literature of French expression is in effect, according to Khatibi, a "narrative of translation": translation from a familiar, yet other, language, and translation from French into French." (My translation).
12  "Pour une économie et une politique de la traduction de et vers l'arabe".
13  Tahar Ben Jelloun, *La Nuit Sacrée*, Paris: Éditions du Seuil, 1987.
14  Tahar Ben Jelloun, *L'Enfant de sable*, Paris: Éditions du Seuil, 1985.
15  Bobby Sayyid, *A Fundamental Fear*, London & New York: Zed Books, 1997, 1.
16  Ovidio Carbonell (1996) "The Exotic Space of Cultural Translation", in *Translation, Power, Subversion* (eds), Román Álvarez & Carmen-África Vidal, Clevedon: Multilingual Matters, 1996, 81.
17  *Orientalism*, 1995, 97.
18  Tahar Ben Jelloun, *Laylatu-l-Qadr* (The Night of Destiny), translation by Mohammed Sharghi. Casablanca: Toubqal/Éditions du Seuil, 1987.
19  "Translation and the Post-colonial experience", 128.
20  Lawrence Venuti, *The Scandals of Translation*, London and New York: Routledge, 1998.

21 *La Nuit sacrée*, 105: "So it would be better to laugh ... all we do is pass by ... We should not allow time to be bored with our presence; doing sorts to give it some satisfaction, with a little fantasy, with colour for example; the Consul adores the subtleties of colours; it is not strange that this passion is that of a blind person," (My translation).
22 Said Faiq, "A Semiotic solution to the intricacies of translation into Arabic, in Anghelescu", in N. and A. Avram (eds), *Proceedings of the Colloquium on Arabic Linguistics*, Bucharest: Center for Arab Studies, 1995, 145-65.
23 Talal Asad, "A Comment on Translation, Critique, and Subversion", in *Between Languages and Cultures*, 331.
24 Abdelkebir Khatibi, *Amour Bilingue*, Casablanca: Editions Eddif, 1992, 131. "Teach me how to speak in your languages." (My translation).
25 "Pour une économie et une poétique...", 157. "These documents are well received because they simultaneously confirm the otherness of the other culture (backward, authoritarian...), and the representation the French culture bestows upon itself (modern, democratic...); a confirmation, emanating from the other, is utterly gratifying". (My translation).
26 Edward Said, *Covering Islam*, London: Vintage 1997 (first published by Routledge and Kegan Paul, 1981).

## 15.
## THE IMAGINARY QUAY FROM WATERLOO BRIDGE TO LONDON BRIDGE: TRANSLATION, ADAPTATION AND GENRE

In the early 1990s a study was undertaken on behalf of the Commission of the European Communities into the circulation of books within the CE. As far as the United Kingdom was concerned, this report does not make for very satisfactory reading. Although the UK had the second largest publishing industry in Europe (being narrowly pipped by that of Germany), it also had the lowest rate of translation of the eleven member states. More concretely, some 67,628 books were brought out in 1993, of which translation was represented by a mere 1,689 titles (3%). Even countries such as Greece and Portugal, both with considerably smaller publishing industries, brought out almost as many or more books than the UK in translation. In the case of Greece, whose total output was only 4,693 books, translation was represented by 1,667 titles (36%); while in the case of Portugal, with a slightly higher output of 6,430 titles, 2,809 books were translations (44%). Germany had a translation rate of 14% (of 67,890 books published); Spain of 24% (of 43,896 books); and France 18% (of 39,535 books).[1]

This situation has not changed dramatically since the Commission's study was published. Gordon Fielden, citing figures published in *The Bookseller* of 20th February, 1998, puts the total number of books published in the UK at around 100,000 with a translation rate of 2-3%. Writing primarily for an audience of professional translators, the author tries to find a cause for some optimism in these statistics: "Well, the figures themselves are not quite as bad at they look. Since 100,000 new titles were published last year [1997], even 2% means that there were 2,000 translations up for grabs."[2] Perhaps. But for those whose interest lies primarily in literary translation, there is little cause for rejoicing. Of those 2,000 titles, something in the region of 29% will be in the field of science and technology; 31% in social sciences; children's books and school books will account for 12%; a further 9% will be of a miscellaneous nature — leaving approximately 19% (or a maximum of 380 titles) in the literary domain (including poetry). Of these 380 or so titles, a significant proportion will be published by small or cultural presses with inadequate resources for marketing or distribution; a couple of dozen will doubtless appear in the form of high quality paperbacks intended for sixth-formers and undergraduates; and a certain number will comprise American translations published under UK imprints. The number of contemporary European novels published by mainstream publishing houses with access to proper marketing and channels of distribution will be extremely small.

In short, there is not a great deal of activity happening in Britain as far as literary translation is concerned. What activity there is tends to be poorly remunerated as far as the translator is concerned; will often be published in small print runs (some high quality paperback imprints sell as few as 1,000 copies per annum, below that point titles tend to be dropped from the list, while a 2,000 print run can be a substantial investment for a small press); and is often aimed as specialist markets. Indeed, it would not be far wide of the mark to claim that literary translation represents a place apart from the mainstream of publishing in the UK. Translators have specific organisations representing their interests (even if one of the most important is a subsidiary group within the Society of Authors); their publishers tend to occupy positions in niche markets; and it is generally felt that their work does not receive the recognition it is due in the form of press coverage or reviews. Equally significant is the fact that there is little synergy between literary translation and other art forms: television and radio adaptations of foreign works are few and far between and, outside the subsidised theatre, stage plays in translation are the exception rather than the rule.

In order to understand the current status and practices of literary translation in the UK it is necessary to have an idea of the status and practices of translation in the recent past. The current precarious foothold that literary translation has in the UK marketplace would have astonished a Victorian theatre reviewer or literary critic. How can we account for the cultural change?

In 1900, towards the end of his career, the journalist and writer Henry Sutherland Edwards published his memoirs: *Personal Recollections*.[3] Although now largely forgotten, in his day Sutherland

Edwards (1828-1906) was a figure of some substance in Victorian literary circles. It would appear that his career commenced in the late 1840s with occasional articles and illustrations for *Punch*, the satirical weekly magazine. By the mid-1850s he was Russian correspondent for the *Illustrated Times*; in 1869 he became the first editor of the newly-founded *Graphic*; and in 1870 covered the Franco-Prussian War on behalf of *The Times*. In addition to this he also penned, probably in collaboration with his wife, a string of novels which would seem to have enjoyed some success in the circulating libraries. Among these works is an early historical mystery novel, *The Missing Man* (1885). He also wrote a number of plays and opera libretti.[4] All in all, Sutherland Edwards might be considered — with his combined journalistic, literary and dramaturgic interests — a fairly typical example of the successful Victorian man-of-letters.

One might expect his memoirs to deal mainly with matters of purely domestic interest: his relationship with newspaper proprietors, publishers and theatre managers in Victorian London, anecdotes concerning famous actresses and politicians, and so on. However, although these matters are all touched upon, occasionally in some detail, Sutherland Edwards's autobiography is surprisingly cosmopolitan in outlook. In the opening chapter, for example, we are informed of the origins of the "polka" (apparently, it came to London in 1846 and before long was introduced into "every imaginable" stage performance); regaled with a history of the moustache (said to be a French importation about the time of the Crimean War); and provided with an analysis of why Englishwomen were reluctant to travel in hansom cabs (to do so was not only potentially dangerous for one's reputation but also, given the proneness of such vehicles to overturn, to run a risk of physical injury). Only with the introduction of the continental four-wheeler about the time of the 1851 Great Exhibition, claims the author, did respectable women begin to make use of cabs in any shape or form. Even so, for a considerable time the opinion was that for a woman to be seen in a hansom was to make her appear among "the most unconventional, the most daring, the fastest of their sex." Not only did the Continent provide the more respectable (and safer) four-wheeler however, but contact with France also contributed to the gradual liberation of mores which ultimately made it acceptable for women to be admitted into restaurants and hotels, even to ride bicycles without public censure.

On this evidence alone the author would stand convicted of being a Europhile, but when it comes to describing the cultural life of the country it would seem as if he was virtually cut off from any specifically English art forms. With regard to the opera, he discusses the work of Meyerbeer, Rossini, Bellini, Donizetti and Verdi; for light music he prefers Strauss; while in passing he refers to a light comedy by Meilhac and Halévy concerning lady cyclists. Even the arrangement and pricing of seats in theatres is claimed to demonstrate a continental influence: "Stalls were the invention of the ingenious Mr. Benjamin Lumley, who doubtless borrowed the idea from the *fauteuils d'orchestre* of the Paris Opera House and the Théâtre des Italiens."[5] (11) All this, remember, is in the opening chapter of his memoirs. Not only this though, but on the basis of subsequent chapters it would seem that even such traditional icons of English culture as Shakespeare were out of fashion for much of the nineteenth century. In the mid-century, Sutherland Edwards informs us, many theatre managers considered that "Shakespeare spelt ruin". A distinguished theatre critic of the period is cited who is claimed to have written: "If Shakespeare were alive and produced a new piece, we would go with pleasure to see it. But we know *Hamlet, Othello,* and *Macbeth* by heart, and we would rather sit at home and stare for four hours at a bare wall than see either of them performed." Elsewhere he asks: "How many first-rate five-act comedies are there in the English language? Only one, [Sheridan's] *The School for Scandal.*" (175)

Even when Sutherland Edwards discusses the works of his contemporaries, the influence of the continent, and particularly France, is never very far away. Take the case of Charles Reade (1814-80), the English playwright and novelist. "His plays [...] were adaptations from the French", claims Edwards, "and by the last of these, *Drink* [based on Emile Zola's *L'Assommoir*], he must have realised a small fortune." (45) Paradoxically, however, we learn that Reade was apparently the first British author to buy the rights to a play from the French author (prior to international copyright agreements the custom was to simply make unauthorised adaptations and translations) and even publicised the fact in a book on the rights of authors entitled *The Eighth Commandment* (1860). But it was not only Reade's theatre which was mainly inspired by French sources, his prose fiction generally had similar origins too. The 1869 novel *Foul Play* (written in collaboration with Dion Boucicault), for example, is said to be based on a French melodrama entitled *Le Portefeuille Rouge*.

Henry Sutherland Edwards's *Personal Recollections* are more than a little inconvenient as far as present day translation theory is concerned. Firstly, he presents a view of British culture as not only vastly inferior to that of France but also, and especially with respect to the stage, enormously receptive to foreign influences. Indeed, but for the fact that Britain was never economically or politically dependent on France, he might almost be mistaken for describing a relationship which would nowadays be termed post-colonial. Certainly, the French stage, French painting, and French music receive considerable praise: Britain, he claims, was "no more a dramatic nation then [in the mid-century] than we are a musical nation now [in 1906]." (175) Secondly, merely in quantitative terms, Sutherland Edwards provides a picture of a Britain in which a considerable amount of translation was occurring across a range of art forms. If this picture of the second-half of the nineteenth century is accurate, translation theory needs to be able to account for the considerable changes which have taken place during the intervening period. Thirdly, Edwards describes a culture in which not only translation flourished but which also saw a considerable amount of adaptation. Indeed, it might well be claimed, at least as far as the stage was concerned, that virtually every translation involved to a greater or less extent a process of adaptation. Not only this though but the adaptation practices he describes frequently involve issues of intermediality — French plays may be turned into English novels (as was the case with Reade's *Foul Play*); French novels may be turned into English plays (as was the case with the same author's *Drink*). Hitherto, translation theorists have tended to avoid not only the issue of adaptation (perhaps because the issues involved cannot be described as linguistic) but also those of intermediality. These questions — the extent of French cultural hegemony in the nineteenth century and its displacement; adaptation; and intermediality — cannot and should not be ignored.

To what extent is Sutherland Edwards' analysis correct though? With regard to the stage at least the situation has long been recognised. "Indeed, so strong is the influence exerted by the French theater", wrote the biographer of Charles Reade's friend and occasional collaborator Tom

Taylor (1817-1880), "that some understanding of it is a prerequisite to an analysis of the development of nineteenth-century English drama."[6] Less hesitant in his pronouncements elsewhere, the same author claims that the French influence was at its height between 1850 and 1870 — so much so that a number of newspapers systematically misprinted the title of T. W. Robertson's 1866 play *Ours* as *L'Ours*.[7]

In fact, the French theatre defined the four most common theatrical forms of the mid-century: the *féerie*, the *mélodrame*, the *comédie-vaudeville*, and the *pièce bien faite*. The *féerie* was a type of spectacular show (the staple form of the early Victorian theatre) reliant on magical, fantastic or supernatural elements. Imported directly from France, it is a form which is surprisingly undocumented given its importance in the development of the early cinema. The *mélodrame* (as distinct from the English *melodrama*) was a hybrid form which included spectacle and music combined with an exciting story, pathos, humour and mystery. The first stage adaptation of John Polidori's *The Vampyre* (1819), for example, relocated the action to Scotland and introduced a number of musical interludes. Appropriately, the stage adaptation was the work of three French authors (P.F.A. Carmouche, A.F.L. de Jouffroy d'Abbans and Charles Nodier) — the English version representing an adaptation by James Robinson Planché of the French adaptation. As Taylor's biographer remarks, "Almost all the melodramas produced on the English stage before 1825 were based on French pieces or on novels and tales."[8] Even, as in this case, where the work being dramatized was British in origin, the process of dramatization was initially engaged abroad. As early as 1830 however, the *mélodrame* was a form which had been entirely domesticated — i.e. English writers had learned and absorbed the techniques of stagecraft associated with the form such that it had been internalised within the British theatrical tradition.

Historically, the *féerie* and the *mélodrame* were less important than the *comédie-vaudeville* (a farce studded with songs set to popular tunes) and the related form of the *pièce bien faite*. It is the playwright Eugène Scribe who is generally credited with having refined the crude two-act *comédie-vaudeville* into relatively sophisticated five-act "comedy drama". "A Scribe play, long or short, is a masterpiece of plot construction", wrote Tolles. "It is as artistically put together as a master watch; the smallest piece is perfectly in place, and the removal of any part would ruin the whole."⁹ When Sutherland Edwards asks how many first-rate five-act comedies there are in the English language, he is implicitly thinking of the *pièce bien faite* in the manner of Scribe. From the point of view of Translation Studies, however, it is not only the fact that an enormous number of such plays were translated, adapted and performed on the British stage in the period in question. Equally important was the fact that it was by means of translation and adaptation that English playwrights mastered the craft of constructing works in the same style. As Tolles again remarks: "Nothing in them was so deeply embedded in French life that it could not be transferred easily to an English setting. The alteration of a character's name made him as English as he had been French; a drawing-room in London had as many doors for opportune exits and entrances as one in Paris. The art of arranging the incidents, although difficult to duplicate, was easy to imitate."¹⁰

As we shall see, Tolles's distinction between *duplication* and *imitation* is perhaps a specious one. Certainly, the process by which French plays (and, indeed, prose works) were turned into English plays was by no means quite so simple as he suggests. Sutherland Edwards provides an interesting example of this in relation to Charles Reade's adaptation of Auguste Maquet's *Le Château de Grantier*. Reade bought the copyright to Maquet's play from him for forty pounds during a visit to Paris in 1851.¹¹ This was an extremely unusual step, unique even, at the time. Maquet, who was conversant both with publishing practices and the theatre (for many years he had been the principal ghost-writer for Alexandre Dumas), was clearly embarrassed and even insisted that a clause should be inserted in the agreement between them that if Reade should not succeed in getting the play put on within two years half the money he had advanced would be returned to him. Reade assured him that this was unnecessary. In the event, the play remained unstaged until 1867 when, as *The Double Marriage*, it opened at the new Queen's Theatre in Long Acre with Ellen Terry in the lead role. Even then it was not a success. Apparently, when Rose de Baurepaire, the character played by Terry, admitted to being the mother of her sister's baby, the audience "instead of being awed [...] burst into derisive laughter."¹²

Meanwhile, Reade, despairing no doubt of having the play staged, had adapted it into a serial for *The London Journal* (beginning in July

1857), then edited by Mark Lemon. But, as *White Lies*, it proved as disastrous there as it would later prove on the stage. Indeed, the drop in circulation was said to be so great that the new proprietors of *The London Journal* sold it back to its former owners as a considerable loss.[13]

The lack of success of Reade's adaptation, either as a play or as a novel, cannot be attributed to the fact that it was a translation however. A few blocks away, Tom Taylor had a string of successes at the Olympic Theatre with plays adapted from the French, including *Still Waters Run Deep* (1855) and *The Ticket-of-Leave Man* (1863). Indeed, claims have been put forward for both plays as the most popular to be produced on the British and American stages during the nineteenth century. Maquet's play had proved popular enough in France; Reade's adaptation is considered solid enough; and Alfred Wigan, the manager of the Queen's Theatre, had learned his trade at a number of other theatres. In fact, it is difficult to determine precisely the number of French plays performed on the London stage during the period in question. In 1856, Reade was in the news again when, having bought the English rights to a play by Edouard Brisebarre and Eugène Nus entitled *Les Pauvres de Paris*, he placed an announcement in *The Times* threatening legal action against anyone who should endeavour to produce another version or imitation. Within a short while he was embroiled in three legal actions: one with a certain Ben Barnett and J. B. Johnstone, authors of a drama entitled *The Pride of Poverty, or the Real Poor of London*, and two with the manager of the Strand Theatre who had commissioned the play. The costs of these actions amounted to £270, of which Reade only recovered some £60 (and that after further legal action). On the positive side, another manager voluntarily offered Reade £20 for the right to stage an adaptation entitled *Fraud and its Victims* by a certain J. Stirling Coyne. It is unlikely that either of these plays would be linked to the French original had it not been for Reade's litigious crusade. Reade's own version, as *Poverty and Pride*, was presented in 1857. But there was at least one other English version, Dion Boucicault's *The Streets of London* (1864), which was staged in New York and London.[14] In other word, one original work spawned at least four English versions.

Indeed, there was no real consciousness amongst those involved in the theatre between original authorship, adaptation and translation.

## The Imaginary Quay from Waterloo Bridge to London Bridge: Translation, Adaptation and Genre

Tom Taylor, writing in 1871, claimed, for example, that the term "a play" meant that the work was translated; "a new play" meant that the material had been reworked (i.e. adapted); and that "a new and original play" indicated that the work in question only bore the slightest hint of a resemblance to another work.[15] Convenient though such a taxonomy may be, it is not even reliable with regard to the author's own work as a playwright.

Much of Reade's discussion of the question of intellectual rights is based on a pecuniary argument. Why should an author be deprived of the reward for his labour simply because his work is performed outside his own country? But this is not the only issue involved, as the analysis of the prose fiction of many of Reade's contemporaries consistently demonstrates. M.E. Braddon (1835-1915), whose relationship with the publisher Tinsley is the subject of an important chapter in Sutherland Edwards's *Personal Recollections* (a source, incidentally, which would not seem to be generally known to Braddon scholars), is a case in point. Remembered primarily for *Lady Audley's Secret* (1862), an extremely successful example of the emerging sensation novel (and considered by some to be the earliest example of the detective novel in the English language), in the course of a long literary career Braddon published more than eighty novels and collections of short stories (excluding unacknowledged works). Of these, at least five are either translation or adaptations of French works (a more detailed examination of Braddon's *oeuvre* would undoubtedly reveal other examples): *The Doctor's Wife* (1864) is clearly indebted, as we shall see, to Gustave Flaubert's *Madame Bovary* (1857); *Circe* (1867), the subject of a lively controversy in *The Pall Mall Gazette*, was quickly recognised as being based on Octave Feuillet's *Dalila*, a Parisian box-office hit of ten years previously; *Dead Sea Fruit* (1868) is taken (at the author's own admission in her correspondence) from an unidentified French play; *The Golden Calf* (1883) is modelled on Zola's *L'Assommoir* (1877), though the author no longer tells the story of a workman's ruin by drink but that of a young English barrister; and *Gerard; or, The World, the Flesh, and the Devil* (1891) is the result of a long-standing desire (first mentioned in a letter of 1866) to write "a semi-supernatural novel, a humble and popularized — you will say vulgarized — imitation of *Zanoni* and the *Peau de Chagrin*."[16] Although the authors of the French originals are not noted on the title page of any of these works, or in other prefatory material, the author makes relatively little effort to cover her tracks. *La Peau de Chagrin*, for example, is discussed quite openly on several occasions in the course of *Gerard*.

Of these works, the most important in terms of the development of the English novel is *The Doctor's Wife*.[17] Indeed, critics have claimed that much of the plot of George Eliot's *Middlemarch* (1872) may be derived from it, while the character of Eustacia Vye in Hardy's *The Return of the Native* (1878) could well have been modelled on that of Isabel Sleaford.[18] Interestingly, the author of *The Doctor's Wife* was engaged in an extensive correspondence with the author Edward Bulwer-Lytton during the composition of the novel. That correspondence suggests a young writer (though her tenth novel it was the one which exemplifies the greatest artistic integrity she had achieved so far — as is indicated by the later enthusiasm of writers such as George Moore for the work) consciously striving for certain kinds of effects and nuances, discussing the literary technique of Flaubert, Balzac, and Bulwer-Lytton himself, and subject to doubts about the dénouement.[19] In other words, though Braddon may have thoroughly anglicized Flaubert's novel, the process was not undertaken from purely cynical motives. Rather we see an English writer anxious to engage and experiment with a new set of narrative and stylistic devices.

The extent of M.E. Braddon's personal investment in the adaptation of *Madame Bovary* as *The Doctor's Wife* is revealed in a number of ways. First, through the relocation of the novel from the Rouen area (which Flaubert knew so well and where, indeed, he was born) to the London suburb of Camberwell (where Braddon herself lived as a schoolgirl). Secondly, through the author's close identification of her younger self with the heroine, both with regard to her family background and her mental development. Thirdly, through the creation of the character Sigismund Smith, a hack author, though a relatively successful one, who makes a living from the penny dreadful market. In fact, Smith represents another portrait of the author, this time as she was in her mid-twenties (when she was writing serial fiction for periodical publications such as the *Halfpenny Journal*). Not surprisingly, there is no character in *Madame Bovary* corresponding to Smith. And fourthly, and perhaps more arguably, in the empowerment of the heroine. Unlike Emma Bovary, who commits suicide in particularly atrocious circumstances, Isabel Sleaford is rewarded by at the end of the novel by relative financial and intellectual independence. It would also be true to say, however, that some changes were forced on Braddon by the moral climate of the period. Even had she wanted to, it is unlikely that she could have got away with actually depicting an adulterous liaison (the same problem Reade had had to confront when adapting *Le Château de Grantier*) — but the evidence would seem to suggest that Braddon had more subversive ideas for the English *Madame Bovary*.

The character of Sigismund Smith is particularly interesting because he has a considerable amount to say on the question of popular authorship and the use of French sources. Early on, he provides an interesting example of the reliance of English serial fiction on the French *roman feuilleton*:

> What the penny public want is plot, and plenty of it; surprises and plenty of em; mystery, as thick as a November fog. Don't you know the sort of thing? "The clock of St Paul's had just sounded eleven hours;" — it's generally a translation, you know, and St Paul's stands for Notre Dame; — "a man came to appear upon the quay which extends itself the length between the bridges of Waterloo and London." There isn't any quay, you know; but you're obliged to have it so, on account of the plot.'" (45)

The author Braddon particularly had in mind here was probably G.W.M. Reynolds whose *Mysteries of London* and its sequel *The Mysteries of the Court of London* outsold Dickens in the mid-century. Both works are greatly indebted to Eugène Sue in terms of plot construction, narrative devices and characterisation. However, to refer to works of this kind as "translations" is, in the light of our present-day understanding of the word, an unusual use of the term. Braddon, or rather Sigismund Smith, goes on to contrast "translation" with the slightly different practice of the "combination story":

> "Why, you see, when you're doing four great stories a week for a public that must have a continuous flow of incident, you can't be quite as original as a strict sense of honour might prompt you to be; and the next best thing you can do if you haven't got ideas of your own, is to steal other people's ideas in an impartial manner. Don't empty one man's pocket, but take a little bit all round. The combination novel enables a young author to present his public

with all the brightest flowers of fiction neatly arranged into every variety of garland. I'm doing a combination novel now — *The Heart of Midlothian* and the *Wandering Jew*.[20] You've no idea how admirably the two stories blend. [...]" (45)

It would be interesting to know how Miss Braddon would have typified — as "translations" or as "combination novels" — the seven or eight such works she penned for *The Halfpenny Journal* in the four years between 1861 and 1865.[21] Although the remuneration that Sigismund Smith received for his work in this vein may have been adequate, there was little prestige in writing for the newly literate urban working-class. Like his creator, Smith had a mind to the next rung up the literary ladder — the triple-decker novel. This was the staple fare of the Victorian circulating library, and one to which the heroine of *The Doctor's Wife* is patently addicted.

The lower end of the audience for fiction in penny instalments had, of course, no access to French. The same would not seem to have been true of the middle classes and, indeed, at least to some extent, the lower middle classes. Like the heroine of *The Doctor's Wife*, M.E. Braddon would seem to have had an interrupted education and not altogether trouble-free childhood in Camberwell. As Wolff notes, Isabel Sleaford's wayward father is clearly modelled on Braddon's own father, a failed solicitor.[22] Braddon at the same age would no doubt have similar educational attainments to those of her heroine:

> Isabel Sleaford was not quite eighteen years of age. She had been taught a smattering of every thing at a day-school in the Albany Road; rather a stylish seminary in the opinion of the Camberwellians. She knew a little Italian, enough French to serve for the reading of novels that she might have better left unread, and just so much of modern history as enabled her to pick out all the sugarplums in the historian's pages, — the Mary Stuarts and Joan of Arcs and Anne Boleyns, the Iron Masks and La Vallières, the Marie Antoinettes and Charlotte Cordays, luckless Königsmarks and wicked Borgias; all the romantic and horrible stories scattered amid the dry records of Magna Chartas and Reform Bills, clamorous Third Estates and Beds of Justice. She played the piano a little, and sang a little, and painted wishy-washy-looking flowers on Bristol board *from* nature, but not at all *like* nature; for the passion-flowers were apt to come out like blue

muslin frills, and the fuchsias would have passed for prawns with short-sighted people.

Miss Sleaford had received that half-and-half education which is popular with the poorer middle classes. She left the Albany-Road seminary in her sixteenth year, and set to work to educate herself by means of the nearest circulating library. (27-28)

Braddon is not kind to her heroine. Significantly, however, not only has Isabel access to French fiction in the original language but she would also seem to know more of French history, especially revolutionary history, than of English history. Of the nine names specifically mentioned in the above extract, six are French historical personages. Significantly, when Isabel begins to feel some form of romantic attachment with the Byronic Roland Landsdell, author of a volume of verse which is described as "refined and anglicised Alfred-de-Mussetism" (129), she tries to translate his work into French. "They were very difficult: how was she to render even such a simple sentence as "My own Clotilde?" She tried such locutions as "Ma propre Clotilde," "Ma Clotilde particulière;" but she doubted if they were academically correct." (157)

Had M.E. Braddon simply wished to ape *Madame Bovary*, she might have let matters stand. But Isabel Sleaford is not Emma Bovary. Unlike the latter, she does not take a lover (let alone two); she does not defraud her husband; she does not seriously contemplate suicide (except as a poetic gesture). In short, she does little which is particularly wicked. Emma's problem is that she is over-educated for her circumstances, as both her own father and her mother-in-law recognise, and utterly cynical in her desire to experience high-life. Isabel, on the other hand, though the dupe of her reading is also protected by it. When Roland Landsell suggests that she should leave her husband for him, she is horrified: "From first to last she had been misunderstood [...]. It was no Dante, no Tasso, who had wandered by her side: only a dissipated young country squire, in the habit of running away with other people's wives, and glorying in his iniquity." (271) Ultimately, Isabel's attachment to Landsell is entirely Platonic.

Feminist critics have for some time been interested in the manner by which Braddon underlines the traditional moral assumptions of the period. "Instead of abandoning the popular conventions," claims Winifred Hughes, "she circumvents them, using them against themselves, investing them with a new ironic significance."²³ Isabel's addiction to popular romance seems a perfect example of this process. Having carefully constructed the expectation that Isabel's downfall will be caused by her excessive reliance on light literature, an expectation perfectly in keeping with repeated warnings of literary critics of the time as to the deleterious effects of reading French fiction, during the climactic scene of Landsell's attempted seduction of the heroine the argument is turned on its head. Isabel's naiveté, fostered by the consumption of popular fiction, acts as shield to her virtue. Likewise, by the end of the novel, Isabel may have lost both her potential lover (killed in a riding accident after murdering her father) and her husband (a victim of typhoid fever), but she has also gained both maturity and independence. With her new acquired wealth, coupled with a strong interest in charity work and model villages, she has exchanged the constructed role of the local doctor's wife for a profession of her own.²⁴ Elaine Showalter has described *Lady Audley's Secret* as "a carefully controlled fantasy of rebellion and power."²⁵ Although lacking the melodrama of the earlier novel, the same remark would hold true for *The Doctor's Wife*.

The three cultural phenomena examined above — Henry Sutherland Edwards's *Personal Recollections*; the work of Charles Reade and other nineteenth-century stage translators, and the creative process behind the transmutation of Gustave Flaubert's *Madame Bovary* into M. E. Braddon's *The Doctor's Wife* — raise a number of important general issues.

The first of these is the centrality of the concept of adaptation to the Victorian experience whether for the stage or in the realm of prose fiction. Although many of these adaptations, especially for the stage, were undertaken hurriedly with a view for making financial profit, it is equally evident that in some cases at least a considerable degree of personal investment was involved. This is certainly the case with *The Doctor's Wife*. Although it could be argued that Braddon's version domesticates Flaubert's novel both with regard to the moral conventions of the time (if only to the extent that the act of adultery itself is avoided) and the British publishing norm of the triple-decker format, it is also clear that the English author was doing more than simply producing a work which was acceptable to the reading-public at large. Domestic conventions were being probed and challenged as well. Not only this but the very act of Braddon's appropriation of the text of another writer seems, even at the distance of more than a century, to represent a violation of cultural hierarchies and a rejection of the concept of aesthetic distance. This feeling is intensified by reading the author's correspondence with Bulwer-Lytton, presumably only one recipient of such communications among many. Nowadays we might refer to such a network as an interpretative community.

In *Textual Poachers* (1992), a seminal study of the contemporary fan subculture, Henry Jenkins proposes ten ways in which such groups rewrite texts whether for their own pleasure, to be circulated within their own groups, to be published in fanzines or posted on the internet.[26] Four of these categories seem of particular relevance here: moral realignment (i.e. the questioning of the moral universe of the primary text); genre shifting (i.e. the reading of a text within different generic conventions); personalization (i.e. the effacement of the gap between the fan's own experience and the fictional space of the primary text); and emotional intensification (i.e. the exploration of moments of emotional crisis). In *The Doctor's Wife* Braddon indulges in all of these tendencies. We have already discussed in detail the changes Braddon made to the "*hideous* morality"[27] of the original (moral realignment) and the use of her own personal experiences in shaping the narrative (personalization). But the displacement of the text from the French realist mode towards English sensation fiction is also, despite Braddon's occasional assurances to the contrary, a form of genre shifting. Given that the three-decker format is considerably longer than the two volume format of the original, Braddon is given ample opportunity for repeated scenes of repentance, confrontation, and emotional suffering.

As Jenkins remarks elsewhere, "concepts of 'good taste,' appropriate conduct, or aesthetic merit are not natural or universal; rather, they are rooted in social experience and reflect particular class interests". Citing Bourdieu, he continues:

> These tastes often seem 'natural' to those who share them precisely because they are shaped by our earliest experiences as members of a particular cultural group, reinforced by social exchanges, and rationalized through encounters with higher education and other basic institutions that reward appropriate conduct and proper

tastes. (16)

Generally speaking, the nineteenth-century writing community was not schooled in a cultural tradition that separated writing for the stage from writing for magazine publication, which considered adaptation and translation as literary hack-work. The editors and correspondents of the more prestigious monthlies (run by university educated men) might make such distinctions, and occasionally authors such as Miss Braddon would get their knuckles rapped for some flagrant breach of such hierarchies. Even Reade was far from consistent in his support of copyright, getting into trouble with Anthony Trollope in 1872 over an unauthorised stage adaptation of the latter's novel *Ralph the Heir*.[28] According to Trollope, Reade simply did not know the meaning of the expression "literary honesty." This confusion is reflected in Tom Taylor's tentative and doomed attempt to differentiate between original, translated and adapted stage plays and M.E. Braddon's curious use of the term "translation" for what might better be described as a pastiche or calque. But whatever the terminology, from the penny dreadful to the triple-decker, every level of British cultural life in the nineteenth century was affected in some degree by French literature and theatre.

This unrestricted access to material waiting to be translated or adapted gave rise to an enormous sense of experimentation among Victorian writers. Indeed, with regard to the stage it allowed the foundations to be laid for the considerable revival in original writing which began with Wilde. But it is not just the amount of translational activity which was occurring that was significant, it was also the manner in which generic rules were internalised and modified: English playwrights learned to write well-made plays in the Scribe manner, serial novelists learned their craft from the *roman feuilleton*, detective novelists studied the technique of Gaboriau (the structure of Conan Doyle's *A Study in Scarlet*, for example, closely follows the French two-part model: in the first part the detective gets his man; in the second part a rationale for the crime is given in the form of a historical flashback). Just as theorists such as José Lambert, Lieven D'hulst and Katrin van Bragt have hypothesised that translation provided the main impulse for the development of French romanticism in the 1820s and 1830s, it could be argued that the assimilation of French literature in the course of the nineteenth century guided the direction that English literature would take.[29]

From the point of view of literary translation, such a culture was capable of mobilising vast energies. As we have seen, French was a language which even those from relatively modest backgrounds (such as that of Miss Braddon following the abandonment of the family by the father) were expected to acquire if they had any social pretensions. Indeed, it enjoyed a similar prestige to that currently enjoyed today by English as the language of social, political and cultural exchange. Highbrow periodicals such as the *Westminster Review* routinely carried critical articles on recent French publications whether in the field of the social sciences, humanities or *belles-lettres*. Equally significantly, the mobilisation of those energies created a system whereby such texts mutually reinforced each other. There were two different translations of Zola's *L'Assommoir* (1877) published in Britain (one for Vizetelly in 1884 and another by Arthur Symons in 1895) and two more in the United States (both in 1879). But even before the first translation was published in Britain, a certain Henry Llewellyn Williams had produced a penny broadsheet entitled *GERVAISE: A Story of Drink* (1878). Compressing the novel into five chapters, it also strove to supply a happy ending with Gervaise retreating at the last minute from the abyss of alcoholism. By 1879, Reade's stage adaptation was well on its way to earning him a reputed £20,000.[30] In 1883, Braddon added to the list of adaptations with her story of the briefless barrister, *The Golden Calf*. Although all these different versions were vying with each other for sales, they also served to create a market for each other, the more acceptable versions also receiving attention in the newspapers and elsewhere.

By the end of the century such unregulated behaviour was subject to greater control due not only to changes in copyright legislation but also as a result of more active censorship following the Vizetelly trial. Perhaps of even greater significance has been the steady shift of hegenomic power from France to the United States during the course of the twentieth century. The consequence of these phenomena, however, has been the gradual separation in the twentieth century of the function of the writer and the translator — a separation belatedly formalised in the UK by the establishment of the Translators Association in 1958. The rise of the universities, with the careful control of the cultural hierarchies, has led to not only translation being marginalised but also, and perhaps to a greater extent, such practices as adaptation. That translation and adaptation were linked in the context of the nineteenth century seems beyond doubt. And any theoretical model which cannot account for the process of adaptation, or refuses to take it into consideration, is necessarily defective.

Terry Hale

**Notes**

1. *Statistical Approaches to Literary Translation in Europe. A study produced at the request of the Unit Cultural Action of DG X of the Commission of the European Communities by BIPE Conseil*, November 1993. All statistics are derived from this report. Only Ireland, with the smallest publishing industry in Europe (producing only 625 books p.a. at the time the report was written) manifested a translation rate as low as that of the UK.
2. Gordon Fielden, "Down to Business. From Principle to Practice — How the TA [Translators Association] tries to help", *In Other Words*, No. 11, Summer 1998, 11-13 (at 11).
3. London: Cassell, 1900.
4. John Sutherland, *The Longman Companion to Victorian Fiction*, Harlow, Essex: Longman, 1988, 207-208.
5. The orchestra-stall is a highly contested part of the theatre. In 1809, Kemble's attempt to raise the price of admission to the pit resulted in rioting, for example. The social composition of the audience which occupies this area (whether artisanal, middle class or "fashionable") has significant implications with regard to the kind of play which is performed. Indeed, one commentator has described this as a "species of class-war". George Rowell, *The Victorian Theatre, 1792-1914*, Cambridge: Cambridge University Press, 2nd ed. 1985, 3.
6. Winston Tolles, *Tom Taylor and the Victorian Drama*, New York: AMS, 1966, 19. (This study was first published in 1940).
7. *Ibid.*, 20.
8. *Ibid.*, 22.
9. *Ibid.*, 22.
10. *Ibid.*, 23.
11. Malcolm Elwin, *Charles Reade*, London: Jonathan Cape, 1931, 130.
12. *Ibid.*, 193.
13. *Personal Recollections*, 47.
14. *Charles Reade*, 123-126, 195.

15 *Tom Taylor and the Victorian Drama*, 20.
16 Letter to Sir Edward Bulwer-Lytton, January 16, 1866. In Robert Lee Wolff, "Devoted Disciple: The Letters of Mary Elizabeth Braddon to Sir Edward Bulwer-Lytton, 1862-1873", *Harvard Library Bulletin*, Vol. XXII, No. 1, January 1974, 1-35; Vol. XXII, No. 2, April 1974, 129-161 (at 130). (Hereafter cited in the text as *Letters*.) For a detailed consideration of M.E. Braddon's literary career, see also Robert Lee Wolff's *Sensational Victorian. The Life and Fiction of Mary Elizabeth Braddon*, New York and London: Garland, 1979.
17 All page references are to the Oxford World Classics edition, edited by Lyn Pykett: Oxford and New York, Oxford University Press, 1998.
18 See the following articles by Christopher Heywood: "*The Return of the Native* and Miss Braddon's *The Doctor's Wife*: A Probable Source", *Nineteenth Century Fiction*, Vol. 18 (1963), 91-94; "Miss Braddon's *The Doctor's Wife*: An Intermediary between *Madame Bovary* and *The Return of the Native*", *Revue de littérature comparée*, Vol. 38 (1964), 255-261; and "A Source for *Middlemarch*: Miss Braddon's *The Doctor's Wife* and *Madame Bovary*", *Revue de littérature comparée*, Vol. 44 (1970), 184-194.
19 See particularly her letters of January 17, 1864; June 24, 1864; two undated letters of summer, 1864; September 7, 1864 ("I always meant Sleaford to kill Roland, but to the last I was uncertain what to do with George."); and December 9, 1864 ("I gave my best thoughts [*to The Doctor's Wife*] — such as they are".) Letters, 18-28.
20 Almost certainly intended as a reference to Eugène Sue's *Le Juif errant* (1844-1845), a vast feuilleton which enjoyed the same level of popularity as his earlier *Mystères de Paris* (1842-1843). The story essentially concerns the criminal attempt made by the Jesuits to procure an enormous trust fund which has been accumulating interest for many centuries. Among the many imitations, George Lippard's *New York. Its Upper Ten and Lower Million* (1853) is the most distinguished.
21 See Robert Lee Wolff's *Sensational Victorian. The Life and Fiction of Mary Elizabeth Braddon*, New York and London: Garland, 1979, 118-126. The volatility of the translation market at the time is exemplified by an anecdote concerning *The Banker's Secret* (1865), Braddon's last *Halfpenny Journal* contribution. Translated into French in the pages of the *Journal pour Tous*, it was translated back into English by the *New York Sunday Mercury*.
22 *Ibid.*, 28.
23 Winifred Hughes, *The Maniac in the Cellar*, Princeton: Princeton University Press, 1980, 120.
24 Another expectation that is defeated is that the force of hereditary instinct will make Isabel follow her father's footsteps into some form of criminal activity. In a sense, Emma Bovary's fraudulent conduct is shunted off by

Braddon into a subplot concerning Mr Sleaford.
25 Elaine Showalter, *A Literature of Their Own. From Charlotte Brontë to Doris Lessing*, London: Virago, 1991, 163.
26 Henry Jenkins, *Textual Poachers. Television Fans and Participatory Culture*, New York and London: Routledge, 1992, 162-177.
27 *Letters*, 22.
28 *Charles Reade*, 1931, 236-242. Reade later made a similar mistake with regard to Frances Hodgson Burnett.
29 José Lambert, Lieven D'hulst and Katrin van Bragt, "Translated Literature in France, 1800-1850", in Theo Hermans (ed.), *The Manipulation of Literature. Studies in Literary Translation*, London and Sydney, Croom Helm, 1985, 149-163.
30 *Charles Reade*, 341.

## Notes on Contributors

**Michel Ballard**, teaches Translation and Translation Studies at the University of Artois in France, where he is the director of Postgraduate studies and the director of a research centre on Translation Studies (CERTA). He is the editor of a series on Translation Studies at the University Press. His research concentrates on the didactics and on the history of translation. His publications include *Le Commentaire de Traduction* (1992), *De Cicéron à Benjamin* (1992), and *La Traduction de l'anglais au français* (1994). He recently edited De Meziriac's address to the French Academy *De La Traduction* (1998), and published *Les faux amis* (1999).

**Susan Bassnett**, is a Pro-Vice-Chancellor at the University of Warwick and Professor in the Centre for British and Comparative Cultural Studies, which she founded in the 1980s. She is the author of over 20 books, including *Translation Studies*, a leading textbook which first appeared in 1980. Recent works include *Studying British Cultures: An Introduction* (1997), *Constructing Cultures* (1998), written with André Lefevere, and *Postcolonial Translation* (1999), written with Harish Trivedi. She writes for several national newspapers, and contributes regularly to the "View from Here" column in *The Independent*.

**Michael Bishop**, is McCulloch Professor at Dalhousie University, Canada, and has published widely in the field of modern and contemporary French literature and culture. He is the author of *The Contemporary Poetry of France* (1985), *Michel Deguy* (1988), *René Char: Les Dernières Années* (1990), *Nineteenth-Century French Poetry* (1993), *Contemporary French Women Poets* (2 vols, 1995), and *Women's Poetry in France 1965-1995: A Bilingual Anthology* (1997). A major translation of Salah Stétié, and a critical study of Prévert are in press.

**Stephen Brewer**, teaches languages and European Culture at Staffordshire University. His research interests are in German and French literature, and he has published on Heinrich Boell. He is currently working with Azzedine Haddour and Terry McWilliams on a translation of Sartre's *Situations, V*.

**Mary Ann Caws**, is Distinguished Professor of English, French and Comparative Literature in the Graduate School of the City, University of New York, and Co-Director of its Henri Peyre French Institute. Author, editor or translator of more than forty books in the fields of poetry and the avant-garde. These include *Surrealism and Women* (1991) and *The Surrealist Look* (1997). Her current projects include a work on Dora Maar, and illustrated biographies of Marcel Proust and Virginia Woolf.

**Said Faiq**, teaches Arabic, Translation/Interpreting, Translation Studies and Linguistics at the School of Languages, University of Salford. His publications include "The Status of Berber", and "Arabic Translation: A glorious past but a meek present". He edited the special edition of *Offshoot* entitled "In and out of Translation", and is editing the forthcoming volumes *Translated: Arabic in other tongues,* and *Cultural Representation and Translation*.

**Terry Hale**, is Research Fellow in translation at the University of Hull. His recent work has been primarily concerned with translation in relation to popular culture, including substantial entries in *The Handbook to Gothic Literature, The Oxford Guide to Literature in English Translation,* and *The Cambridge Guide to Gothic Fiction*. He has edited and translated fifteen books, most recently *The Dedalus Book of French Horror*.

**Jean-Pierre Mailhac**, is Senior Lecturer in French in the School of Languages at the University of Salford, where he teaches French, Linguistics and Translation. His research interests cover Theoretical Linguistics, the syntax of French and Translation Studies. His publications include *Le temps opératif en psychomécanique du langage,* as well as articles on the translation of cultural references, video and numerical material, and on the translation of levels of speech.

**Terry McWilliams**, has taught French and Spanish at Staffordshire University, and University College, Chester, where he is currently Head of the Department of Modern Languages. His research interests lie in French and Spanish Literature and Film, and he is now working with Azzedine Haddour and Steven Brewer on a translation of Jean-Paul Sartre's political essays *Situations, V.*

**Lucy Mazdon**, is Senior Research Fellow at the University of Southampton. Her research interests include film and French and British television, and she has published several papers in both areas. She is currently preparing a book on Hollywood remakes of French film for the British Film Institute.

**Myriam Salama-Carr**, is Senior Lecturer in French and Translation Studies in the School of Languages at the University of Salford. She has published *La traduction à l'époque abbasside* (1990), on the development of medieval Arabic translation, and several articles on the history, theory and didactics of translation, including an entry on the French tradition in the *Routledge Encyclopedia of Translation Studies* (1998), and a chapter in *Translators through History* (1995), published under the aegis of the Fédération Internationale des Traducteurs.

**Emily Salines**, is Senior Lecturer in French at Middlesex University, where she teaches Translation Theory and Practice. She is the author of a PhD thesis on *Alchemy and Amalgam: Translation in the Works of Charles Baudelaire*, and has published articles in comparative literature and translation studies.

**María Sánchez-Ortiz**, is Lecturer in Spanish in the School of Languages at the University of Salford, where her main research interest is in Literary Translation. She is the author of an article on sociolinguistic problems of translation, and of *Translation as a(n Im)Possible Task*.

**Martin Sorrell**, is Reader in French and Translation Studies at the University of Exeter. He specialises in modern French poetry and theatre, areas in which he has published and broadcast widely. His recent work includes *Modern French Poetry* (1992), *Molière: The Hypochondriac* (1994), *Elles: A Bilingual Anthology of Modern French Poetry By Women* (1995), and *Verlaine: Selected Poems* (1999).

**Peter Tame**, is Reader in French Studies at Queen's University, Belfast. His research interests include twentieth-century French literature and Political Ideology. He has published widely and is the winner of several prizes in his specialism. His recent work includes *The Ideological Hero in the Novels of Brasillach, Vailland and Malraux* (1998), and he was nominated for the 1999 Aldo and Jeanne Scaglione Prize for French and Francophone Studies.

**Isabelle Vanderschelden**, is Senior Lecturer in French at Manchester Metropolitan University. Her research lies in the fields of the contemporary French cinema and Translation Studies. Her forthcoming publications deal with social Class and Subtitling, and the family in French Films of Chatiliez.

# GENRES AS REPOSITORIES OF CULTURAL MEMORY

Ed. by Hendrik van Gorp and Ulla Musarra-Schroeder

Volume 5 of the Proceedings of the XVth Congress of the International Comparative Literature Association "*Literature as Cultural Memory*", Leiden 16-22 August 1997. Amsterdam/Atlanta, GA 2000. 568 pp. (Textxet 29)
ISBN: 90-420-0440-1                    Hfl. 225,-/US-$ 121,50

This volume deals with the inherent relation between literary genres and cultural memory. Indeed, generic repertoires may be regarded as bodies of shared knowledge (a sort of 'encyclopaedia' or 'museum' of stocked culture) and have played and still play an important role in absorbing and activating that memory.
The contributors have focused on some specific memory-linked genres that prove especially relevant in remembering and transforming past experiences, i.e. the (post)modern historical novel and various forms of (post)modern autobiographical writing. They deal with such renowned authors as Carlos Fuentes, Vargas Llosa, Umberto Eco, Antonio Tabucchi, John Barth, Julian Barnes, Michel Butor, Nathalie Sarraute, Alain Robbe-Grillet, Claude Simon, Georges Perec and Marguerite Yourcenar. The volume, thus, constitutes an attractive and representative sample of (post)modern forms of rewriting and problematizing individual and collective pasts.

---------------------------------                    *Editions Rodopi B.V.*
**USA/Canada:** 6075 Roswell Rd., Ste. 219, Atlanta, GA 30328, Tel. (404) 843-4314, *Call toll-free* (U.S.only) 1-800-225-3998, Fax (404) 843-4315

**All Other Countries:** Tijnmuiden 7, 1046 AK Amsterdam, The Netherlands. Tel. ++ 31 (0)20 6114821, Fax ++ 31 (0)20 4472979
orders-queries@rodopi.nl —— http://www.rodopi.nl

# POETRY AND OTHER PROSE/ POÉSIES ET AUTRES PROSES

Edited by/edité par Matthijs Engelberts,
Marius Buning, Sjef Houppermans

Amsterdam/Atlanta, GA 2000. 222 pp.
(Samuel Beckett Today/Aujourd'hui 8)
ISBN: 90-420-0700-1         Bound Hfl. 160,-/US-$ 88.50
ISBN: 90-420-0690-0         Paper Hfl. 40,-/US-$ 22.-

Table of Contents/Table des Matières: Matthijs ENGELBERTS: Avant-Propos/Introduction. John PILLING: Beckett and "The Itch to Make": The Early Poems in English. Thomas HUNKELER: "Cascando" de Samuel Beckett. Mary Ann CAWS: Samuel Beckett Translating. Mary LYDON: Beyond the Criterion of Genre: Samuel Beckett's *Ars Poetica*. Jean-Michel RABETÉ: Beckett et la poesie de la zone: (Dante...Apollinaire. Céline...Lévi). Christophe WALL-ROMANA: Beckett au parloir: Poétique du transvoisement. Michael STEWART: The Unnamable Mirror: The Reflective Identity in Beckett's Prose. Yann MÉVEL: *Molloy:* Jeux et enjeux d'un savoir mélancolique. H. PORTER ABBOTT: Beckett's Lawlessness: Evolutionary Psychology and Genre. Catherine LAWS: Performance Issues in Composer's Approaches to Beckett. Emmanuel JACQUART: Beckett et la forme sonate. Wilma SICCAMA: Beckett's Many Voices: Authorial Control and the Play of Repetition. N.F. LÖWE: Sam's Love for Sam: Samuel Beckett, Dr. Johnson and *Human Wishes*. Bruce ARNOLD: From Proof to Print: Anthony Cronin's *Samuel Beckett: The Last Modernist* Reconsidered.

------------------------------                    *Editions Rodopi B.V.*
**USA/Canada:** 2015 South Park Place, Atlanta, GA 30339, Tel. (770) 933-0027, *Call toll-free* (U.S.only) 1-800-225-3998, Fax (770) 933-9644

**All Other Countries:** Tijnmuiden 7, 1046 AK Amsterdam, The Netherlands. Tel. ++ 31 (0)20 6114821, Fax ++ 31 (0)20 4472979
orders-queries@rodopi.nl — http://www.rodopi.nl

F